Sin Tax Reform in the Philippines

DIRECTIONS IN DEVELOPMENT
Countries and Regions

Sin Tax Reform in the Philippines

Transforming Public Finance, Health, and Governance for More Inclusive Development

Kai Kaiser, Caryn Bredenkamp, and Roberto Iglesias

WORLD BANK GROUP

Contents

Boxes

Figures

Map

Photo

Tables

Foreword

Maraming nag-isip na imposibleng maipasa ang Sin Tax Reform Bill: malakas ang kalaban; maingay, organisado, at malalim ang bulsa ng mga kumukontra.

Pero gaya po ng paulit-ulit nating napatunayan: Walang imposible sa Pilipinong suma-sagwan sa iisang direksyon, nasa tamang lugar ang puso, at handang manindigan para sa kanyang mga prinsipyo.

From the speech of President Benigno S. Aquino III at the signing of the Sin Tax Reform Act, December 20, 2012, Malacañang Palace

Translated from the Filipino language, the President's words encapsulate a story of unity and achievement amidst adversity: "Many thought it was impossible to pass the Sin Tax Reform Bill: the enemy is strong, loud, organized, and has deep pockets. But, as we have proven time and again, nothing is impossible with the Filipino nation rowing in one direction, heart in the right place, and ready to stand up for its principles."

Indeed, the Philippines' sin tax reform—a significant simplification and increase in tobacco and alcohol excise taxes, and the earmarking of revenue increases to fund universal health care—exemplifies how the nation seized a rare opportunity to make a decisive and tangible difference in the lives of millions of Filipinos, against the odds. Before the passage of Republic Act 10351, or the Sin Tax Reform Act of 2012, restructuring excise taxation of tobacco and alcohol in the Philippines was a protracted crusade against powerful vested interests that had long benefited from the old system's inefficiencies. Previous efforts languished in the hands of those opposed to change, and the merits of reform were lost to private profit at the expense of the people's welfare.

Now, three years since the sin tax reform, we have seen its considerable gains in finance, health, and good governance. Moreover, it serves as an example of how to bring about reforms in the face of strong vested interests. From our experience, we learned that unwavering leadership and support from the highest levels, a whole-of-government approach, and the constructive engagement of all stake-holders is the formula for success of any reform.

The Department of Finance and the Department of Health stood side by side in pushing for and defending the sin tax reform as a public health measure that promised fiscal returns. We had like-minded legislators steer enlightened deliberations on the measure in Congress. No less than President Aquino himself certified the bill as urgent and called on Congress to enact it into law. Development institutions including the World Bank Group and the World Health Organization provided us with analytical support and international experience to bolster the technical bases of our proposal. Civil society groups—the "white armies" of the medical community, economic reform activists, and tobacco control and health advocates—mobilized to publicize information on the sin tax reform. These actions, both spontaneously and proactively coordinated, were so sustained that even parties who felt that sin tax reform was not in their short-term interest were brought into the dialogue and became convinced that the reform will serve the greater good.

Further, building momentum to secure reform required more than good intentions and solid analysis. We found that strategic communications, starting with how to frame the issue, was critical. When we framed sin tax reform as being in the interest of public health, few could argue against it. Taking the initiative to create a close coalition across the government, private sector, and civil society was also crucial. Listening and reaching out to all stakeholders made for a broadly agreed on and, ultimately, better reform. In the final analysis, the nation fully owned the reform, with every concerned sector helping to make it happen.

Under the Sin Tax Reform Act, the excise tax on cigarettes will plateau in 2017 following four years of progressive increases. Cigarettes will then be taxed at a single unitary rate with annual increases of 4 percent. Although this ensures an automatic upward adjustment in the excise tax, it may not be sufficient to keep pace with the increasing real incomes of Filipinos, who have enjoyed years of sustained economic growth. Beginning in July 2016, after the end of this administration's term, a congressional committee is mandated to review the impact of the Sin Tax Reform Act. This will provide an opportunity not only to show the Filipino people what the reform has achieved, but also to identify further ways to strengthen our tax and expenditure regime in the service of better health for all Filipinos.

This publication methodically showcases the concrete gains achieved by sin tax reform. At the same time, it affirms our continuing responsibility to monitor the impact of the reform, sustain the gains, and seek to further enhance the regulatory framework. In sum, these pages show that what was thought impossible has truly become reality.

Cesar V. Purisima
Secretary of Finance
Government of the Philippines

Preface

Tobacco taxation … can play a critical role in turning the tide on the alarming increase in chronic conditions and injuries we see today in so many developing countries. Helping countries advance universal health coverage is a strategic priority across the World Bank Group. Through our Bank loans and technical assistance, we are partnering with middle-income countries to design and implement tough health sector reforms and contain costs, while at the same time expanding and sustaining coverage.[1]

—World Bank Group President Jim Yong Kim, Global Conference on Universal Health Coverage (UHC) for Inclusive and Sustainable Growth, Tokyo, Japan, December 2013

Reducing extreme poverty and boosting shared prosperity start with healthy populations. Tackling noncommunicable diseases, such as those associated with smoking and excessive drinking, is intrinsically linked with making government finances more sustainable and equitable and scaling up programs to improve the lives of the bottom 40 percent of the world's population.

Development successes such as the Philippines' sin tax reform deserve to be widely shared. They serve as an inspiration for tackling other similar challenges. The sin tax reform demonstrates that getting results is not only about undertaking robust technical analysis, but also about weighing political economy considerations, building reform coalitions, and monitoring implementation and impact. This means helping to create the conditions by which politicians secure majorities for making legislative reforms happen; by which the executive branch ensures that reforms are implemented as well as possible; and by which the private sector, citizens, and civil society play their part in delivering on the letter and spirit of the law.

The 2012 sin tax reform will stand as one of the landmark policy reforms of the administration of President Benigno Aquino. Upon his coming to office in 2010, his government promised good governance and improved service delivery for the poor, articulated in a "Social Compact with the Filipino People." The Sin Tax Law, along with the government's commitment to implementing it well, is very much a testament to the efforts of the Aquino administration.

The World Bank Group is pleased to have played a small part in bringing about the effective implementation of the sin tax reform. One of our greatest strengths is our ability to bring together people with diverse expertise and backgrounds to deliver results for clients. The sin tax reform is one such example of this. We were able to support the government of the Philippines through working simultaneously on issues of fiscal sustainability and revenue mobilization, tackling noncommunicable diseases, scaling up universal health care through earmarked financing, and improving good governance, notably transparency and accountability.

The sin tax reform is also a model of how to ensure the effectiveness of reforms by prioritizing monitoring and harnessing new technologies for better results-tracking. Early tracking provides opportunities to make policy and implementation corrections as needed, and impact evaluations allow one to learn lessons for further reforms, whether in the Philippines or elsewhere.

This publication is written very much in this spirit, offering a results monitoring framework for the sin tax reform that is both comprehensive and detailed. It also highlights how information and communication technologies, including those built on mobile crowdsourcing, can help protect reforms such as the Sin Tax Law.

With implementation of the World Health Organization (WHO) Framework Convention on Tobacco Control included as a target in the Sustainable Development Goals (SDGs) for 2030,[2] we know that government and development partners will be eager to learn the lessons of the sin tax reform in the Philippines. Improving health and well-being are very much at the heart of the post-2015 development agenda, and excise taxes, starting with tobacco, can be a way for all countries, at whatever level of development, to finance some of the SDGs.

We hope that this publication serves both to spread the word about this commendable reform and to support its continued success.

Mara Warwick
Country Director, Philippines
The World Bank Group

Notes

1. The Global Conference on Universal Health Coverage (UHC) for Inclusive and Sustainable Growth, December 2013, http://www.worldbank.org/en/news/speech/2013/12/06/speech-world-bank-group-president-jim-yong-kim-government-japan-conference-universal-health-coverage.

2. http://www.un.org/sustainabledevelopment/sustainable-development-goals/.

Acknowledgments

The passage of the Sin Tax Law involved the unprecedented collaboration of reform advocates from public health, public finance, academic, civil society, and development partner communities. This report describes the design of the Sin Tax Law, documents the technical and political processes by which it came about, and assesses the impact that the reform has had after three years of implementation. We hope that it will be of value to all Filipino citizens who wish to see the health, public finance, and good governance objectives of the Sin Tax Law attained, as well to those who are pursuing similar efforts internationally.

This report was prepared by Kai Kaiser (Task Team Leader and Senior Economist, Governance Global Practice), Caryn Bredenkamp (Senior Economist, Health, Nutrition and Population Global Practice), and Roberto Iglesias (Consultant). Overall guidance was provided by Rogier van den Brink and Alexandra Posarac (Program Leaders, Philippines Country Management Unit), Robert Taliercio (Practice Manager, Governance Global Practice), Toomas Palu (Practice Manager, Health, Nutrition and Population Global Practice), Motoo Konishi (former Country Director, Philippines), and James Brumby (Director, Governance Global Practice). We would like to thank Reina Cuarez (Consultant) for indispensable support in fact-checking and coordinating the review of the report by government agencies; Patricio Marquez for excellent advice on dissemination; Tom Allen, Graham Glennday, and Toomas Palu for insightful peer review of an earlier draft; Maria Consuelo Sy for unfailingly reliable program support; Jewel McFadden, Aziz Gökdemir, Denise Bergeron, and Rumit Pancholi for efficiently managing the final production and editing process; and Den Fajardo for creative contributions to graphics design.

The report is the culmination of four years of analytical and advisory work on the design, implementation, and monitoring of the Philippines Sin Tax Law that has been provided by the World Bank Group to the Government of the Philippines. It draws on a number of analytical inputs prepared during this period to which many Bank staff and consultants contributed. Chief among these were a set of policy notes prepared in 2012/2013 as part of World Bank assistance to the design of the Sin Tax Law, a series of semiannual sin tax monitoring reports, and an ongoing process of policy dialogue on tax and health reform issues. We would like to recognize the contributions of the following World Bank staff and consultants to these reports and activities: Maria Vida Gomez, Rouselle Lavado,

Roberto Rosadia, and Bakhuti Shengelia on health issues; Rob Preece, Lina Isorena, and Reina Cuarez on tax issues; and Greg Alling for editorial assistance.

This report would not have been possible without the vision and support of Under-Secretary Jeremias Paul Jr. and the Department of Finance's (DOF) Domestic Finance Group. We would like to thank the DOF for not only support-ing the preparation of the report, but also for facilitating collaborations with other agencies and stakeholders for its review and finalization. These include the Bureau of Internal Revenue (BIR), Bureau of Customs, Department of Health (DOH), Department of Labor and Employment (DOLE), Philippine Health Insurance Corporation (PhilHealth), Department of Agriculture's National Tobacco Administration, Philippine Statistics Authority, Technical Education and Skills Development Authority, and the Department of Budget and Management (DBM). In particular, we would like to thank Secretary Cesar Purisima (DOF), Secretary Janette Garin (DOH), former Secretary Enrique Ona (DOH), Commissioner Kim Henares (BIR), CEO Alexander Padilla (PhilHealth), Under-Secretary Lilibeth David (DOH), former Under-Secretary Madeleine Valera (DOH), Under-Secretary Laura Pascua (DBM), Senior Vice President Ruben John Basa (PhilHealth), Director Cristina Classara (DBM), Director Rolando Toledo (DBM), and Director Rosette Vergeire (DOH). At the DOF, we also appreciate the close working relationships with Rowena Sta. Clara, Joanne Guadalupe, Johanna Hortinela, Ramon de Guzman, Kenneth Abante, and Stella Montejo, as well as Magdalena Ancheta (BIR) and Rosie Sta. Ana and Estela De Guzman (Philippine Statistics Authority-National Statistics Office).

Special thanks go to the civil society organizations involved in making the sin tax reform happen and advocating for accountability in its implementation. We would particularly like to acknowledge Filomeno Sta. Ana III and Jo-Ann Latuja of Action for Economic Reform. Various development partners and specialists provided valuable inputs and counsel as we prepared the report, including staff of the Asian Development Bank, World Health Organization, Tobacco Free Kids, Bloomberg Philanthropies, the International Union against Tobacco and Lung Disease, and John Colledge (U.S. Customs Service, retired). We also acknowledge the feedback from industry associations.

Financial support for this report, and the analytical and advisory work on which it is based, was provided by various World Bank programs, many of which benefit from significant donor funding, including the joint DFAT–World Bank Philippines Development Trust Fund, the World Bank's Poverty and Social Impact Analysis (PSIA) Trust Fund, and the World Bank's Global Tobacco Control Program, cofinanced by the Bill and Melinda Gates Foundation and Bloomberg Philanthropies.

Abbreviations and Key Legislation and Regulations

ASEAN	Association of Southeast Asian Nations
BIR	Bureau of Internal Revenue
DA	Department of Agriculture
DBM	Department of Budget and Management
DOF	Department of Finance
DOH	Department of Health
DOLE	Department of Labor and Employment
FIES	Family Income and Expenditure Survey
GATS	Global Adult Tobacco Survey
GDP	gross domestic product
HFEP	Health Facilities Enhancement Program
IRRs	implementing rules and regulations
LGU	local government unit
NDHS	National Demographic and Health Survey
NHIP	National Health Insurance Program
NNHS	National Nutrition and Health Survey
NSO	National Statistics Office
NTA	National Tobacco Administration
PSA	Philippine Statistics Authority
RA	Republic Act
RMC	Revenue Memorandum Circular
SAR	special administrative region
SDGs	Sustainable Development Goals
STL	Sin Tax Law
SWS	Social Weather Stations
UHC	Universal Health Coverage
USAID	United States Agency for International Development
WHO	World Health Organization
WTO	World Trade Organization

All dollar amounts are U.S. dollars unless otherwise indicated. Dollar-peso exchange rates for 2011 ($1 = ₱43.31), 2012 (₱42.23), 2013 (₱42.45), 2014 (₱44.50), and 2015 (₱45.50), from World Bank Data (http://data.worldbank.org/indicator/PA.NUS.FCRF). Estimated dollar-peso rates for 2016 (₱46.80) and 2017 (₱46.10) by World Bank Macroeconomic and Fiscal Management Global Practice estimates.

Key Legislation and Regulations

Republic Act (RA) 7171	1992 Act to Promote the Development of the Farmers in Virginia Tobacco-Producing Regions
RA 8240	1996 Act on Tobacco and Alcohol Taxation
RA 9334	2004 Act Increasing the Excise Tax Rates Imposed on Alcohol and Tobacco Products
RA 10351	2012 Act Restructuring the Excise Tax on Alcohol and Tobacco Products
Joint Circular No. 001-2014	Implementing Rules and Regulations for Section 288, Subsections (B) and (C) of the National Internal Revenue Code, as Amended by RA 10351
Revenue Regulations (RR) No. 17-2012 dated December 26, 2012	Implementing Guidelines on the Revised Tax Rates on Alcohol and Tobacco Products Pursuant to the Provisions of RA 10351 and to Clarify Certain Provisions of Existing Revenue Regulations
Revenue Memorandum Order No. 17-2013 dated June 27, 2013	Creates, Modifies, and Drops Alphanumeric Tax Code on Excise Tax Pursuant to RA 10351 as Implemented by RR No. 17-2012
Revenue Memorandum Circular (RMC) No. 90-2012 dated December 27, 2012	Revised Tax Rates of Alcohol and Tobacco Products under RA 10351 by Amending Sections 141, 142,143,144, 145, 8, 131 and 288 of RA 8424
RMC No. 3-2013 dated January 8, 2013	Clarifies Certain Provisions of RR No. 17-2012 Implementing the Provisions of RA 10351 as Well as the Provisions of RMC No. 90-2012 Providing the Initial Tax Classifications of Alcohol and Tobacco Products
RMC No. 18-2013 dated February 15, 2013	Further Clarifies the Taxability of Distilled Spirits Provided under RMC No. 3-2013

RR 7-2014 dated July 4, 2014, as amended by RR 8-2014 dated October 1, 2014; RR 9-2014 dated October 31, 2014; and RR No. 9-2015 dated December 2, 2015

Prescribing the Affixture of Internal Revenue Stamps on Imported and Locally Manufactured Cigarettes and the Use of the Internal Revenue Stamps Integrated System for the Ordering, Distribution, and Monitoring Thereof

Overview

The 2012 Philippines Sin Tax Law (STL) brought about long-overdue reforms to tobacco and alcohol taxation to promote better health, improve financial sustainability, and good governance. The STL greatly simplified and increased excise taxes, especially on cigarettes. In 2012, cigarettes were widely sold at ₱1 apiece or even less—an amount equivalent to a couple of U.S. cents. Falling real taxes and growing incomes in the Philippines meant that tobacco and alcohol products were widely accessible and affordable. The prevailing excise regime had resulted in a significant decline in revenues, from 0.9 percent of gross domestic product (GDP) in 1997 to under 0.5 percent of GDP in 2012. This is equivalent to "losses" of over $2.5 billion per year in 2012 terms. The excise regime granted special low grandfathered rates to certain cigarette producers, suffered from a lack of inflation indexing, and fostered an increasingly monopolistic market. The multiple excise tiers—which varied by price—created the temptation for down-shifting (reclassification) to lower price tiers to avoid taxes. The taxation of spirits, meanwhile, was being challenged by the international community in the World Trade Organization for allegedly being overtly discriminatory by favoring a few major local producers.

The STL raised and simplified tobacco and alcohol excises, increasing government revenues and reducing smoking. After only one year of implementation, excise tax collections from tobacco and alcohol products shot up to approximately ₱103.4 billion ($2.44 billion), an increase of more than 86 percent from the previous year's collections of ₱55.7 billion ($1.25 billion). In 2015, total sin tax collections reached ₱141.8 billion (over 1 percent of GDP), with tobacco accounting for ₱100 billion. Retail prices for cigarettes increased significantly because of the reform, prompting consumers to cut down and even stop smoking, with early data suggesting some declines in smoking prevalence.

The reform scaled up health care financing, nearly doubling the Department of Health's (DOH) budget in its first year of implementation and financing the extension of fully subsidized health insurance to the poorest 40 percent of the population. From 2013 to 2014, the number of poor and near-poor families enrolled in the National Health Insurance Program increased from 5.2 million to

14.7 million. This grew to 15.3 million by end-2015, almost tripling the coverage of the poor and near-poor. Sin tax revenues were also subsequently used to subsidize the insurance coverage of senior citizens, further expanding access to care among the vulnerable. By 2016, the DOH budget was triple its 2012 level (in nominal terms), reaching ₱122.6 billion.

The STL strengthened governance arrangements on the tax and expenditure sides. This was done through the simplification of tax rates (for example, moving to a unitary excise tax); by promoting greater transparency and accountability in the allocation of health insurance subsidies by using an existing official poverty-targeting mechanism; and by mandating annual accountability reports on the implementation of the STL by all concerned agencies to the Congress of the Philippines.

Although the initial impact of the STL was felt immediately, it is a multiyear transition to a new tax regime, and its full implementation stretches to 2017 and beyond. By 2017, all cigarettes will be subject to a single unitary excise tax of ₱30 ($0.70) per pack after a quadrupling of the lowest excise tax tier of ₱12 in 2013 from ₱2.72 in 2012. After 2017 the excise tax will be increased automatically by 4 percent per year. Higher cigarette prices should improve population health by curbing smoking. The STL retained revenue earmarking for tobacco-growing regions (almost equal to 15 percent of tobacco revenues), with a major increase in these transfers slated for 2015, based on 2013 revenue realizations. In July 2016, which coincides with a new political administration, a Congressional Oversight Committee is mandated to review the impact of the tax rates provided under this Act.

The STL overcame a challenging political economy characterized by pronounced rent seeking and elite capture. Dubbed as a "clever marriage of technical virtue and political pragmatism," the STL navigated a political economy in which special interests had often proved hostile to major reforms seeking to serve the broader public interest. Framing the reform as a health measure rather than tax measure helped its success. Together with a range of additional drivers as varied as sovereign debt ratings and international trade disputes, the cause of good health helped fuse a winning political coalition amid formidable opposing lobbies. The Philippines' bicameral legislative structure meant the STL needed to be passed in the House of Representatives and the Senate, and then both versions reconciled by a bicameral committee. The reconciled law was finally passed in December 2012 by only one vote in the Senate, highlighting just how precarious reforms can be in the Philippines.

The STL helped the Philippines shed its historical label as the "sick man of Asia." It helped the Philippines achieve an investment-grade sovereign debt rating. Overall tax mobilization, at 12.4 percent of GDP in 2011, was low by international standards. The tobacco and alcohol excise regime epitomized the exemptions, complexity, and lack of inflation indexing that stood in the way of improving revenues to finance the administration's "Social Contract with the Filipino People" and bring down government debt. Lowering this to sustainable levels, supported by better sovereign debt ratings, would in turn also bring down the cost of financing debt. A decisive tax reform would signal to the markets that the Philippines could deliver on better tax and expenditure policies. The STL stands as one of the main legacy legislative policy reforms of President Benigno Aquino's administration.

The STL and its implementation can be understood through both a "technical" lens and a political economy/institutional reform lens. This report contributes to our understanding of the STL by (1) providing an overview of the key health, revenue, and governance motivations of the reform and the corresponding features of the law; (2) analyzing how the political economy and institutional dynamics were married with technical analysis to bring about the law's passage; and (3) setting out a monitoring framework by which the implementation and results of the tax and earmarking aspects of the STL can be tracked.

A cross-cutting question of this report is the extent to which the STL is both demonstrational and transformational. By demonstrational, we mean whether key aspects of its technical design, as well as the political reform process, can provide lessons for reforms in similarly challenging situations—whether related to tax or otherwise—in the Philippines and elsewhere. By transformational, we mean the extent to which the STL is part of a deeper institutional transformation in the Philippines, from policies and programs driven primarily by patronage and personalism to ones anchored in principles, evidence, and citizen entitlement.

The Sin Tax Law's Key Features

Figure O.1 illustrates the key changes brought about by the STL.

The law simplified and increased excise taxes on cigarettes. It did away with complex tax tiers and rates that catered to a narrow set of special interests. It helped set a floor price for all brands of cigarettes, raising the minimum tax more than fourfold (341 percent) from 2012 levels of only ₱2.72 ($0.06) per pack of 20. It also moved from a multitiered ad valorem system to a specific structure with only two tiers, converging to a unitary rate over four years. This did away with the administrative difficulties of classifying cigarettes by declared value and allowed the Bureau of Internal Revenue (BIR) to focus on more easily observed volumes. To counter risks of tax evasion and smuggling, the BIR also introduced a holographic tax security stamp in 2014. Simplicity and transparency served good governance and tax administration. It is expected that by 2016, floor prices for an individual cigarette will increase further to ₱2 ($0.04).

Spirits and beer taxes were also simplified, but the increases were less than for cigarettes. The World Trade Organization brought an adverse ruling against the Philippines on spirits, specifically that the excise tax system discriminated against international producers. With the STL, all spirits are subject to a ₱20 specific tax-per-proof liter (with automatic adjustments after 2016), as well as a 15 percent ad valorem tax, which increased to 20 percent in 2016. The diversity of the Philippine spirits market—which is spread across a large, low-cost domestic segment and characterized by increasing consumption of premium brands—made the additional complexity of the law necessary. This was not only to secure a floor price for alcohol that would be appropriate from a health perspective, but also to gain revenue through the ad valorem component. A liter of beer will be subject to a unitary specific excise of ₱23.5 by 2017, a nominal doubling of the prevailing rates in 2012.

Revenue earmarking for government health programs and for tobacco-growing regions are important features of the STL. From a public finance perspective, earmarking carries the risk of introducing unnecessary distortions into the budgeting process. Why should one expenditure item by default trump the annual appropriations process? In the Philippines, the combination of limited fiscal space due to a low revenue effort and poorly implemented spending, as well as widespread patronage politics at the national and local levels, had historically undermined the state's ability to deliver effective and broad-based poverty reduction, social protection, and health programs. In this environment, earmarking for health promised to be politically popular, but it also provided a means to ensure the scaling-up of health programs and to improve the targeting of these programs, especially health insurance, as promised in the administration's "Social Contract."

Figure O.1 Key Features of the Sin Tax Law

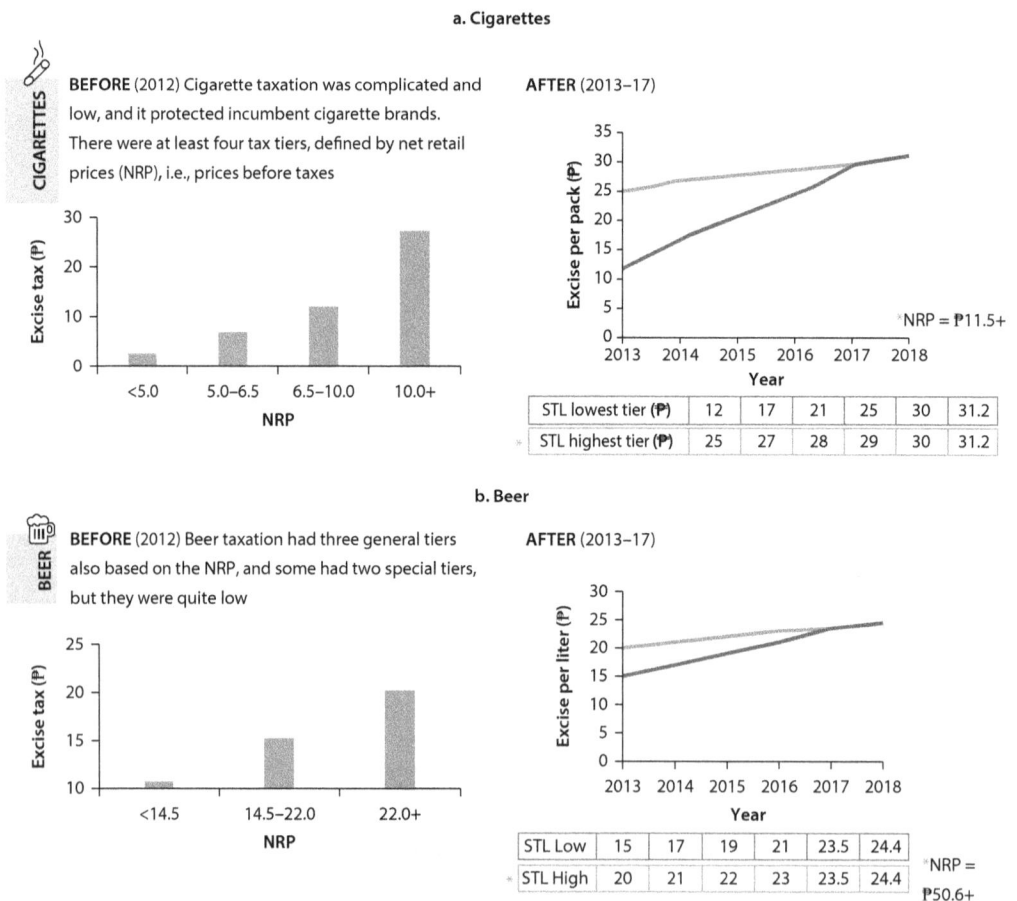

a. Cigarettes

CIGARETTES

BEFORE (2012) Cigarette taxation was complicated and low, and it protected incumbent cigarette brands. There were at least four tax tiers, defined by net retail prices (NRP), i.e., prices before taxes

AFTER (2013–17)

*NRP = ₱11.5+

STL lowest tier (₱)	12	17	21	25	30	31.2
STL highest tier (₱)	25	27	28	29	30	31.2

b. Beer

BEER

BEFORE (2012) Beer taxation had three general tiers also based on the NRP, and some had two special tiers, but they were quite low

AFTER (2013–17)

STL Low	15	17	19	21	23.5	24.4
STL High	20	21	22	23	23.5	24.4

*NRP = ₱50.6+

figure continues next page

Figure O.1 Key Features of the Sin Tax Law *(continued)*

c. Spirits

SPIRITS

BEFORE (2012) Spirits taxation was complicated, low for cheap spirits, and allegedly discriminatory against foreign producers. Spirits that used "domestic inputs" (e.g., sugarcane, nipa) attracted a lower excise tax. In reality, even those that imported their inputs received this benefit. Distilled spirits produced with other materials paid taxes according to NRP (NRP = ₱ 14.8 per proof liter)

AFTER (2013–17)

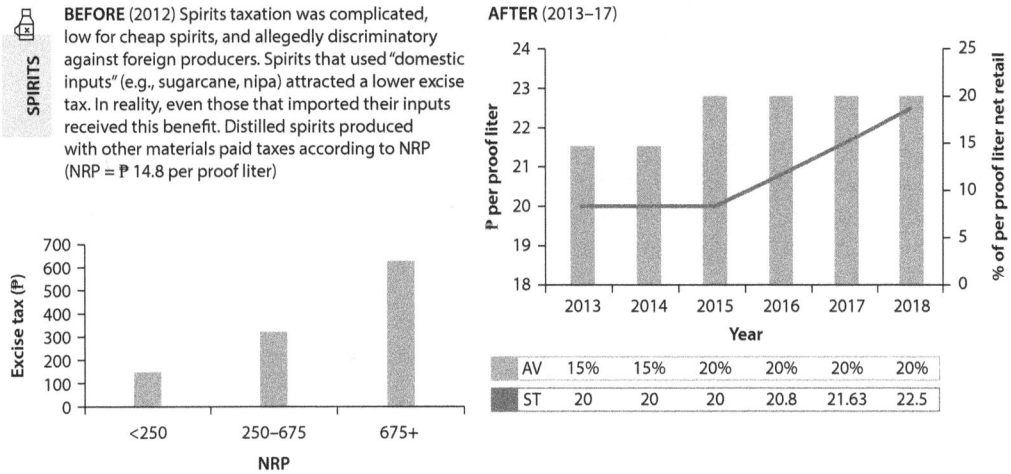

	2013	2014	2015	2016	2017	2018
AV	15%	15%	20%	20%	20%	20%
ST	20	20	20	20.8	21.63	22.5

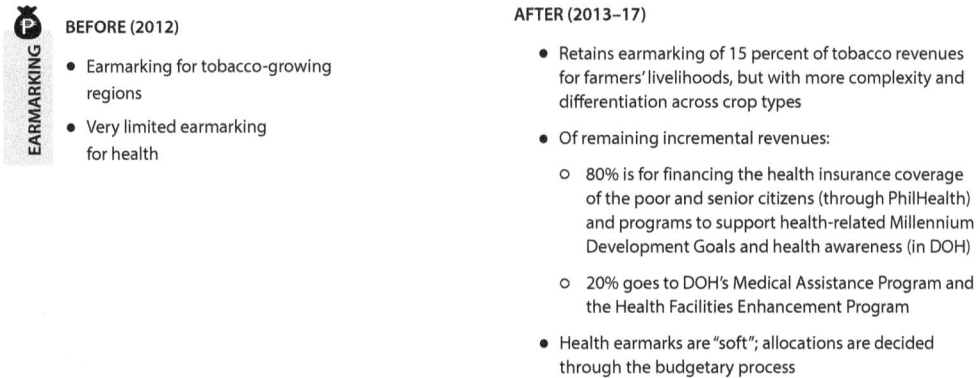

d. Earmarking

EARMARKING

BEFORE (2012)

- Earmarking for tobacco-growing regions
- Very limited earmarking for health

AFTER (2013–17)

- Retains earmarking of 15 percent of tobacco revenues for farmers' livelihoods, but with more complexity and differentiation across crop types
- Of remaining incremental revenues:
  - 80% is for financing the health insurance coverage of the poor and senior citizens (through PhilHealth) and programs to support health-related Millennium Development Goals and health awareness (in DOH)
  - 20% goes to DOH's Medical Assistance Program and the Health Facilities Enhancement Program
- Health earmarks are "soft"; allocations are decided through the budgetary process

Note: AV = ad valorem; DOH = Department of Health; NRP = net retail price; ST = specific tax; STL = Sin Tax Law.

Meanwhile, earmarking almost 15 percent of tobacco excises for domestic tobacco farmers, largely located in the northern Philippines, had been a long-standing feature of excise taxation. Consequently, it was retained for political purposes, but the targeting, transparency, and accountability of these transfers to local governments were improved. The earmarking of STL revenues is "soft" earmarking, though STL revenues are allocated through the annual budgeting process, and annual allocations are considered simultaneously with the overall budgets of the government agencies concerned.

The STL contributed to attaining universal health coverage. This was done through the expansion of health insurance coverage and through investments in health facilities and other health programs; and accompanied by improved targeting, accountability, and transparency mechanisms. The STL's incremental revenues, net of allocations to tobacco-producing regions, are reserved for the government's health program. Of this, 80 percent is allocated to universal health care and, specifically, the National Health Insurance Program, health-related Millennium Development Goals, and health awareness programs. The remaining 20 percent goes to the DOH's Medical Assistance Program, which deposits funds at hospitals to cover the medical bills of patients who cannot afford to pay, and the DOH's Health Facilities Enhancement Program (HFEP), which funds additional infrastructure investments in underserved areas. The National Health Insurance Program share is transferred from the DOH to the Philippines Health Insurance Corporation, known as PhilHealth, a Government-Owned and/or Controlled Corporation, effectively providing free health insurance to the poorest 40 percent of the population (currently at a premium/subsidy of ₱2,400, or $55, per family). Importantly, beneficiaries are identified using the National Household Targeting Survey for Poverty Reduction, a targeting list originally designed for the government's conditional cash transfer program. This ends the practice of leaving the targeting of the poor to the discretion of local government units and replaces it with a national entitlement and transparent targeting.

The additional earmark for tobacco-growing regions was scheduled to be allocated starting in 2015. The law, in effect, retains earmarking of 15 percent of tobacco revenues, but with some complexity and differentiation across crop types (that is, Virginia, Native, and Burley). The revenues are transferred to local governments whose farmers produce the yields, but with a two-year lag. In the 2015 budget, the allocations to tobacco-growing regions roughly doubled on aggregate to over ₱10 billion ($250 million). However, a major scandal concerning the Priority Development Assistance Fund, which provided lump sums for legislators to allocate to projects of their choosing, led to the Supreme Court's decision in 2013 to declare these types of lump sum appropriations unconstitutional. This meant that new guidelines were needed to allow for the release of the tobacco-earmarked revenues for 2015 and 2016. At the time of writing, this issue was not yet resolved.

Reconciling Technical Analysis with Political Realities

The successful passage of the STL was made possible not only by rigorous technical analysis, but also by careful consideration of political economy issues from all angles—health, tax, and governance. Despite being a good governance reform with strong presidential backing, and a win-win proposition from health and public finance perspectives, the STL ultimately passed by only one vote. The intense political wrangling that preceded the vote is reflected in the number, and substantively different content, of the STL bills that were submitted throughout the legislative process of the bicameral Congress. This, in turn, speaks to the deeper political economy and institutional issues that need to be addressed by any legislative reform intended to make headway on the inclusive growth agenda in the Philippines.

One obvious lesson from the STL experience is that it is not enough to simply do technical analysis on a first-best bill and then hope that the political process

will yield a good-enough bill. The nature of the legislative process in the Philippines is such that the output of the process could actually undermine the very core of the reform initiative. Several versions of a bill can be introduced at any time during the legislative process in the House of Representatives and Senate. Success is not guaranteed until both houses have voted on their respective versions of a bill and those versions have been reconciled by a bicameral conference committee. Special interests pervade the legislative process; just a month before the passage of the final sin tax bill, the chair of the Senate Ways and Means Committee resigned amid charges of conflict of interest in favor of the cigarette industry.

Setting clear objectives, principles, and non-negotiables was an important part of anchoring the strategic choices made in finalizing the bill. These included (1) significant streamlining of the excise tax structure (that is, converging to a unitary rate for cigarettes); (2) setting a minimum floor tax for cigarettes to discourage smoking; (3) ensuring a level playing field for producers; (4) generating sufficient revenues to scale up universal health care, notably for the bottom 40 percent of the population; and (5) ensuring that the reform as a whole was pro-poor. Consequently, the key design choice on the tax side centered on excise structure (specific, unitary, or multitiered; ad valorem or hybrid); rates and phasing through 2017; and the relative treatment of cigarettes, beer, and spirits. Expenditure decisions focused on earmarking specifications (that is, for what and how "hard"), and whether the STL would generate sufficient revenues to finance universal health care in both the short and medium term.

Passing the STL involved a host of technical and political trade-offs and uncertainties. Achieving a measure that was a win for both health and revenues meant effectively dealing with the technical "devil in the details" while ensuring the integrity of the reform package and satisfying the key principles, objectives, and non-negotiables of the players. Revenue projections were also subject to a range of modeling uncertainties since it was unclear at the time how consumers and firms would react to the changes in excise tax structure. This report describes the approach taken to deal with these trade-offs and uncertainties, and highlights the extent to which the reform team often had to make do with incomplete information. As with any other political bargaining process, the passage of the STL required having the reform coalition rally around the details that really mattered for health, taxation, and governance, while yielding on less critical points. This also included making a judgment on what needed to be tackled as part of the law versus what could be left to be described downstream in the implementing rules and regulations. From a health perspective, it also made sense to avoid having the STL derailed by the objective of collecting maximum revenues for both tobacco and alcohol and, instead, to keep the focus on cigarettes where the health gains would be the greatest.

International norms and theory were instructive, but special work was needed to ensure an effective fit with the local context. Recommended norms on tax incidence (such as the World Health Organization's recommendation to set cigarette tax at 70 percent of the retail price) provided some general guidance on a desirable rate setting. However, norms and theory were less helpful in showing how a better-structured excise should be initiated and phased in. In the Philippines' case, analyzing the market structure of the tobacco and alcohol industries (and their associated industry markets) was critical. The behavior of firms toward protecting their profits and maintaining their market share shaped their lobbying efforts and how they would later pass tax increases on to the consumer. Another critical part of the STL's design was ensuring that it could be effectively implemented, especially in settings with a history of policy capture and weak and corruption-prone bureaucracies. In this regard, keeping the tax design simple and transparent was critical, even though more sophisticated reform designs might have been technically better or politically easier. A simple design also made it easier to communicate the details of the STL to the reform coalition, and mitigate the risk of capture and weaker implementation through complexity.

Mobilizing and sustaining a multisectoral reform coalition is vital in a setting such as the Philippines. The coalition included various actors across the executive (Department of Finance, DOH, Office of the President). It also included the private sector and international development partners. Importantly, it included the "white armies" of medical professionals, coupled with civil society activists, who pushed the STL to be pro-health, pro-poor, and pro-good governance. While this particular coalition of actors was specific to the reform issue of sin taxes, it also suggests a number of important strategic and tactical considerations that are important for building effective coalitions more generally. What is clear is that no single actor can bring about such a major reform alone.

The STL leveraged existing pro-poor and good governance reforms. The rapid scale-up of health insurance to the bottom 40 percent of the population was only possible because a national list of the poor already existed for the government's conditional cash transfer program. The decision to use the National Household Targeting Survey for Poverty Reduction rather than build yet another agency database created a precedent, and other government programs in the Philippines are now also using a common and more transparent list. The STL experience shows that reforms are easier and stronger if they are able to build on existing mechanisms, even if they are only pilots. Few truly transformational reforms come purely from "stroke of the pen" changes.

Monitoring the Implementation of the Sin Tax Law

Open and systematic monitoring will be critical to the success of the STL and ensuring effective implementation. Public legitimacy of the STL will be a beacon for advancing further reforms in the health sector and beyond. Just as health advocates rallied around securing extra resources for the health sector through the STL, they need to coalesce to make sure that it is well-implemented so that the tangible impacts of the law are felt by all people, and especially those in the bottom 40 percent. In this regard, monitoring awareness of health insurance coverage, changes in health care utilization, and health spending is important. On the tax side, monitoring of cigarette and alcohol prices and tax stamp roll-out

Figure O.2 Sin Tax Monitoring Framework for Tax and Expenditure Earmarking

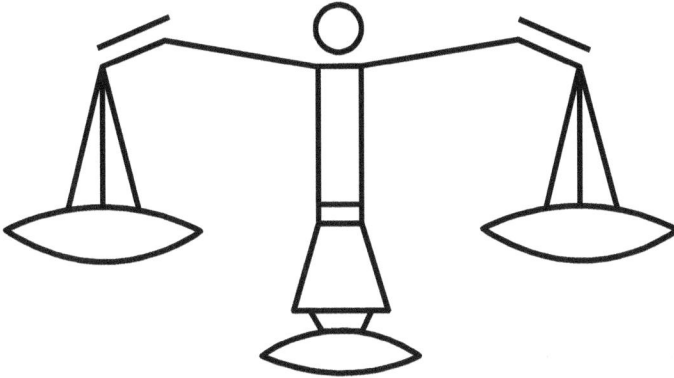

**Tax implementation
and impacts**

**Expenditure earmarking
implementation and impacts**

**1. Retail prices of tobacco
and alcohol products**
Positive: end of the one-peso cigarette

**1. Disbursements to tobacco-producing
local government units (LGU)**
Positive: budgets increase for 2015,
but not yet disbursed

2. Domestic sales/removals
Mixed: declines, but some
increase in cheap cigarette sales

2. LGU project selection, appraisal, and monitoring
Unclear

3. Excise tax collections
Positive: significant increase in revenues

3. LGU reports on utilization and impact evaluation
Unclear

4. Revenue gaps (licit)
Mixed: continued front-loading
prior to year of tax increase

4. Health budget, releases, and accountability
Positive as overall budget has increased,
but some reporting gaps

5. Tax avoidance mechanisms (illicit)
Uncertain, but some control
actions implemented by Government

**5. Overall utilization of the
amounts earmarked for health**
Mixed: apparent limitations in
absorptive capacity

**6. Consumption and prevalence
behavior (smoking and drinking)**
Positive/uncertain: decline in smoking;
no data on excessive drinking

**6. National Health Insurance Program-
sponsored coverage of poor/near-poor**
Positive, but need to validate whether poor know their
entitlements and inform those who don't

7. Impact on tobacco farmers
(as evidenced by domestic tobacco
leaf prices and demand)
Positive: no evidence of major adverse impacts

7. Improved access to and use of health services
Uncertain: increase in availability of PhilHealth-accredited
health facilities, but data to measure changes in
utilization not yet available

Figure O.3 Cigarette Prices Following Sin Tax Reform

The reform eliminated the one-peso cigarette

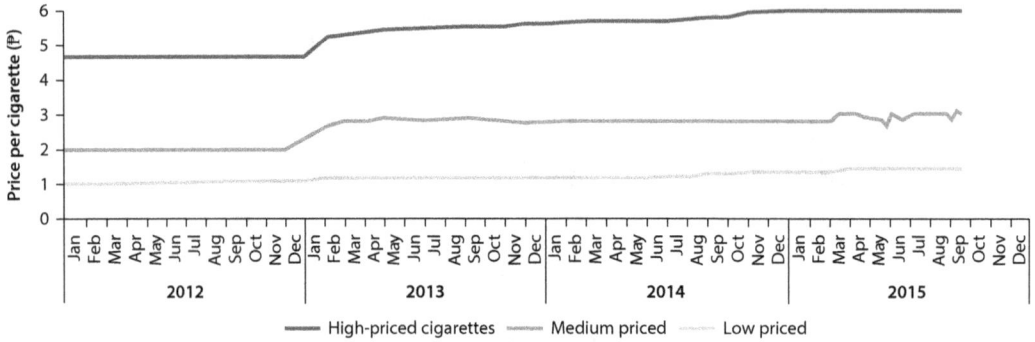

Sources: Philippine Statistics Authority; Premise; AC Nielsen.

Figure O.4 Sin Tax Revenues, 2009–15

Revenues doubled as a share of GDP

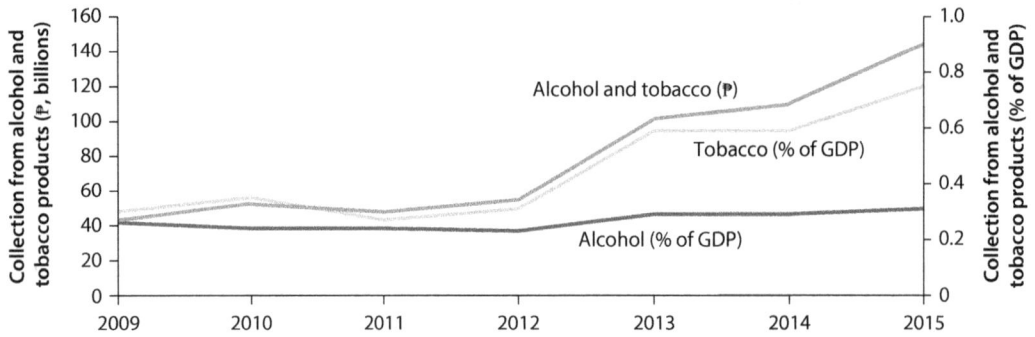

Source: Department of Finance.

Figure O.5 Coverage of Holographic Tax Stamps, 2015–16

The rollout of cigarette tax stamps protected revenues

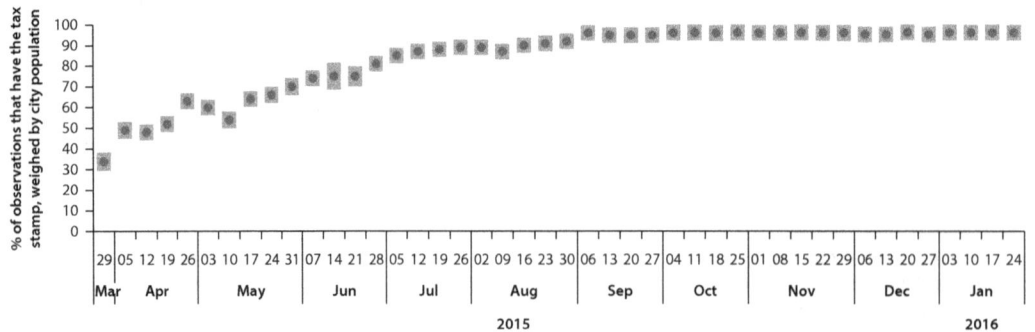

Source: Premise.

Figure O.6 Smoking Prevalence since Sin Tax Reform

Smoking prevalence declined

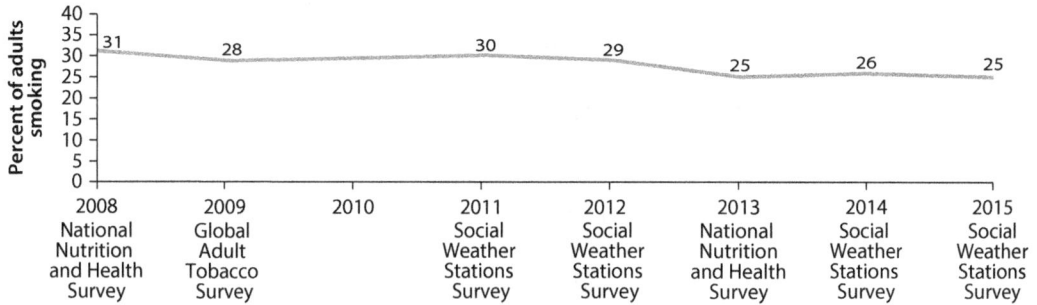

Sources: Department of Health; Global Adult Tobacco Survey; National Nutrition and Health Survey.
Note: The Social Weather Stations Surveys were commissioned by the Department of Health.

Figure O.7 Department of Health Budget, 2007–16

Budgets for the health sector increased dramatically

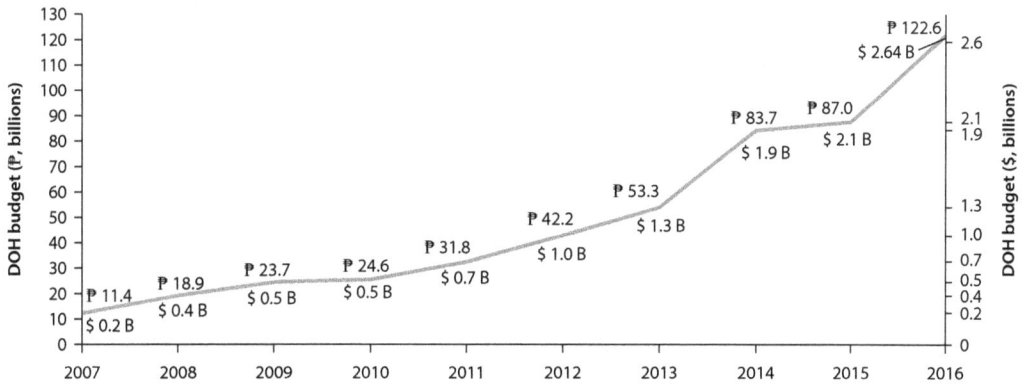

Sources: Department of Budget and Management; General Appropriations Act (GAA).
Note: DOH = Department of Health.

Figure O.8 National Health Insurance Program Coverage of Families since Sin Tax Law

National health insurance became near-universal

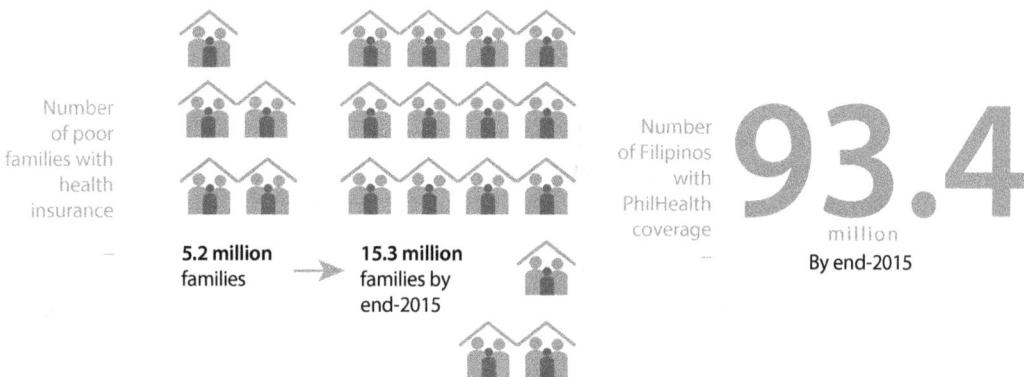

Source: PhilHealth (Philippines Health Insurance Corporation).

will help to ensure industry compliance with the law. In light of the historical weaknesses of administrative data in the Philippines, ex-ante efforts were needed to put in place additional data collection mechanisms to ensure that data for an evidence-based dialogue would be available down the line, whether from official or third-party sources.

The report sets out a monitoring framework for the implementation of the STL, emphasizing regular data collection, evaluation, communication, and feedback. Regular reporting using this framework will serve as a litmus test of the government's commitment and ability to track, in an evidence-based manner, the impact of this flagship reform. The monitoring framework summarized in figure O.2 consists of 14 indicators: seven on the taxation side and seven on the expenditure earmarking side. These cover, among other things, prices, revenues, leakage, process reforms, smoking and drinking incidence, and earmarking for health programs and tobacco farmers. The monitoring framework can be used to assess, and further influence, the STL's implementation until the end of the Aquino administration in 2016 and even beyond. The implementation issue that each indicator seeks to address is identified in the figure, as are the information gaps. A short summary of the experience during the first three years of implementation is also provided.

The first three years of implementation of the STL have been a success. Of particular note is that (1) prices of the cheapest brands of cigarettes have increased by more than 50 percent (figure O.3), (2) total revenues have increased (figure O.4), (3) holographic tax stamps are now on over 95 percent of packs (figure O.5), (4) the BIR has taken legal action to address concerns of tax evasion in the sector, and (5) smoking prevalence has fallen (figure O.6). On the expenditure side, the DOH's health budget has tripled in three years and the poorest 40 percent of the population, as well as senior citizens, receive free health insurance (figures O.7 and O.8).

As in any major reform of this size, some initial implementation and monitoring challenges are likely to emerge. Some outcomes, such as smoking prevalence and access to health services, are subject to both an effect lag and a measurement lag, so that the impact will only be fully captured by the results framework in later years. A priority at this stage of the law's implementation, therefore, is ensuring that timely monitoring mechanisms are in place for an annual evidence-based review (see box O.1). Where the official administrative and statistical systems are not able to monitor implementation promptly, third-party efforts and data collection innovations (for example, crowdsourcing) are already helping.

Informed consultation and continual feedback will make the STL reform stronger. The following three chapters of this report provide a fuller account of the motivations and content of the STL, the technical and political considerations that yielded the law, and a discussion of the results on the tax and earmarking sides. The STL's overall success depends on both tax and expenditure impacts. The significant increase in the DOH's budget from STL revenue allocations has raised concerns about absorptive capacity. Questions are also being asked about the level of benefit awareness among PhilHealth's newly entitled members and

---

Box O.1 Seven Recommendations for Strengthening the Sin Tax Law's Implementation

Considering progress made on the implementation of the Sin Tax Law (STL) to date, we recommend the following priority actions for consideration:

1. Conduct an annual review of the monitoring framework, and take early action on data gaps or concerns about the STL's implementation on both the tax and expenditure side. The analysis will require timely disclosure by the government of key data on tobacco and alcohol markets, revenues collected from the sin tax, and direct and indirect health expenditure impacts.

2. Ensure the continued success of the tax stamp system, complemented by enhanced administrative oversight of the tobacco industry and strengthen security features as any vulnerabilities emerge to reduce the potential for smuggling and domestic-based tax evasion.

3. Make sure that the poor and near-poor who are eligible for free health insurance are informed of their entitlements and benefits. Providing them health insurance cards could be a quick win.

4. Ensure financial sustainability of STL earmarking by strengthening PhilHealth's actuarial capacity and information systems, and institutionalizing a rolling three-to-five-year Medium-Term Expenditure Framework in the Department of Health.

5. Design and implement health awareness campaigns to reinforce the health objectives of tax increases, namely to reduce smoking incidence and excessive drinking, especially among the youth.

6. Enhance transparency and accountability of budgets and expenditures for investments in tobacco-growing regions financed by sin tax earmarks.

7. Sustain a broad coalition of civil society and continue the legislative engagement and support for the effective implementation of the STL and its objectives related to health, social contract financing, and good governance.

---

the extent to which they are actually using health services. Also, the respective roles and responsibilities of members of Congress, governors, mayors, and the national tax authority will need to be effectively balanced to ensure that the scaled-up earmarks from the STL reform will provide sustainable livelihood outcomes for the citizens of the benefiting tobacco-producing localities.

This report should be of interest to all Filipinos concerned with making the STL and other reforms like it a success. We hope it will also be of interest to a wider audience in the Philippines and other countries grappling with similar reform contexts and initiatives to enhance good governance. The implementation of the STL's earmarking provisions have had to confront the challenge of national and local governments that are prone to patronage, capture, and corruption. Concerned Filipino citizens will therefore easily understand why the success of the reform is not only important in and of itself, but also as a barometer of a deeper struggle for better governance in the Philippines.

Overview of the Report

Photo O.1 Signing Ceremony of the Sin Tax Law on December 20, 2012

Source: © Lauro Montellano, Jr./Malacañang Photo Bureau. Used with permission; further permission required for reuse. The photo shows President Benigno Aquino (sixth from left in the front), surrounded by members of Congress and government, after signing into law Republic Act 10351, the Sin Tax Law, at the Rizal Hall, Malacañang Palace on December 20, 2012.

Chapter 1: Why and How Sin Tax Reform Happened

What motivated the reform? The affordability of cigarettes and alcoholic drinks had been increasing, especially because of decreasing real tax rates. Moreover, prevailing excise taxes were poorly designed and failed to ensure a level playing field for all producers. Sin tax reform was an opportunity to curb smoking and excessive drinking, and to generate financing for expanding access to basic health services, mainly through increasing health insurance coverage, especially among the bottom 40 percent of the population. The successful passage of the Sin Tax Law (STL) would also demonstrate the government's commitment and ability to pass significant and decisive reforms.

How was the reform presented? Proponents framed the STL primarily as a health measure, but also as one that would make up for lost revenues due to a lack of automatic real excise rate adjustments in past administrations.

What were the key reforms of tobacco and alcohol excise taxes? These included a minimum and ultimately unitary specific tax for cigarettes by 2017, a unitary specific tax for beer, and a hybrid specific and an ad valorem rate for spirits. These are expected to increase revenues, and reduce smoking and excessive drinking.

How will incremental revenues be used? About 15 percent of incremental revenues from tobacco products go to tobacco-growing regions, supplementing the current allocation; the STL's remaining incremental revenues go to investments in health care, especially expanding health insurance.

Chapter 2: Reconciling Technical Analysis with Political Realities

What was the political context in which the final version of the STL evolved and was passed? Its passage was uncertain until the very end because of significant opposition from vested interests involved in the legislative process. And even that was a close shave—the STL's final bicameral version passed by just one vote in the Senate.

What were the key elements of the STL that needed to get political support? The reform was not just about increasing excises, but involved a constellation of choices. Key decisions involved the minimum rate for cigarettes, beer, and spirits; when and whether to achieve a unitary rate; and the balance of revenues that would come from cigarettes versus beer or spirits. The extent and design of revenue earmarking for health and tobacco-growing regions was important. In addition, the amount of leeway that would be provided in the STL's implementing rules and regulations—and the subsequent legislative review—needed to be given consideration.

What role did technical analysis play? Robust modeling and analysis ultimately led to a stronger STL. Technical analysis provided real-time inputs on the revenue, health, and equity implications of various policy choices. It also helped to lay out the consequences of, and thus further shape, priorities and "nonnegotiables" on health, public finance, and governance reform objectives.

What was needed beyond technical analysis? Careful attention had to be paid to the prevailing political economy, notably the vested interests that could potentially scuttle reform. This needed to be complemented by a committed reform coalition across the executive and civil society, equipped with an effective communications strategy. Delivering on the passage of the STL and its ensuing implementing rules and regulations depended on champions with a strong command of the institutional processes involved in getting work done in the House of Representatives and across the bureaucracy.

Is the STL demonstrational or transformational within the context of the Philippines' political economy? What lessons does the STL hold for other reform efforts confronting vested interests? Does the law help shift the implementation of public policy from one dominated by personal politics and patronage to one based on principles and that is representative of the wider interests of the population, particularly the poor? The STL provides insights into strategy and tactics that can be used to pass major reform in a democracy characterized by patronage politics. Its transformational legacy now hinges mainly on implementation, notably on how frontline prices contribute to quitting smoking and responsible drinking, and on the way the National Health Insurance Program delivers for the bottom 40 percent of the population.

Chapter 3: Tracking Implementation: Setting the Baseline

What are the key measures that will be used to assess the impact of the STL? On the tax side, they include prices, removals and revenues, consumption patterns, illicit sales measures, and domestic raw tobacco prices and sales. Measures also include indicators to assess how the earmarks for tobacco-growing regions and health are spent, and the impact of this spending. In short, success depends on results being delivered, and balanced, across both the tax and the expenditure earmarking parts of the law.

How should these measures be monitored? Ideally, comprehensive monitoring should be done annually, if not semiannually. This would allow for any data and implementation gaps to be addressed in a timely manner.

Are current information sources adequate? Despite contributions to the monitoring framework by all relevant government agencies, including the Philippine Statistics Authority, gaps remain. The accuracy of existing sources, the timeliness of data availability, and rules around data disclosure all need to be looked at. Special efforts have been made at additional data collection, including using special surveys and crowdsourced technology for price monitoring and health insurance utilization. The question is how these can be scaled up and institutionalized.

CHAPTER 1

Why and How Sin Tax Reform Happened

Introduction

On December 20, 2012, President Benigno Aquino signed into law a reform of the Philippines' tobacco and alcohol excise tax: Republic Act 10351, popularly known as the Sin Tax Law (STL). Its final design greatly simplified and increased tobacco and alcohol taxation, especially on spirits and beer. Key highlights included an immediate shift to a two-tiered excise in the first year of the law with a ₱12 ($0.28) minimum excise per pack of cigarettes, followed by a unitary excise of ₱30 ($0.70) in 2017, with automatic percentage increases thereafter. This is a great improvement over the complex and weak excise taxation that was in place in 2012, when the minimum excise was ₱2.72 ($0.06), less than a fourth of 2013's level. A transition to a unitary excise in 2017 is also being implemented for beer, although the rate increases are less than those for cigarettes. The reformed taxation on spirits provides a balance of a single specific excise "floor" based on alcohol content and an ad valorem component (based on value). The latter increased to 20 percent of the net retail price in 2015 (from 15 percent in 2013 and 2014) to capture revenues in the more premium segments. The sin tax reform also involved earmarking the bulk of incremental revenues (about 85 percent) to finance universal health care, especially the insurance premiums of the poor, while retaining earmarks for domestic tobacco-growing regions (about 15 percent) that were in place under existing legislation.

The STL, which took effect on January 1, 2013, and its accompanying implementing rules and regulations, were the culmination of over a decade of reform efforts. The final package successfully navigated a variety of political economy challenges, as illustrated in the various congressional, Senate, and bicameral drafts that preceded the final law. It also addressed international trade issues, including a dispute brought before the World Trade Organization (WTO) on spirits. The STL was a litmus test of the Aquino administration's ability to deliver on the social priority of universal health care, its willingness to make social investments and reforms sustainable, and its fundamental commitment to improve governance and transparency. With the law now under implementation, attention is shifting to (1) the quality of tax administration and associated public spending; (2) the achievement of health objectives of reducing smoking, excessive drinking, and youth drinking; and (3) whether health insurance earmarks are resulting in improved access to health care.

The reform rationale for the STL was straightforward: a win-win for health and revenues, including remedying distortions that had accumulated over decades. The health consequences of smoking and excessive drinking are well documented in developed and developing countries. Increasing the price of "sin products" through tax increases will curtail demand and improve public health. For the Philippines, the increasing prevalence of smoking and excessive drinking, particularly among the youth, were clear motivations for sin tax reform.

New, higher tax rates were expected to augment domestic revenues. In the Philippines, the tax yield from tobacco and alcohol had actually fallen by over 0.6 percent of gross domestic product (GDP) since the last substantive tobacco and alcohol excise tax change in 1997. Because the previous tax design did not allow excise rates to be adjusted for inflation, introducing this design feature, coupled with a streamlined and more transparent tax structure to increase efficiency gains, could yield additional revenues. The new STL promised to generate, at a minimum, an additional 0.3 percent of sin tax excise revenues per year, from a baseline of 0.5 percent in 2012.

The STL should help level the playing field and ensure fairer competition because the pre-STL tax code incorporated an elaborate set of grandfathering clauses that protected incumbent tobacco producers from newcomers. Fairer competition will limit the ability of a small number of firms to capture and control the market for cigarettes, earn excess profits (rents), and reduce the risks of concentrated lobbying and regulatory capture. The removal of preferential tax treatment that had no obvious policy objective also provides a clear signal of the government's commitment to economic governance and a tax policy that is designed to advance the public interest and does not give preference to particular market actors and vested interests. The successful international challenge by the WTO against the Philippines' previous alcohol excise tax structure lent further urgency to the need for a new law. In sum, a well-designed and carefully implemented STL offered a win-win reform from a health, public finance, and economic perspective.

The repeated failure of past sin tax reform efforts underscored the political challenges of advancing these reforms. Opponents argued that the reform would adversely affect the poor and domestic tobacco farmers, and trigger widespread smuggling and tax evasion. To address this, a reform coalition, backed by strong presidential leadership, needed to be mobilized in the run-up to the law's passage in 2012. Government departments came together across ministerial lines and in partnership with civil society. The "white armies" of doctors were an active and vocal front pushing for meaningful reform. Even so, the risk of failure was real, right up to the very end. In October 2012, the then chair of the Senate Finance Committee resigned amid allegations of conflict of interest when he proposed a highly watered-down draft reform proposal (Legaspi 2012). On December 11, 2012, following its passage through the House of Representatives and the bicameral committee, the Senate finally approved the bill by the narrowest of margins, 10–9.

This chapter documents the main motivation for, and final key features of, the STL. The final STL has a number of tax features that can be considered "best practice." Among them: a simplified and more transparent structure of excise taxation for cigarettes, beer, and spirits; a transition path to a unitary and inflation-adjusted single excise tax rate by 2017; and a commitment to annual public disclosure of progress in implementation. Through earmarking of revenues for health, the STL was also expected to significantly increase the short- and medium-term fiscal space for health by an estimated 0.2 percent of GDP per year—a level that after a few years of implementation it quickly exceeded. Despite the risks of budget rigidities and entitlements that lack rigorous prioritization through annual performance and prioritization review (see, for example, Bird 2015), earmarking prospective incremental revenues for health was critical for getting the STL more broad-based public support and, ultimately, getting it passed in 2012. To satisfy certain political constituencies and to allay concerns about the livelihoods of tobacco farmers, the STL retained earmarking for tobacco-growing regions. All in all, the STL needed to produce a comprehensive package that tackled cigarette, beer, and spirits tax structure, as well as generate sufficient revenues for earmarked expenditure goals. One advantage of such a broad-based package of reform principles was that it could overcome the opposition often inherent in more narrowly focused packages. Appendix A summarizes STL earmarking for tobacco-growing regions; appendix B summarizes STL earmarking for health.

Growing Pressure for Sin Tax Reform, 2010–12

For years, the tax regime suffered from shortcomings under the prevailing regulations, in place since 1997. Until the STL's imposition of a simplified two-tier structure in 2013, which is scheduled to transition to a unitary tax by 2017, excise taxes on cigarettes had multiple tiers. Lower-priced cigarettes attracted lower tax levels and reduced the price of "entry level" cigarettes, thereby undermining efforts to discourage smoking through increases in retail prices. Moreover, grandfathered rates for specific brands under special "annexes" of previous laws protected a number of incumbent producers and discouraged competition. Excise taxation was also low by global standards and not adequately indexed to inflation, causing further real erosion of sin tax revenues. Complex tax structures and fragmented oversight increased the risk of tax leakages. Figure 1.1 highlights the decline in sin tax revenues until the STL reversed the trend, and, as figure 1.2 shows, the Philippines was also a lagging international outlier in relative tobacco excise taxation.[1]

The Philippines was also under pressure to reform its alcohol tax regime, particularly for spirits, which was being challenged under WTO rules. Before the challenge, alcohol excise rates were significantly lower for spirits produced domestically with local inputs, such as the sap of nipa palm, coconut, and sugarcane.

Figure 1.1 Sin Tax Revenues, 1997–2015

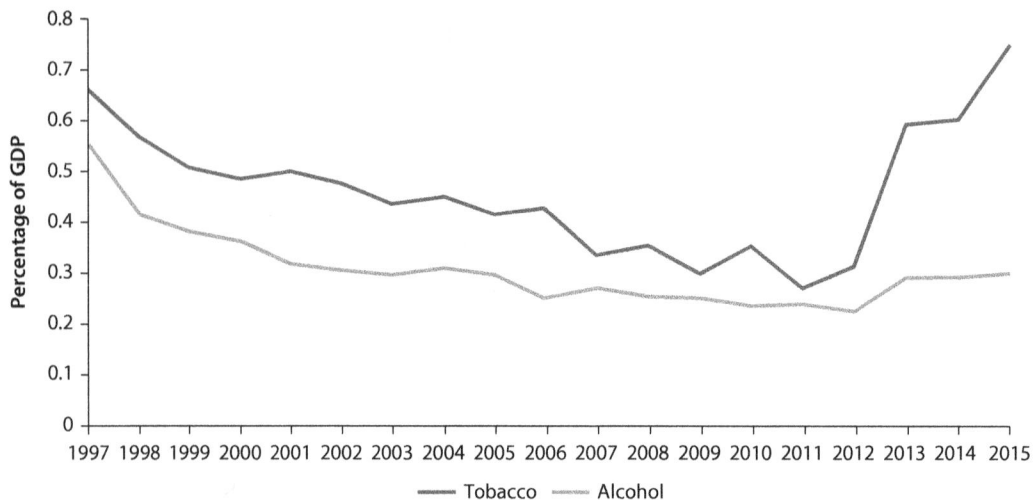

Sources: Bureau of Internal Revenue; Department of Finance.

Figure 1.2 Excise Tax as Share of Retail Sale Prices in Selected East Asian Countries, 2012

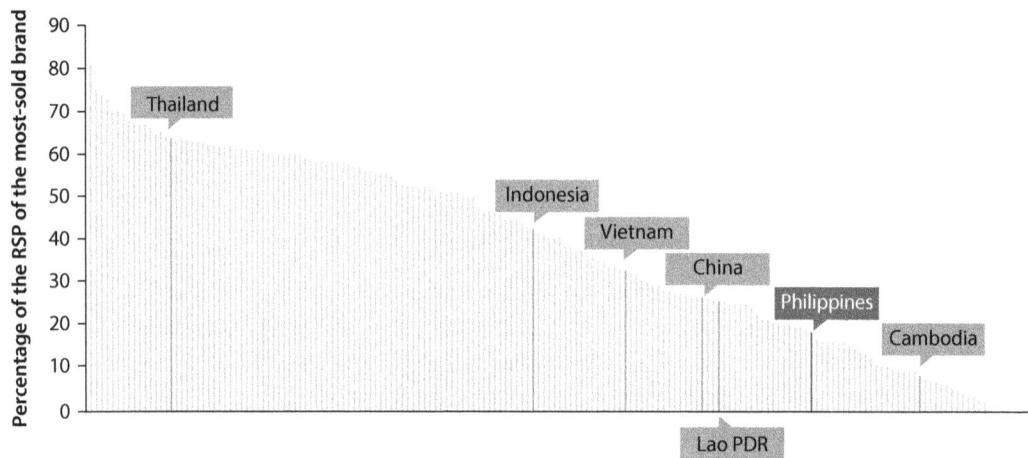

Source: WHO 2015.
Note: RSP = retail selling price.

This implied discrimination, through higher excise rates, against products produced with foreign-processed inputs and foreign products, and violated the WTO principle of equal "national treatment" under a country's laws. The prevailing alcohol tax regime also included multiple tiers, which in effect meant that lower-cost domestic spirits incurred lower tax rates than premium and more expensive international brands. Some foreign brands, to circumvent higher rates on their finished products, imported raw materials and bottled them locally to create "cheaper" and lower-taxed versions that were sold under their international brand names. The WTO ruling set deadlines for the Philippines to remove the discriminatory measures against foreign producers of distilled spirits, and this added urgency to the need for STL reform.

The Aquino administration made a commitment to scale up social investments for the poor and near-poor when it came into office in 2010. Its so-called Social Contract with the Filipino People[2] also placed a strong emphasis on measures to improve governance, especially eradicating corruption. However, the country's low tax-to-GDP ratio clearly constrained the administration's ability to deliver on its promises of social investments (World Bank 2013, 88).

The administration was also seeking an investment grade sovereign debt rating, which would help lower its borrowing costs. Its ability to push through an important tax reform would therefore be an important signal for investors seeking stability and predictability in the country's markets.

On the health side, the need for STL reform was underscored by high tobacco and alcohol consumption rates, especially compared to other countries in the region. Cigarette sales per capita had been on the increase until about 2005 and then hovered around 1,000 cigarettes per capita per year. Compared with other lower middle-income countries with a similar GDP per capita during 2009–11, such as Morocco and Mongolia, the Philippines' per capita cigarette consumption was high, as it was in regional comparators Vietnam and Indonesia (figure 1.3). When it comes to alcohol consumption, the Philippines is also an outlier; its consumption levels lie high above that of other countries with a similar GDP per capita (figure 1.4).

Figure 1.3 Cigarette Consumption versus per Capita Income in Selected Countries, 2009

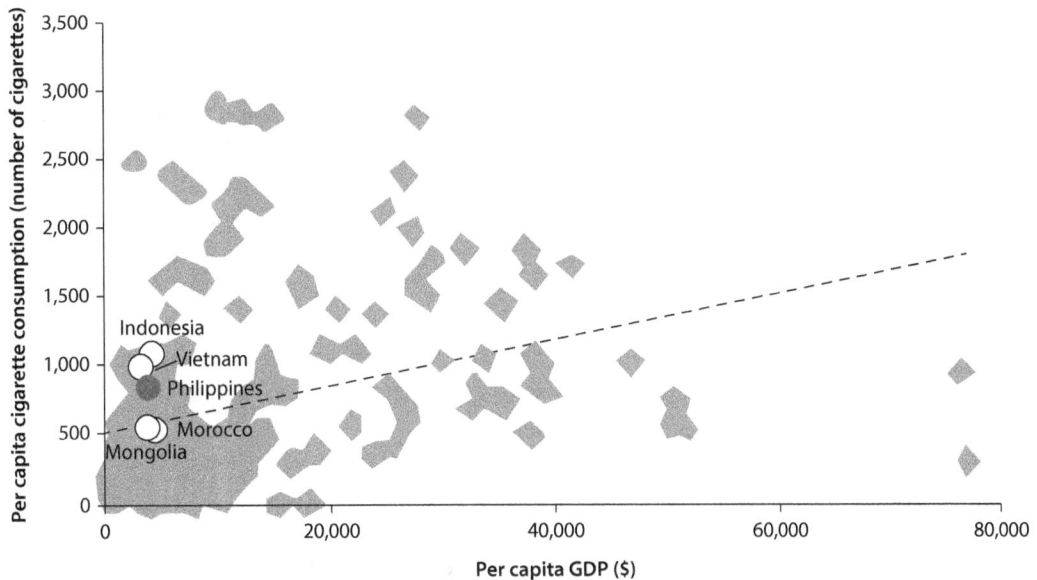

Source: Eriksen, Mackay, and Ross 2012.

Figure 1.4 Alcohol Consumption versus per Capita Income in Selected Countries, 2012

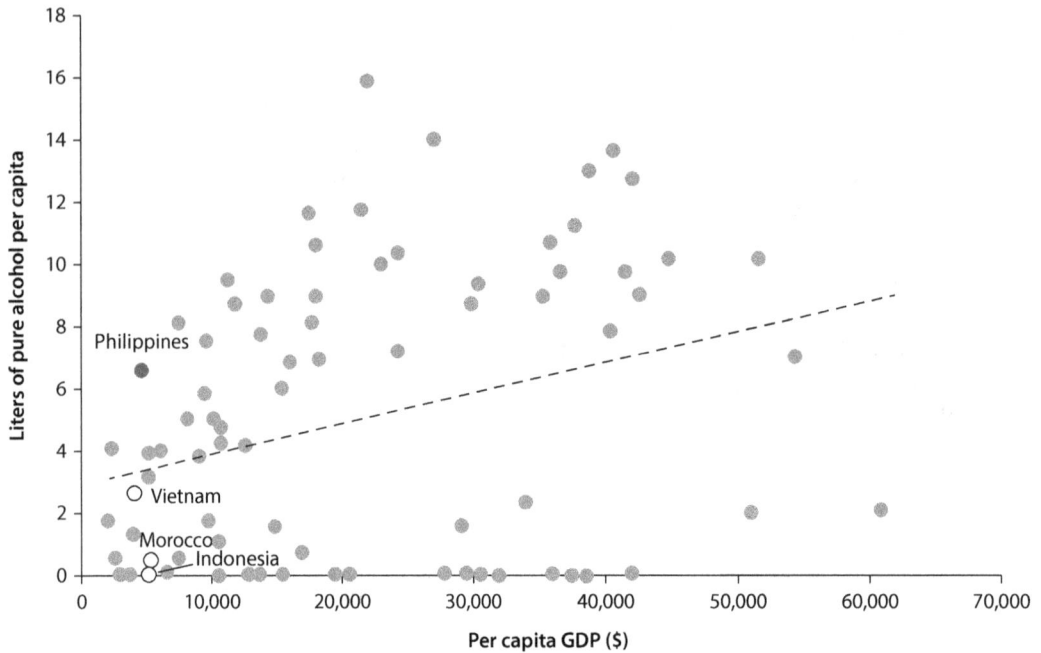

Source: WHO 2011.

Policy makers were also taking note of the growing evidence that smoking and excessive alcohol use were compromising the nation's health. Data on the burden of disease in East Asia and the Pacific show that 12 out of the 20 top diseases causing premature death and disability among Filipino males were associated with tobacco use and alcohol abuse to differing but significant degrees (World Bank and IHME 2013) (figure 1.5). In the Philippines, smoking is the second most important risk factor for disease (and the highest among men), accounting for about 9 percent of disability-adjusted life years lost. Alcohol, meanwhile, was the fifth most important risk factor, accounting for just under 5 percent of disability-adjusted life years lost. Between 1990 and 2010, the increase in the disease burden of both of these public health risk factors contrasted with the progress made in reducing the incidence of communicable diseases. The increased prevalence of diseases caused by smoking and alcohol abuse was also putting excessive financial pressure on the health system and on individual households, as these diseases require costly chronic care and can significantly limit the productivity of the adult population.

Concerns that the oligopolistic market structure for tobacco and alcohol sales in the Philippines—where only a few firms dominated the market—was becoming increasingly concentrated was a further motivation for sin tax reform. Before 2010, local firm Fortune Tobacco Corporation produced most of the

Figure 1.5 Burden of Disease Attributable to 15 Leading Risk Factors in the Philippines, 2010

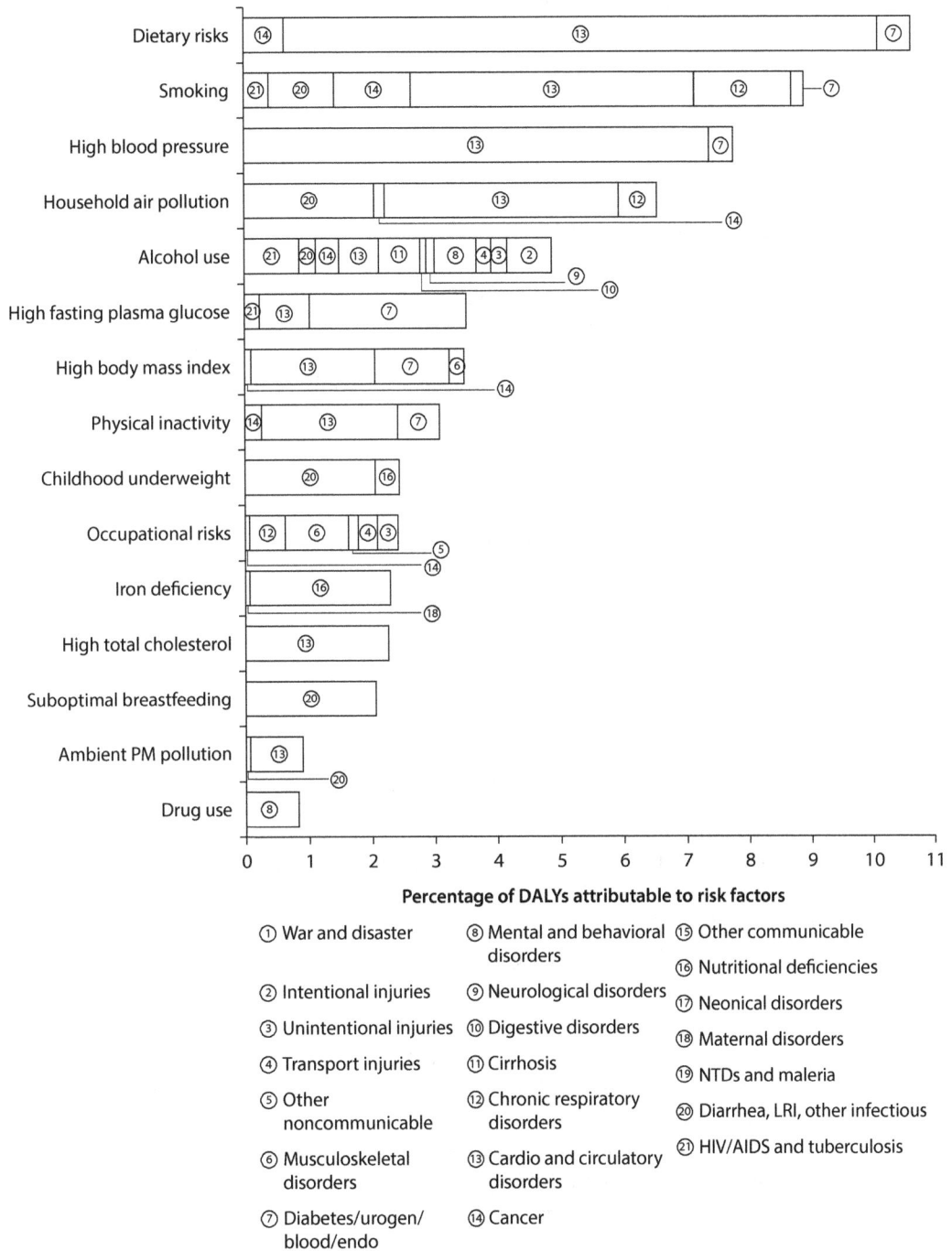

Percentage of DALYs attributable to risk factors

① War and disaster
② Intentional injuries
③ Unintentional injuries
④ Transport injuries
⑤ Other noncommunicable
⑥ Musculoskeletal disorders
⑦ Diabetes/urogen/blood/endo
⑧ Mental and behavioral disorders
⑨ Neurological disorders
⑩ Digestive disorders
⑪ Cirrhosis
⑫ Chronic respiratory disorders
⑬ Cardio and circulatory disorders
⑭ Cancer
⑮ Other communicable
⑯ Nutritional deficiencies
⑰ Neonical disorders
⑱ Maternal disorders
⑲ NTDs and maleria
⑳ Diarrhea, LRI, other infectious
㉑ HIV/AIDS and tuberculosis

Source: World Bank and IHME 2013.
Note: DALYs = disability-adjusted life years; LRI = lower respiratory tract infection; NTDs = neglected tropical diseases; PM = particulate matter.

lower-cost cigarette brands. Philip Morris International's local subsidiary Philip Morris Philippines Manufacturing made and sold the bulk of higher-end brands, including Marlboro. Some local producers, especially Fortune Tobacco, enjoyed protection under the 1997 grandfathering clauses and were taxed at lower excise rates than newer market entrants. In 2010, Fortune Tobacco and Philip Morris Philippines Manufacturing formed a joint partnership, Philip Morris Fortune Tobacco Corporation.[3] The new arrangement (inclusive of affiliated subsidiaries) accounted for over 90 percent of domestic production for the Philippine market. Other producers of lower-priced cigarettes included Mighty Corporation and La Suerte.

Tobacco production in the Philippines is for both the domestic and international markets, and both domestic and international leaves are used to make cigarettes. Factories in Batangas province, a two-hour drive south of Manila, produce most of the country's cigarettes. The bulk of domestic leaf is produced in northern Luzon, the country's largest island where Manila is located. The beer sector, meanwhile, is dominated by San Miguel Corporation, followed by Asia Breweries at a distant second. San Miguel is also the main spirits producer (for example, San Miguel Gin).

The impetus for the sin tax reform was also connected to regional taxation trends. For tobacco and alcohol, countries in East Asia had recently seen a wave of reforms intended to tax products in a way that increase revenues and provide positive public health outcomes, in line with global trends. Box 1.1 provides an overview of approaches that have been taken in the region to increase and reform excise taxation on tobacco and alcohol products.

Sin Tax Reform Involved Difficult Policy Choices

It is clear that the declining real revenue receipts (figure 1.1) associated with the prevailing sin tax structure were harming the government's fiscal position. However, the Aquino administration had promised not to introduce any new taxes until all efforts to improve expenditure efficiency and tax administration were exhausted. Consequently, tax reform advocates had to be careful that the STL was not perceived as a new tax, and they were successful in casting it as a remedy for the tax regime's growing problems.

Reform advocates were also successful in framing the STL as a much-needed health measure. As well as a policy that would be effective in directly reducing the harmful health effects of smoking and excessive drinking by making prices higher and curbing demand, sin tax reform was sold as a way to finance a major expansion of universal health care, especially subsidized health insurance through the Philippines Health Insurance Corporation (PhilHealth). Specifically, the national government promised to use sin tax revenues to fully fund the health insurance coverage of the bottom 40 percent of the population, expanding national subsidies for health insurance well beyond the 5.2 million families that it was financing at that time. The financing gap was estimated to be, at minimum, equivalent to 0.3 percent of GDP annually.

Box 1.1 Sin Tax Trends in East Asia at the Time of the Sin Tax Law

In East Asia, tobacco and alcohol are taxed on either an ad valorem or a specific rate basis—and, in some cases, a composite of ad valorem and specific rates. Specific rates can be based on either volume of a particular spirit, or the product's volume of alcohol. The latter would mean that higher proof spirits attract a higher excise by liter.

For tobacco, specific rates are set per gram, per kilogram, per cigarette, or per pack. Generally, less-developed economies in the region apply their excise taxes on an ad valorem basis, and the more developed ones apply specific-rate taxation. A number of economies in transition use a mix of ad valorem and specific rates. The reason that ad valorem rates, which are generally considered progressive taxes, are often preferred in least-developed economies is that they allow for a range of affordable products to be available to all income groups and capture greater revenues from premium-end products consumed by the more affluent. However, specific taxation is the "optimal" for tobacco and alcohol taxation because it treats all products of equal harm equally, rather than taxing equivalent to value. The use of a composite of specific and ad valorem rates is, thus, often a transitional policy to move excise systems from the taxation of value to the taxation of harm.

In several countries, an additional feature of the excise system is the use of some type of earmarking of tobacco and alcohol revenues, often for the purposes of health promotion.

Where economies use ad valorem excise taxation, a range of tax bases are used. Ex-factory (or cost, insurance, and freight plus import duties for like imports) is the most common, though Thailand uses the "last wholesale" price. The Philippines, meanwhile, bases the value component on "net retail" price (that is, sales price excluding value added tax and excise), as set by the Bureau of Internal Revenue based on a retail outlet survey. Retail prices are also used for classification purposes in Indonesia and the Philippines.

Most East Asian countries now levy a general value added tax on cigarettes, beer, and tobacco. Indicative rates range from 7 percent in Thailand to 16 percent in Myanmar; the Philippines falls roughly at the midpoint at 12 percent. Excise taxes vary both in structure and level across the region. Before the Sin Tax Law's passage, tax tiers in the Philippines ranged from a single tier to four or more. Only a few countries in the region have converged to unitary tax tiers, as the Philippines will. Cambodia, the Lao People's Democratic Republic, Malaysia, Myanmar, Thailand, and Vietnam all levy ad valorem rates on cigarettes. A concern about ad valorem rates is that they are more demanding from an administrative standpoint and require more accurate measurement of the base than specific taxes. Indonesia, the Philippines, and Singapore all restrict cigarette taxation to specific excise taxes; Malaysia maintains a hybrid system.

Customs duties vary significantly across East Asia. Most countries impose customs duties on a cost, insurance, and freight basis. The Association of Southeast Asian Nations (ASEAN) has long had a free trade agreement within the region even before the ASEAN Economic Community came into effect at the end of 2015. With integration, intraregional alcohol and tobacco trade tariffs should be reduced to zero, although some countries including Malaysia have placed alcohol and tobacco on a "sensitive list" where tariffs will remain. Within ASEAN,

box continues next page

Box 1.1 Sin Tax Trends in East Asia at the Time of the Sin Tax Law *(continued)*

the so-called CLMV countries (Cambodia, Lao PDR, Myanmar, Vietnam) will be able to keep import tariffs on alcohol and tobacco until 2018.

Like in the Philippines, trade disputes have triggered sin tax reforms in a number of countries. This was the case for tobacco in Thailand, and is also a potential issue for wine and distilled spirits in Indonesia and Thailand.

A number of important sin tax reforms have been undertaken in the region in recent years. China increased taxes on high-strength alcohol in 2009, and Indonesia significantly increased taxes on alcohol in 2009 and 2013. Thailand completely restructured alcohol taxation in 2013. But the Philippines stands out because of its significant structural change in cigarette, beer, and spirits taxes, as much as for its tax rate changes.

A further choice for how these taxes are used involves the extent of earmarking for health or other programs, such as farmers' livelihood initiatives. Indonesia for example, allocates 2 percent of revenues to health, assigned to local governments by location of collection. The Republic of Korea provides for hard earmarking of alcohol taxes to education; Thailand allocates alcohol and tobacco taxes to health, local provincial management, and public TV broadcasting.

Because the STL had to address both revenue and health concerns, the key policy choices in excise tax design were even more difficult than would ordinarily have been the case and involved trade-offs. To maximize revenues and also achieve health objectives, the key tax design decisions were (1) whether to opt for specific or ad valorem taxes, or a hybrid of both; (2) which rates to apply; and (3) whether to retain multiple tax tiers. Given the structural distortions and low starting tax rates, it was also clear that any increases would need to be phased in, thus raising the issue of how to design a transition path. The issue of equitable "burden sharing" of tax increases across the alcohol and tobacco industries also featured prominently in the STL debates.

For tobacco, setting minimum and unitary specific tax rates was attractive to decision makers. Multiple tiers, with lower taxes on cheaper brands, create an incentive for producers to downshift their products to lower-taxed tiers; meaning, in effect, that the lowest tier of excise taxation would define the cheapest cigarette in the country. Multiple tiers would also encourage smoking by lowering the price of entry-level cigarettes for new (and especially young) smokers and/or blunt the effect of tax increases by creating an opportunity for price-sensitive smokers to continue the habit at the same intensity by switching from more expensive to cheaper brands. A unitary tax structure, however, would in effect put a "floor price" on cigarettes. Health priorities, therefore, were a good argument for streamlining the four existing rates, as well eliminating the grandfathered rates, while moving to a higher uniform excise tax rate for all cigarettes.

For alcohol, the objective was a minimum price through a specific excise rate, but the debates on this recognized that not all products are the same—including with regard to alcohol content and market segment, both of which have important health and equity implications. Given how widespread beer consumption is, beer tax increases would provide a solid revenue base because modest tax increases could be easily absorbed by producers and consumers alike without reducing consumption. For spirits, which range dramatically in quality, price, and market segments, a hybrid specific plus ad valorem structure was introduced. The specific component provided a "floor price" for alcohol; the ad valorem component ensured higher revenues from premium brands. The hybrid was calibrated to consider the nature of the existing mass domestic market, which would not be able to tolerate an increase beyond a certain threshold, and ensuring there were no net revenue losses from premium imported brands. Other Southeast Asian countries around that time had also implemented mixed excise tax schemes for alcohol around that time (see box 1.2). Despite the added difficulty of ad valorem tax administration (because it requires price estimates for all products), these taxes were seen as a good way to generate more revenues from premium or luxury brands. A uniform excise tax for spirits (which have, by far, the lowest unit price of any alcohol in the Philippines by alcohol volume) coupled with an ad valorem rate also appeared to respond adequately to the WTO challenge.

STL opponents argued that increasing cigarette taxes would adversely affect domestic tobacco producers. The earmarking of a share of tobacco tax revenues for tobacco-growing regions had already been a long-standing practice in the Philippines, largely to address this concern. The preexisting legal framework allowed for a share of cigarette revenues (up to 15 percent) produced by particular types of leaf (Burley and Virginia) to be allocated to tobacco-growing regions, especially in the northern part of the country. Over the years, questions had been raised about the transparency and accountability of these funds. Even so, removing or reducing earmarking for farming regions was not a political option.

STL opponents also voiced concerns that the poorest would suffer the most from the tax increases, and used this to argue that tax increases on the lowest-priced and lowest-taxed brands should be limited. It was also pointed out that one possible response of consumers at the cheapest end of the market might be to shift to informal (or "homebrewed" or home-produced) sin products, which could have higher potential health risks than manufactured products. However, STL proponents countered that the public health gains of reduced consumption, coupled with free health insurance for the poor and near poor, would offset the potentially regressive effect on households of increased taxes on cheap cigarettes and alcohol.

The design and implementation arrangements of the STL reform needed to be both technically sound and politically viable. Table 1.1 summarizes the key issues, objectives, prevailing tax structure, and the STL's final features. The law's architects needed to simultaneously address issues related to the taxation of cigarettes, beer, and spirits; domestic revenue mobilization; import and customs

---

Box 1.2 Examples of Recent Tax Reforms in East Asia and the Pacific

Significant structural reforms of tobacco and alcohol tax systems have been undertaken in East Asia and the Pacific since 2012, with most countries increasing tobacco and alcohol tax rates. Some of these changes include:

Thailand (2013): Undertook structural reforms of all alcohol taxation, moving from the "greater of an ex-factory ad valorem calculation and a specific rate calculation" to a mixed system in which an ad valorem component is calculated against a "last whole price" and a specific rate comprising the greater of "per liter" or "per liter of alcohol" rate. The Thai reforms also included the introduction of a "high-strength alcohol" surcharge on products with alcohol strengths exceeding 45 percent alcohol per volume (spirits), 40 percent (white spirits), 15 percent (wine), and 7 percent (beer). For distilled spirits, the tax structure was simplified from four categories to two. For wine, the category was "split" into products above and below a "last wholesale price" of B 600 ($18) per bottle.

Indonesia (2012 and 2014): In 2012, the tobacco tariff moved from a 19-tier value/factory capacity method of production structure to a 15-tier one, still based on value, capacity, and whether products were produced by machine or by hand. The restructuring was accompanied by an increase of 9–15 percent in excise rates. In 2014, a 10 percent tax earmarked for distribution to the regions was implemented. The same year saw increases in alcohol excise rates of 15 percent for beer, 10 percent for wine, and 6 percent for distilled spirits.

Solomon Islands (2013): A restructuring of alcohol tax created a three-tier tariff based on alcohol strength, with tiers set at up to 7 percent alcohol per volume, 7–14 percent, and above 14 percent. The reform also removed discrimination against imported alcohol, which had been taxed higher than domestically produced alcohol.

Brunei Darussalam (2011): Increase of 339 percent in tobacco excise duties from B$56.90 ($42) per thousand cigarettes to B$250 ($185) per thousand cigarettes.

General tobacco and alcohol tax increases: All countries in East Asia and the Pacific have increased tobacco and alcohol taxes—ranging 10–25 percent—in recent years except for the Republic of Korea, Lao People's Democratic Republic, and Timor-Leste. Australia is particularly noteworthy: it made two significant increases to tobacco excise—25 percent in 2010, followed by 50 percent in four annual installments of 12.5 percent, the first being in December 2013. These increases are in addition to the biannual indexation of tobacco excise rates which, beginning March 2014, was based on average weekly ordinary time earnings to prevent tobacco becoming more affordable over time.

---

duty reform; expenditure earmarks; implementation capabilities; governance concerns; and effective monitoring and evaluation mechanisms.

The Final 2012 Sin Tax Law

The final STL was responsive to both the health and revenue objectives pursued during the reform process. The law mandated a single excise rate for all cigarettes of ₱30 per pack by 2017, which will subsequently be adjusted by an annual

Table 1.1 Reform Objectives and Final Features of the Sin Tax Law

Key issue	Key objectives	Starting point	Final Sin Tax Bill
Structure and level of cigarette taxation	Reduce the prevalence of smoking by reducing affordability. Raise revenues to expand universal health care for which an annual financing gap of a minimum 0.3 percent of GDP (approximately ₱34 billion or $791 million) was estimated. Ensure acceptable "burden-sharing" of tax increases across tobacco and alcohol industries.	Four tiers of taxation, grandfathered rates for incumbent producers, lack of inflation indexation.	Lowest tier at ₱12 ($0.28) per pack in 2013; unitary tier by 2017 at ₱30 ($0.70). Rates adjusted by 4 percent annually afterward. From 2013 to 2016, tobacco expected to contribute on average 67.3 percent of the projected incremental revenue, with 17.4 percent from beer and 15.3 percent from spirits.
Structure and levels of beer taxation	Decrease excessive and youth drinking. Raise revenues for universal health care.	Multitiered structure with relatively low rates.	Higher and simplified rates for beer. ₱15 ($0.35) and ₱20 ($0.46) per liter with cut-off at ₱50.6 ($1.18) in 2013. Unitary tier at ₱23.5 ($0.55) in 2017. Rates adjusted by 4 percent annually afterward.
Structure and levels of spirits taxation	Ensure World Trade Organization compliance. Decrease excessive and youth drinking. Raise revenues for universal health care.	Differential treatment for spirits based on local content of raw materials. Price classifications de facto discriminated against imported brands.	Mixed ad valorem and specific tax. Specific tax ₱20/15 percent ad valorem for 2013; specific tax ₱20/20 percent ad valorem for 2015; specific tax indexed by 4 percent annually afterward.
Design and implementation of special tax and customs administration measures	Mitigation of smuggling and tax evasion risks for revenue and health (owing to potentially lower retail prices).	Growing concerns about tax and customs revenues leakages.	Simplified tax structure, coupled with proactive tax administration and oversight measures, including tax stamps.
Earmarking of revenues to health	Scale up the universal health care program. Reduce the financing gap for health.	No significant health earmarking.	Substantial incremental earmarked funds for universal health care (85 percent of incremental revenue).
Earmarking of revenues to tobacco-producing regions and affected areas	Ensure transfers to tobacco-producing regions have maximum impact on farmers' livelihoods, considering 15 percent of particular crop revenues were historically earmarked.	Historic earmarking of tobacco excise revenues by type of leaf and area of production (15 percent of tobacco revenues).	Additional incremental revenues, based on historical shares (about 15 percent of incremental).
Implementation and monitoring	Timely, evidence-based monitoring and assessment of sin tax implementation to ensure transparency and good governance. Take timely action to mitigate risk and ensure that health goals are met, integrity of revenue use, and that producers comply with the tax law.	Limited monitoring as part of mainstream systems and congressional oversight of tobacco revenue earmarking for producing.	Detailed implementing rules and regulations and the requirement of an annual review process, including reporting on utilization of earmarked funds.

Source: Republic Act 10351 and associated implementing rules and regulations.

increase of 4 percent to account for inflation (see figure 1.6). Immediately in the first year of the reform (that is, 2013), the tax structure would be reduced from four to two tiers and the rates for some of the lowest-tax cigarettes would increase from ₱2.72 ($0.06) to ₱12 ($0.28) per pack, a very low rate, which had been locked in under special provisions in the old law, to ₱12. This in effect meant that excise incidence would, on average, be 61.1 percent of the retail price in 2016, with 65 percent for low-end cigarettes and 57 percent for mid- and upper-range ones. This would put the Philippines in the second quartile of countries covered in figure 1.2.

For beer, the reform settled on two excise rates; figure 1.7 shows projected excise taxes until 2018 for beer and fermented liquor. For spirits, the reform introduced a single excise rate to be adjusted for inflation, plus an ad valorem rate (see figure 1.8). The new structure significantly simplified the previous excise structure. It also countered the charges of discrimination in the WTO's challenge against the Philippines regarding discriminatory taxation of higher-priced foreign spirits.

The STL also stipulated that progress on its implementation would be formally reviewed in 2016, and that a set of implementing rules and regulations be issued to define the administrative provisions that would make the law effective in practice (see chapter 2). The STL's tax and administrative provisions are summarized in table 1.2.

The STL maintained prevailing revenue earmarks for tobacco-producing regions. Republic Acts (RA) 7171 (1992) and 8240 (1996) promulgated the earmarking of tobacco excise revenues to support tobacco-growing regions, providing

Figure 1.6 Excise Taxation on Cigarettes, 2013–18

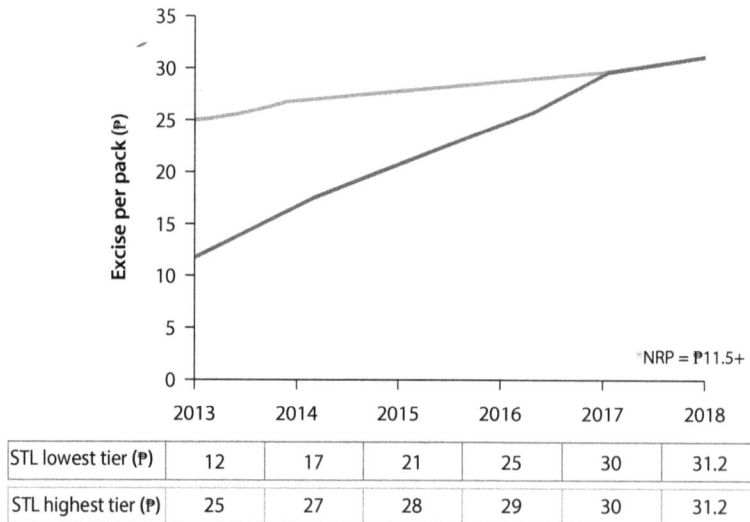

	2013	2014	2015	2016	2017	2018
STL lowest tier (₱)	12	17	21	25	30	31.2
STL highest tier (₱)	25	27	28	29	30	31.2

Source: Republic Act 10351.
Note: NRP = net retail price; STL = Sin Tax Law.

Figure 1.7 Excise Taxation on Beer and Fermented Liquors, 2013–18

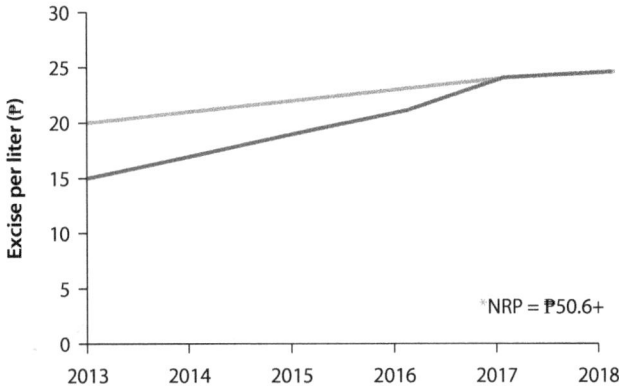

NRP = ₱50.6+

	2013	2014	2015	2016	2017	2018
STL Low (₱)	15	17	19	21	23.5	24.4
STL High (₱)	20	21	22	23	23.5	24.4

Source: Republic Act 10351.
Note: NRP = net retail price; STL = Sin Tax Law.

Figure 1.8 Excise Taxation on Spirits, 2013–18

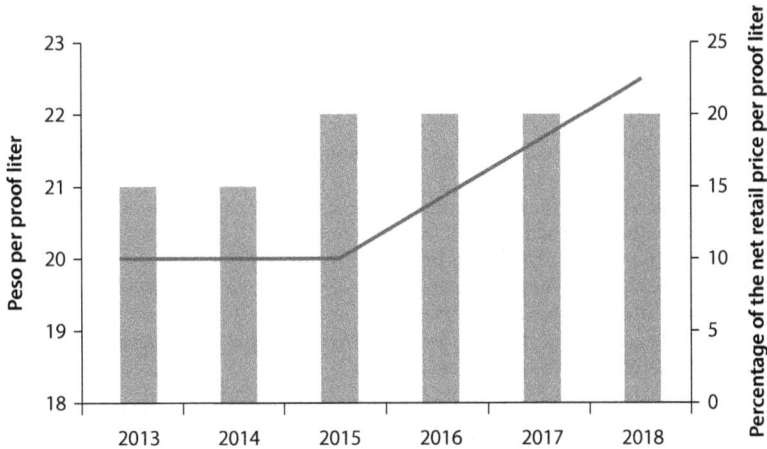

	2013	2014	2015	2016	2017	2018
AV	15%	15%	20%	20%	20%	20%
ST (₱)	20	20	20	20.80	21.63	22.50

Source: Republic Act 10351.
Note: AV = ad valorem; ST = specific tax.

15 percent of total excise tax revenues from locally produced Virginia-type ciga-rettes to Virginia-growing regions under RA 7171, and 15 percent of the incre-mental revenue under RA 8240 to Burley- and Native-producing regions. These revenues are allocated to local government units to spend for the benefit of tobacco farmers. This earmarking remains in place under the STL, but with a small shift in the types of projects that can be funded from those supporting

Table 1.2 Administrative Provisions of the Sin Tax Law

Provision	Machine-rolled cigarettes (20 per pack)	Fermented beverages/beer (specific tax, per volume liter)	Distilled spirits (ad valorem and specific, per proof liter)
Tax tiers	2013–16: Two tiers with low-tier net retail price maximum of ₱12 ($0.27) per pack. 2017 onward: no tiers.	2013–16: Two tiers with low-tier net retail price maximum of ₱50.6 ($1.20), per volume liter. 2017 onward: no tiers.	No tiers.
Rates, see:	Figure 1.6	Figure 1.7	Figure 1.8
Long-term indexation	2018 onward: specific tax increased 4 percent annually.	2018 onward: specific tax increased 4 percent annually.	2016 onward: specific tax increased 4 percent annually.
Other products	Cigars: ad valorem tax of 20 percent and specific tax of ₱5 per cigar, increasing 4 percent annually from 2014. Hand-rolled cigarettes: same as machine-rolled lower tier, with specific tax of ₱12 per pack in 2013, increasing to ₱30 ($0.70) per pack by 2017, and 4 percent annual increases from 2018. Chewing tobacco/other tobacco consumables: ₱1.5/1.75 ($0.03/0.04) per kilogram, and 4 percent annual increases from 2014. Microbrews/restaurant brewers: ₱28 ($0.65) per liter, with 4 percent increases from 2014. Still wine: two tiers with cut-off at 14 percent alcohol by volume; specific ₱30 ($0.70) for lower tier and ₱60 ($1.39) for higher tier, with 4 percent increases from 2014, and tax classification every two years. Carbonated wine: two-tier tax with cut-off at ₱500 retail price; specific ₱250 ($5.80) for lower tier and ₱700 for higher tier, with 4 percent increases from 2014, and tax classification every two years. Fortified wine: more than 25 percent alcohol by volume to be taxed as distilled spirits.		
Domestic sourcing	For cigarettes sold domestically, manufacturers and sellers required to buy at least 15 percent of tobacco inputs from Philippine producers "subject to adjustments based on international treaty commitments."		
Key administrative measures specified in the Sin Tax Law	Net retail price surveys: conducted annually by the Bureau of Internal Revenue with methodology subject to congressional oversight and review; separate surveys set for Metro Manila and other regions. Producer sworn statements of sales: due quarterly; strong potential fines and sentencing for understatement and other violations. New products: same tax treatment as existing products; net retail price validated by the Bureau of Internal Revenue at three and nine months after introduction. Beer: no downward reclassification across tiers. Bonding: various bond measures to discourage diversion of tobacco for exported products clarified; bonding of alcohol imports not mentioned. Tax labeling: "Adequate security features" are required for printing of stamps, labels, and other markings for alcohol and tobacco products. Automated volume counters: now required at packing/bottling locations.		

Source: Republic Act 10351 and associated implementing rules and regulations.

production techniques to also include other livelihood measures, such as investments in alternative crops, social infrastructure, and tourism development.

The balance of incremental STL revenues, net of earmarks for tobacco-growing regions, goes to health. Of total incremental revenues, 80 percent goes to scaling up the National Health Insurance Program (to cover the health insurance subsidies of the poor and near-poor), attaining Millennium Development Goals, and health awareness programs. The allocation to health insurance is accompanied by the requirement that subsidized premiums are allocated only to those households that have been identified as poor by the National Household Targeting System for Poverty Reduction of the Department of Social Welfare and Development, thus improving the targeting of the poor and avoiding the risk of corruption inherent in the previous system of insurance targeting, which was at the discretion of local governments. The remaining 20 percent is allocated to the Department of Health's (DOH) Medical Assistance Program, which are funds placed in hospitals to cover the medical costs of those who cannot afford to pay, and the DOH's Health Facilities Enhancement Program, which funds the construction and renovation of health facilities in underserved areas. The share of funds allocated to each of these programs is determined by the DOH as part of the annual planning and budgeting process.

Table 1.3 summarizes the main earmarking provisions, and table 1.4 summarizes the agencies responsible for them and estimated amounts involved.

Table 1.3 Sin Tax Law Earmarking

Provision	Tobacco farmer protection	Universal health care	Other health
Tax earmark	15 percent of incremental revenues of domestic Virginia cigarette production for Virginia tobacco regions, per Republic Act (RA) 7171 (1992); 15 percent of incremental revenues of Burley and Native production, in line with RA 8240 (1996) for Burley and Native tobacco-producing regions.	80 percent of balance of incremental revenues from RA 10351 after RA 8240 and RA 7171 deductions.	20 percent of balance of incremental revenues from RA 10351 after RA 8240 and RA 7171 deductions.
Listed potential projects	• Inputs and training for production shifts for farmers • Financial support for displaced farmers • Cooperative programs for farmers, alternative crops, and livelihoods • Tourism programs in tobacco-producing regions • Infrastructure projects • Agro-industrial projects incorporating farmer ownership and management	• National Health Insurance Program (PhilHealth), specifically transfers for premiums of indigents • Various programs related to attaining the Millennium Development Goals • Various health awareness programs	• Medical Assistance Program • Health Facilities Enhancement Program
Follow-on actions	Department of Budget and Management (DBM) and Department of Agriculture (DA) have 180 days to issue implementing rules and regulations (IRRs) on allocating and disbursing funds.	The Secretary of Finance, in consultation with DOH, must promulgate IRRs within 180 days.	The Secretary of Finance, in consultation with DOH, must promulgate IRRs within 180 days.
	DBM and DA must submit to the Congressional Oversight Committee a detailed annual report on use of funds.	DOH and PhilHealth must submit to the Congressional Oversight Committee a detailed annual report on use of funds.	DOH and PhilHealth must submit to the Congressional Oversight Committee a detailed annual report on use of funds.

table continues next page

Table 1.3 Sin Tax Law Earmarking *(continued)*

Provision	Tobacco farmer protection	Universal health care	Other health
Key implementation concerns	The baseline for determining "incremental revenues" was unclear under RA 7171 and RA 8240, and fund distribution was delayed. New rules and regulations should include clear calculations and tracking measures. Eligible projects will need close monitoring at national and local levels to ensure funds are used effectively.	The baseline for determining incremental revenues under RA 10351 needed to be clarified and tracking measures put in place. Eligible programs will need close monitoring at national and local levels to ensure funds are used effectively, especially as DOH programs supported by RA 10351 are broadly specified and also covered by existing/other budget allocations.	
Transitory provision for displaced workers	Special provision for unemployment alleviation program and training and retooling programs for displaced workers in the alcohol and tobacco industry to be funded by the general annual budgets for 2014–17 to the Department of Labor and Employment (DOLE) and the Technical Education and Skills Development Authority (TESDA).		
Congressional Oversight Committee	Composition of committee per RA 8240: the chairpersons of the agriculture and health committees of the House of Representatives and Senate shall be included as part of the four members to be appointed from each House. 2016 impact review: the committee is mandated to conduct an impact review of the revised taxes, but the procedures for review are not specified.		

Source: Republic Act 10351 and associated implementing rules and regulations.
Note: DOH = Department of Health.

Table 1.4 Sin Tax Law Expenditure Earmarks

Earmark	Responsible agency	Legal statute	Estimated amounts
1 Farmers and potential industry displacement			
a Allocations to Burley and Native tobacco-producing regions	LGUs	Sec. 8, 288 (B)/(C)	15 percent incremental
b Allocations of 15 percent Virginia	LGUs	Internal Revenue Code Amended, p. 25	15 percent total Virginia production (estimated ₱6 billion) for farmers or 15 percent of incremental
c Displaced workers	DOLE		₱0.75 billion ($17 million)
d Training	TESDA		₱0.25 billion ($5.8 million)
2 Health			
a Health insurance premiums	PhilHealth	Section 10, 289 (B) Internal	₱23 billion ($534.9 million) per year for four years
b LGU district hospitals	DOH	Revenue Code Amended, p. 27	₱0.618 billion ($14.4 million) (618*₱10 million)
c Regional hospitals	DOH		₱3.8 billion ($88.4 million) (16+22*₱100 million)
d Information campaign	DOH		₱0.1 billion ($2.3 million)
Total	₱34.5 billion ($803 million)		

Note: Internal Revenue Code section 8, 288, adopts a more general provision, which is inconsistent with section 10, 289. DOH = Department of Health; DOLE = Department of Labor and Employment; LGU = local government unit; TESDA = Technical Education and Skills Development Authority. The estimated amounts are based on Bureau of Internal Revenue's overall projections of incremental revenues from the sin tax, and consequently the expected budget earmarks.

The STL's implementing rules and regulations (IRRs) provide a solid foundation for accountability in sin tax implementation.[4] Shortly after its passage, the Bureau of Internal Revenue issued the STL-mandated Revenue Regulation No. 17-2012 on the tax rates, tiers, and guidelines for calculating sin tax revenues. Revenue Memorandum Order No. 17-2013, issued in June 2013, further redefined alphanumeric tax codes to facilitate the identification and monitoring of excise tax payments. Revenue Memorandum Circular (RMC) No. 90-2012, issued in December 2012, revised the tax rates of alcohol and tobacco products. RMC No. 3-2013 clarified certain provisions of Revenue Regulation No. 17-2012, and RMC No. 90-2012 provided the initial tax classifications of tobacco and alcohol products. RMC No. 18-2013 further clarified the taxability of distilled spirits. The issuance of the IRRs for RA 10351 on the earmarking and expenditure provisions, Joint Circular No. 001-2014, followed in 2014. The affixture of internal revenue stamps on imported and locally manufactured cigarettes, and the use of the Internal Revenue Stamps Integrated System, was prescribed on the issuance of Revenue Regulation No. 7-2014 in July 2014.

The IRRs, and in particular the expenditure and earmarking IRRs, contain a number of measures intended to ensure good governance. First, they clearly define the roles and responsibilities of different agencies and parties in implementation, including clear reporting deadlines for funds used by recipient local government units. Second, because they are jointly issued by the five government agencies tasked with implementation at the central government level, they reinforce the fact that the STL was the outcome of a multiagency coalition and cement that coalition for the future. And third, they explicitly recognize the participation and contribution of civil society organizations in promoting the STL and monitoring compliance with its implementing rules and regulations.

Conclusion

In designing and promoting the STL, the choices faced by policy makers were complex. The key challenge was to set tax rates at a level that would both be a deterrent to smoking and also generate sufficient revenues to fill the financing gap for universal health coverage. The debates were also informed by (1) what middle-income countries in the region and globally were doing; (2) technical analysis from various health, revenue, and equity vantage points; and (3) the "real" political economy of crafting a reform package that could be successfully pushed through the House of Representatives and Senate.

The reform process also highlighted the role that international trade agreements and disputes are increasingly playing in domestic tax design. The WTO challenge on spirits imposed a clear timeline—and deadline—for reform. At the same time, it raised interesting debates about the health rationale for excise taxation of cigarettes compared to alcohol, such as the relative importance from a health perspective of quitting smoking versus curbing excessive drinking, which informed the relative levels of the final tax rates. The debate also reminded us of what a good potential revenue source beer, spirits, and tobacco can be, particularly for developing countries with less-diversified tax bases.

Today, after more than three years of implementation and with less than a year to go until the transition to unitary tax rates is completed, the STL appears to have been largely successful. It is no longer possible to buy a cigarette for less than one peso (and the average cigarette price is more than double that), revenues have exceeded expectations, 15.3 million poor and near-poor families have free health insurance, and smoking rates are down. The importance of effective implementation as a litmus test of the Aquino administration's commitment to good governance cannot be overstated.

The Philippines' larger tax system is not without its challenges, with myriad exemptions and administrative weaknesses, and it is possible that effective STL implementation could provide impetus for broader tax reform. Indeed, the push for a simpler and more transparent STL was also motivated by a desire to more broadly improve economic governance and create a level playing field for all industries. The fact that the STL could succeed may well be both an example of a desire for more broad-based tax reform and an encouragement to pursue these much-needed reforms.

Some of the lessons of the STL reform that could be applicable to other areas of tax reform areas include the importance of starting early with key reform principles that can be broadly agreed to by all parties, and leveraging technical work to advance an outcome that serves the public interest and is pragmatic about political realities. This is discussed further in chapter 2, which provides an in-depth analysis of the policy choices made during the sin tax reform, including by comparing the final law with the earlier bills passed by the House of Representatives and Senate, and highlights how technical policy and political analysis needed to come together to generate a viable reform package.

Essential to successful STL implementation will be vigilant monitoring and analysis. The STL spans dimensions of both tax reform (related to cigarettes, beer, and spirits) and expenditure reform (including earmarking for health and tobacco-producing areas). Implementation failures in any of these areas would place future sin tax increases and restructuring at risk, and also provide detractors with an argument against other needed tax reforms. The Philippines has many examples of reforms that stalled or became ineffective because of weak administration, or were undermined by vested interests or corruption.

The STL's implementation can and must be different—and government also needs to be able to demonstrate that it is so. To this end, chapter 3 sets out a robust, multivariate framework for monitoring its implementation. The framework is intended to assist in improving the implementation of STL reform, and so protect it for the future, as well as to provide a guide to policy makers and stakeholders in other countries interested in advancing—and monitoring—similar tax and health policy reforms.

Notes

1. For wider treatment of the need for comprehensive tax reform in the Philippines, see Nakayama, Mansour, and Mullins (2012, 69) and World Bank (2011).
2. For more details of the social contract, see http://www.gov.ph/about/gov/exec/bsaiii /platform-of-government/.
3. Fortune Tobacco and Philip Morris Philippines Manufacturing continue to retain affiliated operations for certain assets in addition to Philip Morris Fortune Tobacco. See http://www.pmi.com/marketpages/pages/market_en_ph.aspx?pageNumber=1.
4. Most laws in the Philippines require following implementing rules and regulations (IRRs). These specify operational details of the laws, or clarify issues that emerge in their subsequent application. The STL required a series of IRRs concerning both tax and earmarking/disbursement aspects.

References

Bird, R. 2015. "Tobacco and Alcohol Excise Taxes for Public Health Financing: Marrying Sin and Virtue?" Policy Working Paper 7500, World Bank, Washington, DC.

Eriksen, Michael, Judith Mackay, and Hana Ross. 2012. *The Tobacco Atlas, Fourth Edition*. Atlanta, Georgia and New York: American Cancer Society and World Lung Foundation. Also available at http://www.TobaccoAtlas.org.

Legaspi A. 2012. "Sen. Recto Resigns as Panel Chair amid Charges of Conflict of Interest on Sin Tax Bill." GMA News Online, October 15. http://www.gmanetwork.com /news/story/278344/economy/finance/sen-recto-resigns-as-panel-chair-amid-charges -of-conflict-of-interest-on-sin-tax-bill.

Nakayama, K., M. Mansour, and P. Mullins. 2012. "The Philippines: Tax Policy at a Cross-Roads." Country Report 12/60, International Monetary Fund, Washington, DC. http:// www.imf.org/external/pubs/ft/scr/2012/cr1260.pdf.

World Bank. 2011. "Raising Excise Taxes on Tobacco and Alcohol Products (Special Focus 1). Manila, In Sustaining Growth in Uncertain Times." *Philippines Economic Quarterly* (December). http://www.worldbank.org/en/news/press-release/2011/12 /20/philippines-structural-reforms-needed-boost-growth-above-5-percent-world -bank-report.

———. 2013. *Second Philippines Development Policy Loan to Foster More Inclusive Growth*. Report 70954-PH, Washington, DC: World Bank.

World Bank and IHME (Institute for Health Metrics and Evaluation). 2013. *The Global Burden of Disease: Generating Evidence, Guiding Policy*. East Asia and Pacific Regional edition. Seattle, WA: IHME and World Bank, Human Development Network.

WHO (World Health Organization). 2011. *Global Status Report on Alcohol*. Geneva: WHO.

———. 2015. "WHO Report on the Global Tobacco Epidemic 2015." Dataset. WHO, Geneva.

CHAPTER 2

Reconciling Technical Analysis with Political Realities

Introduction

After years of failed sin tax reform efforts dating back to the Ramos administration in the mid-1990s, the final battles to pass the Sin Tax Bill were fought between June and December 2012. The Philippines' bicameral legislative structure meant that the Sin Tax Law (STL) needed to succeed in both the House of Representatives, with its 236 members, and the Senate, with its 24 members.[1] The first sign of major momentum for the bill was the passage of the "Abaya bill" by the House in June 2012.[2] The final approval of the STL involved five full legislative votes, several legislative proposals over a six-month period, intensive political negotiations, and substantial technical analysis by a range of actors.

Taken at face value a reform of sin taxes should have been easy to pass. Who could argue with a health measure that promised to save lives? Sin tax reform had been repeatedly identified as a win-win for health and revenues (Jha et al. 2012). Moreover, the way the previous STL had favored certain incumbent producers was—or should have been—difficult to defend, even by the most shameless politicians. In reality, sin tax reform took over a decade to achieve, ultimately passing the final hurdle of the Senate vote on December 11, 2012, by just one vote.

The desired higher-level "first best" technical policy objectives of sin tax reform—health, revenues, and good governance—were by and large clear. These objectives included (1) curbing smoking and excessive and youth drinking through an increase in cigarette and alcohol prices; (2) generating additional revenues and, therefore, fiscal space to scale-up social expenditure; and (3) adhering to the principles of good governance through tax policy reforms that are nondiscriminatory to domestic and international producers and equitable to consumers, while reducing the risks for corruption (such as tax evasion and smuggling). From a conceptual and empirical point of view, even this range of policy priorities posed trade-offs. Take curbing smoking from a health perspective, for example.

The ideal would be to impose extraordinarily high taxes, making cigarettes so expensive that very few people would be able to smoke. However, this would result in negligible tax revenue. The trade-off necessitated a compromise position—a more gradual approach that involved slowly increasing taxes while ensuring effective market adjustment and corresponding administrative capacity to collect new taxes.

Although a new STL was a compelling reform cause, it had inherent political and technical complexities. The law had to simultaneously address cigarettes, beer, and spirits as a group because this was the structure of the existing tax legislation. This created both challenges and opportunities in moving the reform forward. Measures were also needed to address the expiration of inflation adjustments. In addition, the World Trade Organization's (WTO) challenge specific to the protectionist taxation of spirits demanded that action be taken on those products sooner rather than later.[3] The broad consensus that there should be "burden sharing" in the bill's design required that the costs of the reform be shared among a wide set of producers across both the tobacco and alcohol industries. But, this also potentially created an opportunity for a more powerful anti-STL lobby to emerge. If both industries had joined forces to veto any meaningful reform in excise taxation, the government's proposal would have been scuttled before the final Senate vote. Even with the strong backing by health advocates and the promise of increased health financing, reform champions still had to navigate treacherous political waters.

A major focus of this chapter is on the technical elements of getting sin tax reform right. Because the bill involved tax design and expenditure management considerations, owing to the prominence of health and earmarking for farmers in the bill, technical analysis was needed to model the anticipated behavior of consumers, firms, and the bureaucracy. This was further complicated by sin tax reform straddling multiple sectors: cigarette production, domestic tobacco leaf production, and alcohol. A big cross-cutting concern was assessing the potential impact of the reform on the extreme poor and the bottom 40 percent of the population as cigarette and alcohol consumers, as producers, and as beneficiaries of universal health care. At the same time, technical work needed to consider the reform's potential impact on those who had the power to undermine, or even veto, it. Consequently, although it was recognized ex ante that compromises would be needed to get the STL passed, the reformers also made the decision that the work would need to be anchored in a clear set of reform principles, objectives, and nonnegotiables from which they would not budge.

Using a political economy lens, this chapter discusses the extent to which the STL was both demonstrational and transformational. By demonstrational, we mean how the way in which the reform was structured and advanced could serve as a model for other reform efforts in the Philippines and internationally in similar contexts. This, in turn, raises further questions. Can the sin tax reform serve as a model for promoting broad-based and comprehensive reforms, especially in areas where vested interests and economic rent-seeking need to be tackled?

What can we learn about how to successfully reconcile technical and political analyses, and how can the impact of Sin Tax Reform be gauged? By transformational, we mean whether the STL's design, passage, and implementation defined a new and different way of bringing about reform in the Philippines?[4] Also, subsequent to the STL, have there been efforts to tackle economic rent-seeking and vested interests in other areas of the economy, building on the Aquino administration's good governance platform and the momentum of the STL? The planned review of the STL shortly after the 2016 elections will be a litmus test of the reform's endurance and its ability to transcend administrations.

The lessons from the STL come from an appreciation of the different elements of the final version of the bill and how they fit together, and also from the context and process that yielded the reform. While chapter 1 gave an overview of the motivations for the STL and a detailed description of its final structure, this chapter delves deeper to illuminate the process by which the final bill was shaped and passed. It draws out the strategic and tactical lessons that can be learned from the technical analysis, strategic communications and engagement, and the political coalition-building of the reform. In providing a more detailed analysis of the final passage of sin tax reform through a political economy lens, this chapter also draws out those aspects of the STL's design and implementation that will likely be remembered as demonstrational and transformational from a governance point of view.

The chapter has five sections. The first reviews the political economy context, legislative process, civil society contributions, and coalition-building that accompanied the passage of the STL. It highlights the importance of President Aquino's support to the STL, especially in a strong presidential political system, and, above all, the complexities involved in passing decisive reforms in the Philippines. The second section summarizes the technical considerations at the center of the process, and how these crystalized into the executive's negotiables and nonnegotiables in the political bargaining over the STL. The third section underscores the value of clearly mapping out, ex ante, the market structure for key product segments when designing excise taxes. Market maps were critical not only in modeling the impacts of different excise structures and implementation trajectories, but also for crystalizing what different stakeholders' interests would be in different reform scenarios. The fourth section examines the pros and cons of revenue earmarking (in this case for tobacco-growing regions and health), and argues for a need to shift toward monitoring performance and value for money for earmarked revenues. The final section sets the stage for chapter 3, with its focus on measuring the impact of the STL on the tax and expenditure sides.

Political Economy, Legislative Process, Coalitions

The governance reforms pursued by the Aquino administration since 2010 attracted international attention because of their apparent success in breaking the Philippines' reputation as the "sick man of Asia."[5] Strong annual economic growth and improvements in the investment climate (including the upgrading of the Philippines' investment grade status by international rating agencies) contributed to this turnaround. The success of the STL in 2012, with its emphasis on health, social, and fiscal impacts, is emblematic of this revival.[6] Also, the policy reform was realized in a challenging political economy and had to traverse a bicameral legislative process. Success required outmaneuvering powerful corporate interests and securing sufficient majorities in both the House of Representatives and Senate. It also required successfully rallying coalitions across the executive and civil society.

The Challenge of Reform in an Oligopolistic Democracy

The sin tax reform was passed against the backdrop of what has been widely characterized as an oligarchical democracy with elite capture.[7] The Philippines is an oligarchical democracy in which presidential executive powers are strong (Sidel 2014, 30), although presidents are limited to a single six-year term. The legislative is based on a bicameral system, which means that bills need to pass both houses (and their respective committees) before being finalized during bicameral reconciliation. Political parties are institutionally weak, with interests strongly rooted in personalistic and local dynastic interests. Montinola (2013, 149–97) notes the prevalence of rent-seeking monopolies across a number of critical sectors of the economy (for example, transport and finance) which, in the post-Marcos era, contributed to the country's subpar economic performance. The cigarette industry is an example of this market concentration, with one manufacturer dominating over 80 percent of the market, and consequently having strong political clout.

Not only do the cigarette and alcohol industries exhibit strong industrial concentration within the sectors themselves, but they are also interlinked with other conglomerates across the rest of the economy. The cigarette industry has also historically mounted a very strong lobby to influence policy and, when policy is deemed hostile to its interests, subvert its implementation. For example, tycoon Lucio Tan, owner of Fortune Tobacco Corporation, has historically enjoyed close relationships with government, starting with the Marcos administration. The tobacco industry has also been able to neutralize a number of government advertising campaigns that sought to curtail smoking (Alechnowicz and Chapman 2004). In February 2010, Fortune Tobacco formed a joint venture with Philip Morris called Philip Morris Fortune Tobacco Corporation, leading it to control an estimated 90 percent of the cigarette market, ranging from low-end mass market brands to premium brands. Tan also controls Asia Breweries, which has about 10 percent of the beer market, as well as rum producer Tanduay. Conglomerate San Miguel Corporation, meanwhile, controls close to 90 percent of the beer market as well as the mass gin market.[8] San Miguel is Southeast Asia's largest publicly listed company, and also has strategic interests in water, power, telecommunications, energy, and infrastructure.[9]

Along with the predominance of conglomerates, the concentration of tobacco farming in five provinces in northern Luzon has also affected the political landscape. A solid voting bloc in the Ilocos region played a role in bringing former president Marcos to power, and some of the earmarking of tobacco revenues dates to that time. The flow of these funds buttress incumbent local politicians, and have been an instrument of discretionary favor for national authorities. The presence of a strong lobby, combined with the legacy of local earmarks, meant that it would have been difficult to abolish this special earmark in the STL.[10]

Legislative Process

After years of protracted efforts, the STL was passed quite quickly in December 2012 once the reform momentum gained strength. Following an election pledge not to raise taxes, President Aquino found his reform agenda strapped for cash, and the administration began to work with Congress and civil society to find a way to bring about the controversial reform.[11] An important trigger for action was the WTO's challenge that the taxation of spirits discriminated against international producers. Even so, getting the STL passed just before the May 2013 midterm elections was an impressive achievement.

After a slow start—sin tax reform was on the agenda of the House of Representatives already in 2011—the STL's passage was helped by the replacement of the chairman of the House Ways and Means Committee with an Aquino ally, Congressman Joseph Abaya, and House Bill No. 5727 was passed in June 2012. Abaya had initially proposed a bill which framed the reform as a way to recoup lost revenues (because of the failure of tax rates to keep pace with inflation, thus eroding real revenues) with a target of about ₱60 billion ($1.4 billion), and with the burden sharing of tax collections split evenly between the alcohol and tobacco industries.[12]

The Philippines' political dynamics, including the executive's practice of using earmarking as a way to get support in the House of Representatives and Senate, is at the core of the nature of the STL reform. Party discipline is weak and personalistic, dynastic politics dominate, money politics is prevalent, and party-switching or "turncoatism" is par for the course.[13] Although the president has strong powers, mustering the majority needed for reform is a challenge, and national expenditure discretion ("pork") is an important mechanism for rallying votes. An example of the institutionalization of this practice is the Priority Development Assistance Fund, one of the sources of discretionary funding available to legislators. The fund was declared unconstitutional by the Supreme Court in 2013 after a major scandal over the diversion of its resources, including through alleged kickbacks to politicians. As will be seen later, scrapping the fund would also have implications for sin tax earmarks. To pass policies in the public interest, especially in the absence of political party majorities or party discipline, reformist executives in the Philippines have had to maintain or promise other programs to entice swing majorities.

These political dynamics explain why the STL did not fundamentally alter earmarks to tobacco-growing regions, and arguably created scope for further discretionary expenditure in the health earmarking; for example, through allocations to the Health Facilities Enhancement Program and the Medical Assistance Program. Whether or not these discretionary earmarks were an appropriate means to an end is debatable, but they do raise the question of whether such compromises were the result of the bill itself or whether they should rather be seen as an outcome—and perhaps unavoidable outcome—of the underlying political dynamics.

Although beyond the scope of this publication, a growing political science literature is documenting the challenging realities, as well as possible reform trajectories, of the Philippines' legislative and electoral politics.[14] One related question is whether STL earmarking—some of which is discretionary and some of which, such as the health insurance premiums, is linked to identifiable recipients targeted by nonpolitical processes—will eventually be viewed as one of the more progressive aspects of the sin tax reform, or as yet another example of opaque and captured financing practices. This is discussed in a later section of this chapter on expenditure earmarking for health and tobacco-growing regions.

The political debates in the House of Representatives and Senate throughout 2012 generated a number of reform permutations. Competing bills differed by the tiers and levels of the excise taxation proposed, the phasing-in of increases and tier changes, and earmarking provisions. Table 2.1 provides an overview of the key bills to highlight the policy choices, possible trade-offs, and potential poverty and social impact implications.[15] For cigarettes, major topics of debate included whether, when, and at which level the restructuring should yield a

Table 2.1 Selected Sin Tax Law House and Senate Drafts

Bill	Date	Vote (for, against, abstain)	Highlights
Original Abaya Bill (House Bill No. 5727)	Jan 2012	No vote held	Unitary rates for both cigarettes and alcohol (3 years after effectivity of Sin Tax Law for cigarettes and distilled spirits, immediate upon effectivity of law for fermented liquor).
Amended Abaya bill	Jun 2012	210–21 (5 abstentions)	Highlights should be two-tiered system for both tobacco and alcohol, lower rates for alcohol relative to the original Abaya bill.
Santiago (Senate report)	Aug 2012	No vote held	Higher alcohol taxation. Same rates for both tobacco and alcohol as the original Abaya bill, but the indexation is based on per capita nominal gross domestic product growth rate.
Recto (draft Senate report)	Sept 2012	No vote held	Same structure as Republic Acts 8240 and 9334, with very low increases in tax rates. Associated with resignation of Senate Ways and Means Committee chairman Ralph Recto.
Drilon (Senate Bill No. 3299)	Nov 2012	Senate: 15–2	Unitary rate for tobacco. Substitute for Recto's committee report.
Sin Tax Law	Dec 2012	Senate: 10–9	Unitary rate for tobacco by 2017.

Source: Various bills, House Journal.

single excise tier. Debates also centered on price increases for the lowest level of excise tier and on abolishing preferential rates for particular producers. It was argued that increasing the level of the lowest tier would imply more assertive increases in taxation and consumer prices. A unitary excise would reduce the risk of having consumers and producers shift to lower excise categories. Similar debates covered the reform of the excise for beer and spirits.

Following the bill's passage through the House of Representatives, it moved to the Senate Ways and Means Committee where the debate intensified. Committee Chairman Ralph Recto presented a much-maligned proposal that mirrored industry positions.[16] To everyone's surprise, Recto suddenly resigned from the committee on October 15, 2012,[17] and an Aquino ally, Senator Franklin Drilon, took the chair. His bill (Senate Bill No. 3299) was passed on November 20, 2012. Voting was sped up by a presidential motion marking the bill as urgent. However, agreement was temporarily delayed because legislators shifted their focus from absolute revenue targets back to the question of equity in burden sharing across tobacco and alcohol industries.

The final legislative step was the negotiation of a bicameral bill for President Aquino to sign. On November 29, 2012, a bicameral session was convened for House and Senate leaders to reconcile both bills. After reviewing and debating various health and revenue outcome scenarios, the bicameral session approved a joint bill containing new tax rates and administrative provisions on December 11, 2012. President Aquino signed Republic Act 10351, the Sin Tax Law, on December 19, 2012, amending the relevant sections of the National Internal Revenue Code of 1997. The new excise tax rates came into effect on January 1, 2013.

The STL's legislative journey highlights a number of the challenges of passing reformist legislation in the Philippines. Bills proliferate, but passing a decisive one requires strong executive backing and an effective legislative strategy by its sponsors in both chambers of Congress. A major success of the STL was not allowing the provisions to be watered down with each legislative milestone. The bicameral process, in particular, deserves special recognition for taking the best elements of the House and Senate bills, especially the progressive excise tax levels, and securing a final joint bill that succeeded. To succeed, a thorough understanding of the main technical design elements, their potential impact on health and revenues, and the corresponding institutional reforms was needed.

Managing Reforms and Building Coalitions

Strong executive leadership, effective positioning of the sin tax reform as a health measure, and revenue earmarking commitments all played important roles in the STL's passage. President Aquino's intervention to clinch the final Senate vote was, by all accounts, a decisive factor. The one-vote margin by which the STL was passed underscores the challenge of passing far-reaching reform measures in the prevailing political environment. For reformers from inside and outside government, as well as contributing development partners (box 2.1), this raises the question of what is needed to advance technically desirable but politically

Box 2.1 How World Bank Technical Analysis Supported the Passage of the Sin Tax Reform

The Philippines has historically suffered from low aggregate revenue effort. This has impaired fiscal stability and its ability to finance development priorities. The continued erosion of tobacco and alcohol excise taxes made this an obvious candidate for reform. To help ensure that a policy reform in this area could be realized efficiently and equitably, the World Bank was asked by the government to analyze policy options and their likely impact.

In 2011, the World Bank published an overview of these options (World Bank 2011), drawing on a more comprehensive analysis of possible tax policy and administration reform options. In 2012, during the Senate and bicameral sessions that led to the final Sin Tax Law, the World Bank provided "just-in-time" advice through a Poverty and Social Impact Analysis in the form of a series of seven multidimensional policy notes. The analyses focused on the projected health and revenue outcomes that could result from different taxation structures. The notes sought to help sharpen the reform objectives and provide objective analysis of the many challenges related to the revenue, health, and good governance dimensions of STL reform.

The seven "just-in-time" notes are Note No. 1: Excise Tax Reform Revenue Projections and Post-Reform Scenarios; Note No. 2: Earmarking "Sin" Excise Tax Revenues for Public Health Expenditures; Note No. 3: Equity/Poor Impacts of Excise Tax: Health and Expenditure Impacts; Note No. 4: Potential Tobacco Farmer Impacts and Policy Options; Note No. 5: Industry Impacts; Note No. 6: Philippines Beer, Spirits, and Wine Excise Reform; and Note No. 7: Cigarette Smuggling Risks.

---

difficult reforms. The challenge of legislative approval means that it may be easier, and even better, to simply take an executive route to policy reforms. However, as the STL showed, policies sometimes become so distorted over time that there is little alternative but to pursue a more comprehensive legislative policy measure.

The STL experience suggests that a mix of opportunism, a rallying of effort, and strategic partnerships and coalitions are needed to advance difficult reforms through the legislature. Two recent case studies have sought to draw out the lessons of the STL experience, in part to inform how development partners can better support the building of coalitions for reform (Booth 2014; Sidel 2014). These studies highlight both the considerable effort and the degree of opportunism that went into making the initiative a success. They underscore the prominence of the informal political economy and personal relationships—both binding but also ever-shifting—in driving reform initiatives forward, and, conversely, sometimes stalling them. They also highlight the importance of the role played by catalyzing civil society coalition builders. In the sin tax reform, Action for Economic Reforms was able to work closely with reformers in the executive and the constructive tension between civil society and government helped to advance the bill and prevent it being hijacked by its detractors. The key role for intermediaries such as Action for Economic Reforms is not to drive a single issue, as civil society often does, but rather to help coalesce the interests of various constituent actors.[18]

Stories of the STL's passage are replete with anecdotes about the strategies and tactics pursued by different actors, as well as their behind-the-scenes motivations and ploys. Today, some three years after the STL's implementation, one can more easily discern which choices and which actors were most critical to the overall process.

Broad-based policy reforms require consensus on core reform objectives and principles. As our review of the STL's passage reveals, the devil was indeed in the details. Any number of the design choices could have doomed the STL politically, or rendered it toothless from a health, revenue, or governance perspective. Framing the bill as a health measure, and one seeking to make up for lost revenues, was an important anchor. As the next section will show, this also needs to be complemented by technical analysis to validate broader framing, including laying out the nonnegotiables for proponents. Although this approach involves compromises that may not always yield ideal first-best policy choices, the passage of second-best measures can often have very significant impacts and serve the public interest almost as well.

Meaningful reforms also require strong institutional building blocks to be successful. Reforms build on previous reforms and the STL might not have been possible without certain previous complementary reforms and institutional changes. One important reform that preceded and enabled the STL was the establishment of the National Household Targeting System for Poverty Reduction (NHTS-PR) in 2011. The NHTS-PR is a listing and ranking of over 10 million households that was completed by the Department of Social Welfare and Development during the previous Arroyo administration for the country's large conditional cash transfer program, Pantawid Pamilya Pilipino Program. With this targeting mechanism in place, the case could be made that the earmarking of funds for free health insurance for the poor under the STL would go only to those who could be legitimately identified as poor, thus positioning the STL also as a good governance reform. This allowed the STL to be transformational in the sense of moving away from health insurance subsidies that had historically been subject to local patronage-based politics (where beneficiaries were identified by local chief executives, such as mayors) toward more transparent and rule-based mechanisms. To be transformational and scalable, the STL needed a set of foundations that had been built up over the previous years, including the Department of Social Welfare and Development's targeting database, a basic health care package that was already being provided by the Philippine Health Insurance Corporation (PhilHealth), and a consensus that targeting should be needs-based rather than discretionary.

Broad-based public support will continue to be needed to sustain and deepen the reform gains made by the STL—and a number of implementation challenges remain. After the 2016 elections, a review of the STL's implementation will be undertaken, and it is conceivable that attempts to reverse or erode some key provisions, (such as on the unitary inflation-adjusted excise for cigarettes) will be made. Further gains, notably those for health, will require progress on other tobacco-control measures, such as tobacco advertising and smoking bans.[19]

The challenge in any economic reform is how to overcome vested interests and rent-seeking to advance the public interest. For the STL, continued effort will be needed to sustain the supporting coalition for the reform inside and outside of government, including through public awareness building and outreach. The STL should not be seen as an Aquino administration reform, but rather one that belongs to the Filipino people. For this to be achieved, people need to feel the impact of its benefits in their daily lives. The extent to which the STL is succeeding in making its impact felt is examined in chapter 3.

Targets, Negotiables, and Nonnegotiables

The STL's passage presented political economy and technical challenges. The primary rationale for the reform was health gains, and, on the surface, the legislative process focused on setting new tax rates to achieve revenue targets that would be sufficient to finance universal health care. Closer examination, however, reveals the myriad design choices that were needed to arrive at the final law. As this analysis will show, policy makers not only had to deliver a viable package of reforms that covered cigarettes, beer, and spirits, but also lay out a multiyear path in which tax rates would be simplified and increased through 2017. The detailed design work needed on rate structure, levels, and earmarks was something that made this dual health and revenue reform particularly challenging, and also particularly noteworthy.

Because the excise tax reform started from a low base, careful modeling was needed to assess its likely impact on the cigarette and alcohol markets. The technical work focused on forecasting demand and revenues, health, equity, and industry responses to the various policy packages. Legislative debates and technical analysis proceeded simultaneously and real-time modeling of proposals was needed in order to be in sync with the political dialogue. The first set of modeling focused on the projected units of consumption and revenues that would be associated with the different excise rates and structures for 2013–17. The second set focused on the anticipated health gains from reduced smoking associated with excise tax and product price increases. The third focused on the likely impact excise changes and associated incremental expenditure programs for the poor will have. The fourth set of analysis highlighted the importance of the dynamic industry responses in passing excise tax changes on to the consumer (by, for example, subsidizing prices of entry-level brands with profits from premium brands).

All models had to consider how demand and revenues would change in response to excise tax changes,[20] and the models were sensitive to assumptions about the elasticities for cigarettes, spirits, and beer. The models also made the trade-offs very clear: health goals would arguably be best served by decreases in consumption, whereas financing the expansion of universal health care would benefit from increased revenues. Dynamic market responses meant that some tax reform packages would be preferable to others.[21] The communication of the options as trade-offs between health (that is, reduces consumption) and incremental revenue projections was perhaps a little crude, but simple messages and clear communication are necessary in a political process.

Another major concern was to better understand the market response of cigarette companies, given that, for competitiveness reasons, they were unlikely to simply pass on all excise taxes equally across brands, and certainly not in the first year of the STL's implementation. Because the degree of pass-through of taxes on retail prices significantly affects revenue and demand forecasts, this required modeling of the profitability and response function of incumbent producers.

A focus on incremental revenue targets was a prominent feature of the sin tax reform. Although the bill was clearly framed as a health measure, much of the technical work led by the Department of Finance was revenue modeling. This was the result of two factors. The first was the government's decision to finance the expansion of its universal health care program through the expected incremental revenues. This objective meant that any proposal would be evaluated in terms of the medium-term financing gap for universal health care. The second factor was the decline in tobacco and alcohol excise tax collections from 1.1 percent to 0.5 percent of gross domestic product (GDP) between 1997 and 2011 (see chapter 1). This meant that policy used recouping this 0.6 percentage-point loss as the starting point for their revenue targets. In 2011, this loss would have been equivalent to about ₱60 billion ($1.4 billion) per year. Because excise taxes had fallen to very low levels, both relative to Philippine retail prices and international comparator markets, changes in excise rates to regenerate 1997 revenue levels would need to be particularly high.

Still, any annual revenue forecasts are subject to a high degree of uncertainty, especially during the first year. Figure 2.1 summarizes the total revenue forecasts of the Department of Finance and Bureau of Internal Revenue for the final STL, as well as the Senate and House bills. For comparison purposes, the top line in the graph shows what revenue yields would have been if tobacco and alcohol excise tax collection had remained constant at 1.1 percent of GDP, which was the percentage achieved in 1997. This line helps to highlight how, without the STL, the revenue gap—amounting to about ₱60 billion ($1.4 billion, or almost 0.6 percent of GDP) annually would have continued to grow as the economy grew. Projections of the revenue yield under the final STL and the preceding bills in 2016 showed that the final STL would contain that gap to ₱40 billion ($1.16 billion, or almost 0.3 percent of GDP), while the Senate and House bills would have left a gap of ₱40 billion ($930 million) and ₱60 billion ($1.4 billion), respectively. The fiscal projections should, however, be treated with considerable caution because modeling assumptions matter significantly for the forecasts. Actual revenue mobilization for 2013 was reported at ₱103.4 billion ($2.4 billion), which was almost 20 percent higher than the initial models suggested, with 68.1 percent coming from tobacco and 31.9 percent from alcohol products.

Figure 2.1 Proposed versus Actual Sin Tax Revenue Projections

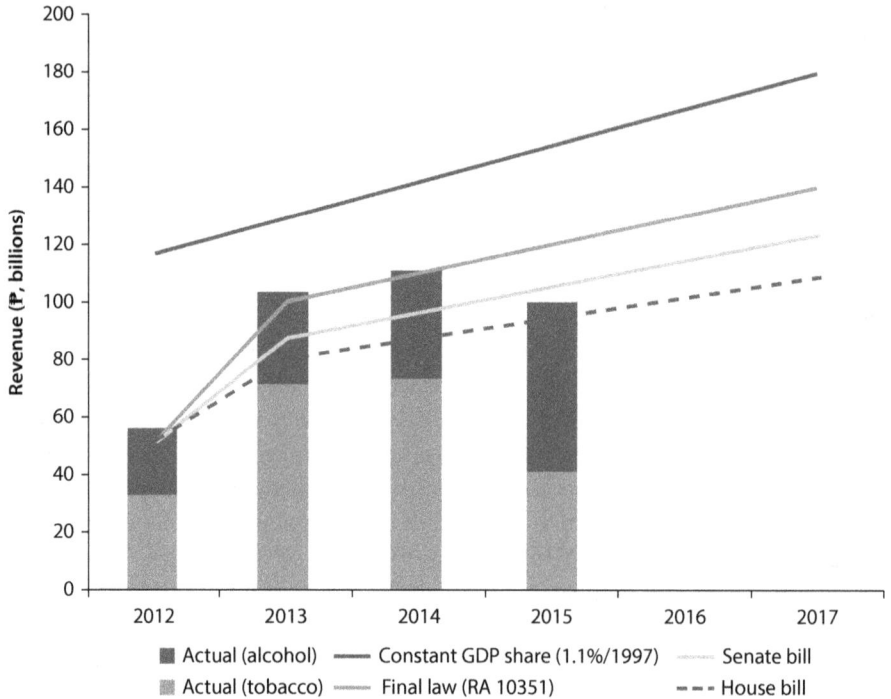

Legend:
- Actual (alcohol)
- Actual (tobacco)
- Constant GDP share (1.1%/1997)
- Final law (RA 10351)
- Senate bill
- House bill

Source: Department of Finance.
Note: RA = Republic Act.

The focus on expected revenues was reinforced by legislative concern over the distribution of prospective increases across tobacco and alcohol products (the burden-sharing argument); and within alcohol, across beer, spirits, and even wine. Health considerations meant that there should be a large increase in tobacco tax rates to reduce the prevalence of smoking, as well as the quantity of tobacco consumed per smoker. Also, while the health consequences of alcohol consumption are less clear-cut than those of tobacco, the health argument in favor of reducing excessive drinking as well as drinking among the youth came up frequently in the policy debate. In terms of the cost per unit of alcohol, spirits are far cheaper than beer in the Philippines,[22] suggesting that substantially higher taxes should be imposed on spirits. However, it was counterargued that the prospect of large excise increases in the lowest tier of spirits may simply result in people, and especially the poor, switching consumption to homebrewed alcohol, which may have even more adverse health implications. From a political point of view, a major concern was that more aggressive rate increases for beer and spirits, while attractive for revenue generation, could have coalesced into an anti-STL alliance across both cigarette and alcohol producers.

From a health perspective, it is useful to examine the relative retail prices (and associated tax incidence) of proof alcohol in beer and spirits products. In 2012, the net retail price per proof liter of the cheapest spirits, namely GSM Wrap-Around and Tanduay 5, ranged from ₱60 to ₱80 ($1.40 to $1.86). In 2012, beer on a per-proof-liter basis was far more expensive; Red Horse, for example, cost ₱183 ($4.25) per proof liter. Table 2.2 shows the different retail rates for a group of representative spirits and beer. These ratios were still in the region of about 20 percent after the STL reform. The implications of this are that, in the future, there is room to further increase the excise tax on spirits to prevent switching (substitution) from beer to spirits, which are after all more harmful to health.

First-year excise rate changes were guided by the twin objectives of generating additional revenues and attaining a fair distribution of the tax burden across tobacco and alcohol products. Cigarettes constituted the largest tax base of the three products, and had the highest potential for additional revenues. In addition, the tax incidence and retail sale prices of cigarettes were clearly out of line with international comparators. Consequently, the argument for increasing tax incidence and prices on tobacco products was persuasive, especially at the lower end of the market where prices were particularly low. For these reasons, the government pursued a large increase in tax rates for the low-price tier of cigarettes in the first year—a 341 percent increase in the specific tax, from ₱2.72 to ₱12.00 ($0.06 to $0.28) for a pack of 20 (figure 2.2). Attaining the specific tax of ₱12 for low-price tier cigarettes was generally a consensus across the House and Senate bills. There was less consensus on beer, however. The executive branch, in providing its revenue and health projections during the bicameral discussions, sought, together with proponents in the Senate, to increase beer rates by more than the rates contained in the House bill (figure 2.3).

The burden-sharing of taxes collected from tobacco and alcohol products emerged as an important issue in the sin tax debates. Much of the political debate centered on maintaining the ratio of tobacco to alcohol in the incremental revenues from increased taxation. The House bill downplayed this and focused on tobacco taxation, proposing a split of 87 and 13 percent. In the Senate, an agreement was reached whereby tobacco products would be expected to provide approximately 60 percent of additional revenues and alcohol products 40 percent by 2017. The final law recognized that any burden-sharing ratio could not necessarily be maintained over time because producer and consumer responses would not be the same in the two sectors. However, a key element of burden-sharing is the anticipated ability of both industries to recapture 2012 profitability levels. Given the large increases in tobacco prices, and the expectation that the quantities consumed would experience a structural downward shift for health

Table 2.2 Per Proof Liter Cost, Spirits and Beer

Product	Old retail/PL	New retail/PL	Old ratio (%)	New ratio (%)
GSM	84	99	18	17
Tanduay	107	129	23	22
Red Horse	475	589	100	100

Note: GSM = Ginebra San Miguel; PL = proof per liter.

Figure 2.2 Cigarette Excise Rate Increases for Low-Price Segment and Market Average, 2013–17

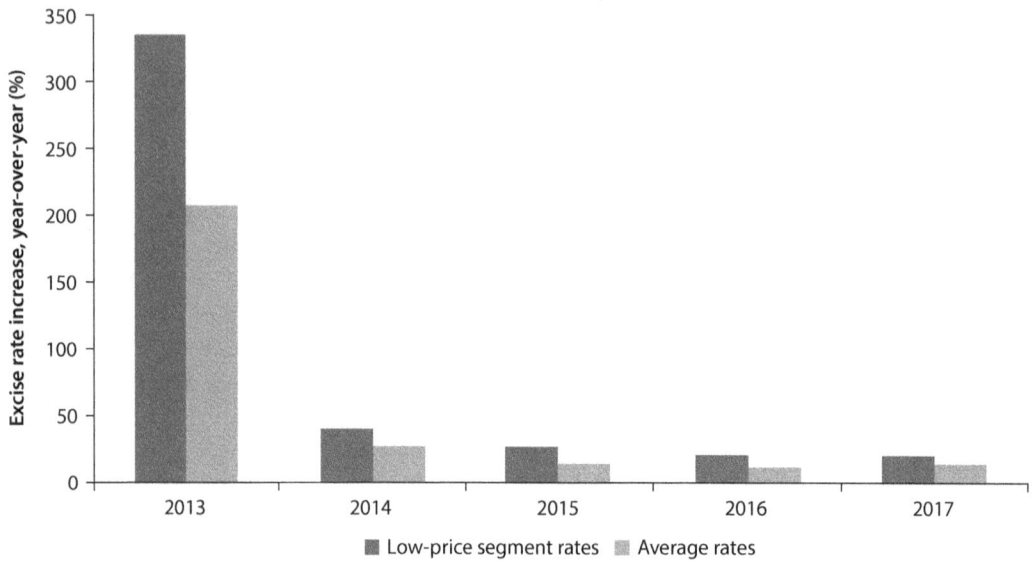

Source: Based on Republic Act 10351.

Figure 2.3 Beer Excise Rate Increases in Relation to the Previous Year for Low-Price Segment, House Bill and Sin Tax Law, 2013–17

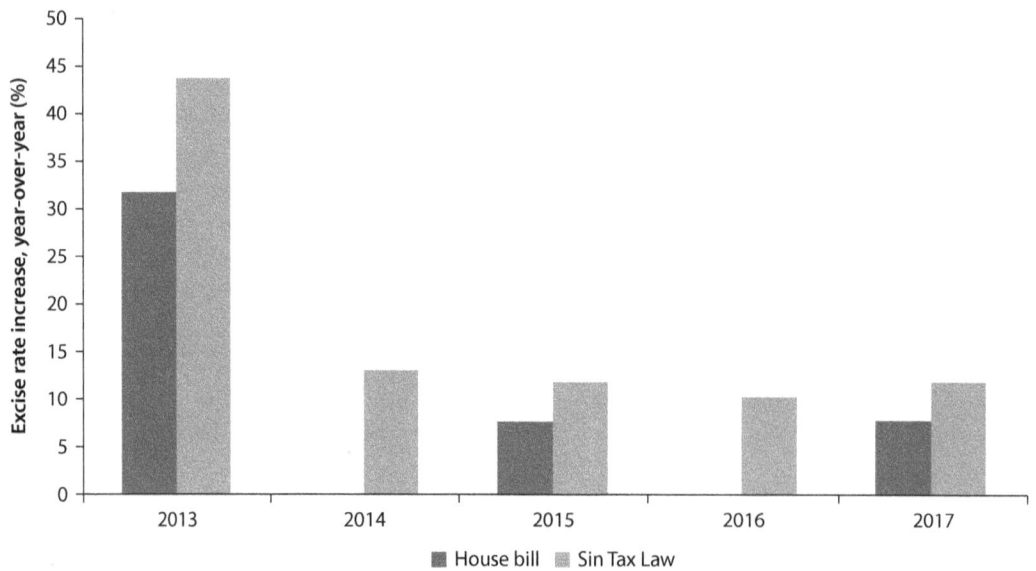

Source: Based on Republic Act 10351.

reasons, a sustained reduction in cigarette industry profitability is expected. This should push up cigarette prices and reduce sales in the coming years, decreasing the share of tobacco in total incremental revenues. During the final revisions of the STL, which focused on the bicameral reconciliation of the House and Senate bills in late 2012, the incremental revenue objective for tobacco and alcohol centered on some 0.3 percent of GDP (approximately ₱40 billion or $930 million), with roughly 60 percent from tobacco, 30 percent from beer, and 10 percent from spirits.

Mind the Market Structure

An early and clear understanding of market structure is vital before undertaking further drill-down analysis. Our ability to construct market visualizations—ranking prices and prevailing market volumes—for cigarettes, beer, and spirits proved extremely helpful in understanding the incidence of different excise tax scenarios, as well as in understanding the different associated market players. Although this began as a static exercise, it formed the basis of more dynamic predictions of the behavior of producers in different segments in response to tax increases, such as whether producers would fully or partially pass-on excise increases in the form of higher prices. Similarly, household survey data, visualized by quintile, allowed us to better assess and communicate the likely impact of taxes on consumption of tobacco and alcohol products, including how the STL might differentially affect poor and nonpoor market segments.[23] One lesson learned in working with different counterparts and with off-the-shelf models was that it is critically important to clearly document the assumptions used across different models so as to fully understand what is driving the forecasts.[24]

Cigarettes

The Philippine cigarette market was characterized by a high degree of concentration and very low taxes. As figure 2.4 shows, the pre-STL cigarette market structure was dominated by one producer, Philip Morris Fortune Tobacco. Lower-priced cigarettes represented almost 64 percent of the market in 2011, but were taxed at only ₱2.72 (less than $0.06) per pack.

In 2011, the average indirect tax incidence (excise tax and value added tax) was 38 percent. However, this concealed a wide difference across market segments. The average indirect tax incidence on medium and premium brands was 42.2 percent and 48.8 percent, respectively. For lower-priced brands, however, the total tax incidence was 30 percent, including only 18 percent excise tax. The Philip Morris Fortune Tobacco joint venture had been able to establish brand presence across the entire spectrum of cigarette prices. The only other significant local cigarette producer was Mighty Corporation, but its sales were concentrated at the lower end of the market. This had implications not only for how different tax structures would affect the different producers, but also for how they would act strategically to keep their market share. For example, Philip Morris Fortune Tobacco would potentially be able to cross-subsidize its low-end brands by

Figure 2.4 Cigarette Market Structure, 2011

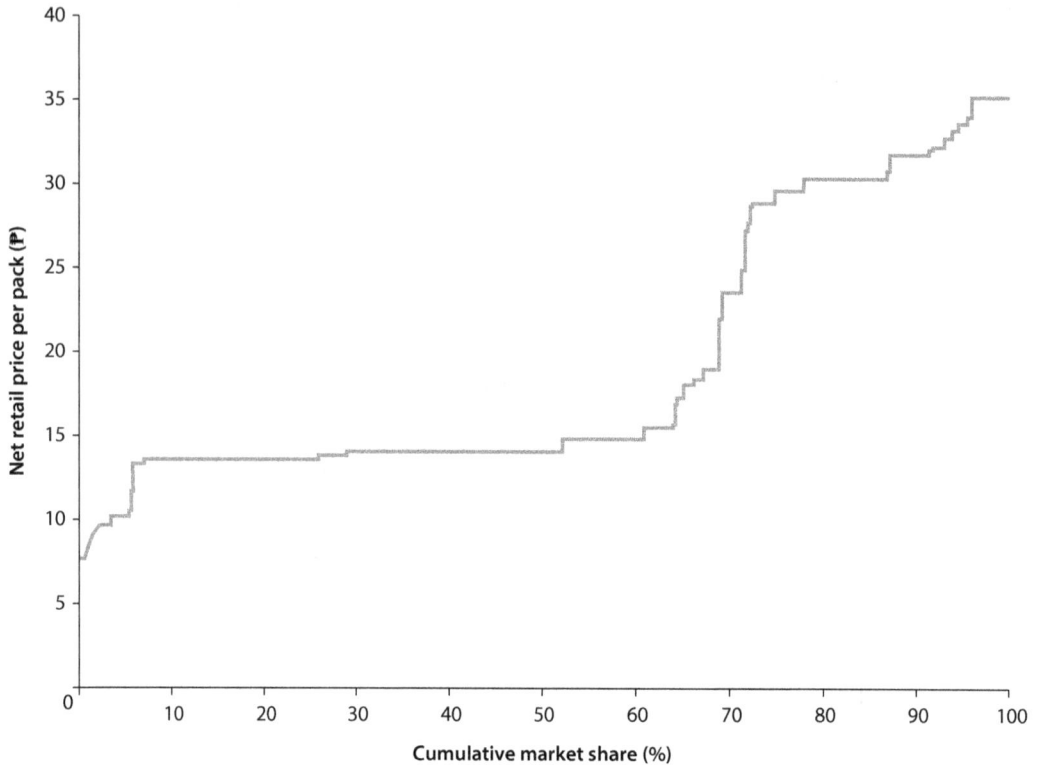

Source: Department of Finance.

high-end ones. Producers concentrating on the lower end of the market, however, would not have that option.

With the affordability of cigarettes increasing in the decade preceding the STL's passage, estimated consumption increased by 40 percent over this period (see figure 2.5). This resulted in the cigarette market growing from a one-year average of 3.55 billion packs of 20 during 1998–99 to 4.93 billion during 2010–11. Over the same period, the amount of excise tax collected per pack declined from ₱8.72 ($0.20) to ₱5.92 ($0.14) (measured in constant 2011 values). The decrease in tax incidence per pack, shown in figure 2.4, allowed cigarette producers to reduce real sales prices by 22.6 percent. The average per-pack price for the entire market in 2011 was ₱19.05, or less than $0.50.[25] The combination of declining real prices and growing income per capita thus resulted in higher cigarette affordability and increasing sales.

The geographic distribution of tobacco growers and cigarette manufacturing facilities also mattered for the allegiances of political actors in the House and Senate. Map 2.1 shows the concentration of domestic tobacco production in northern Luzon[26] and cigarette manufacturing in Batangas. Congressional opposition from these areas was a notable feature of the political debate over sin tax reform.

Figure 2.5 Cigarette Sales and Real Excise per Pack, 1998–2015

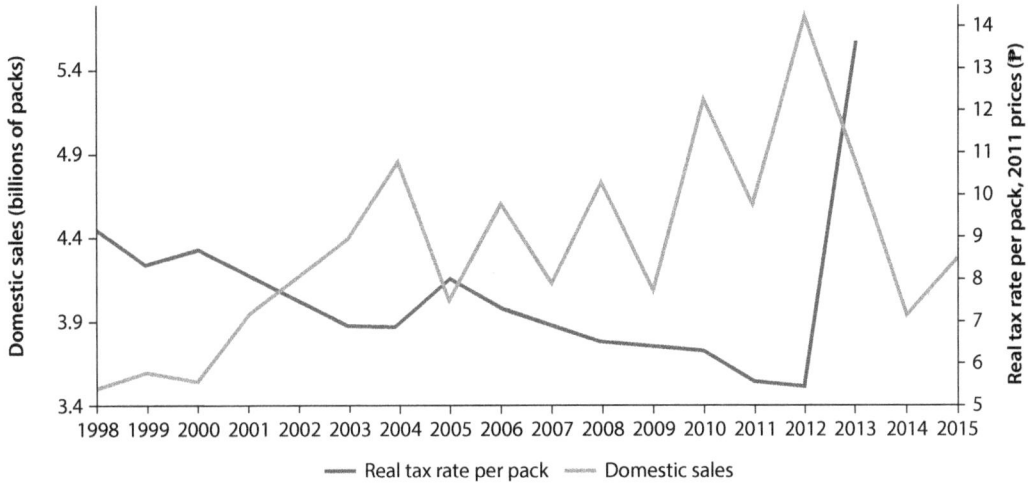

Sources: Department of Finance; Bureau of Internal Revenue.

For instance, Senator Ralph Recto, who early on in the proceedings chaired the Senate Ways and Means Committee, which handled the STL, comes from Batangas. The concentration of tobacco-growing in the north meant that there was a strong veto bloc from lawmakers comprising the "northern Luzon bloc."

A central part of the drill-down analysis was demonstrating that farmers would not suffer from the STL's expected impact on domestic demand because export channels would likely protect their markets and prices.[27] The analysis also needed to show that the current system of earmarked transfers under existing sin tax legislation was likely being captured by local politicians instead of being used to improve the welfare of farmers.[28]

The STL raised excise tax incidence significantly, particularly for cigarettes. However, the effective tax incidence on consumers—a combination of excise taxes and value added taxes—would vary across products depending, primarily, on producer pricing. Using market averages for the low-price segment, excise tax incidence was projected to increase in 2012–16 as follows: from 20.2 percent to 65.1 percent of retail prices for cigarettes, from 17.7 percent to 29.6 percent for beer, and from 13.7 percent to 27.6 percent for spirits. Table 2.3 shows projections of how the excise tax incidence would increase for the low-price segment under the different bills put forward as part of the legislative process, assuming no industry behavioral response other than a straight pass-through of taxes to the consumer. The projected retail price excise incidence was far lower for both beer and spirits.

With the reduction from three to two tiers in 2013 for cigarettes, followed by unitary taxes in 2017, the STL leveraged some of the best reform aspects presented in the House and Senate bills. Key policy choices included (1) the number of tiers in a given year, (2) the net retail prices that would be used to determine

Map 2.1 Number of Tobacco Farmers by Region

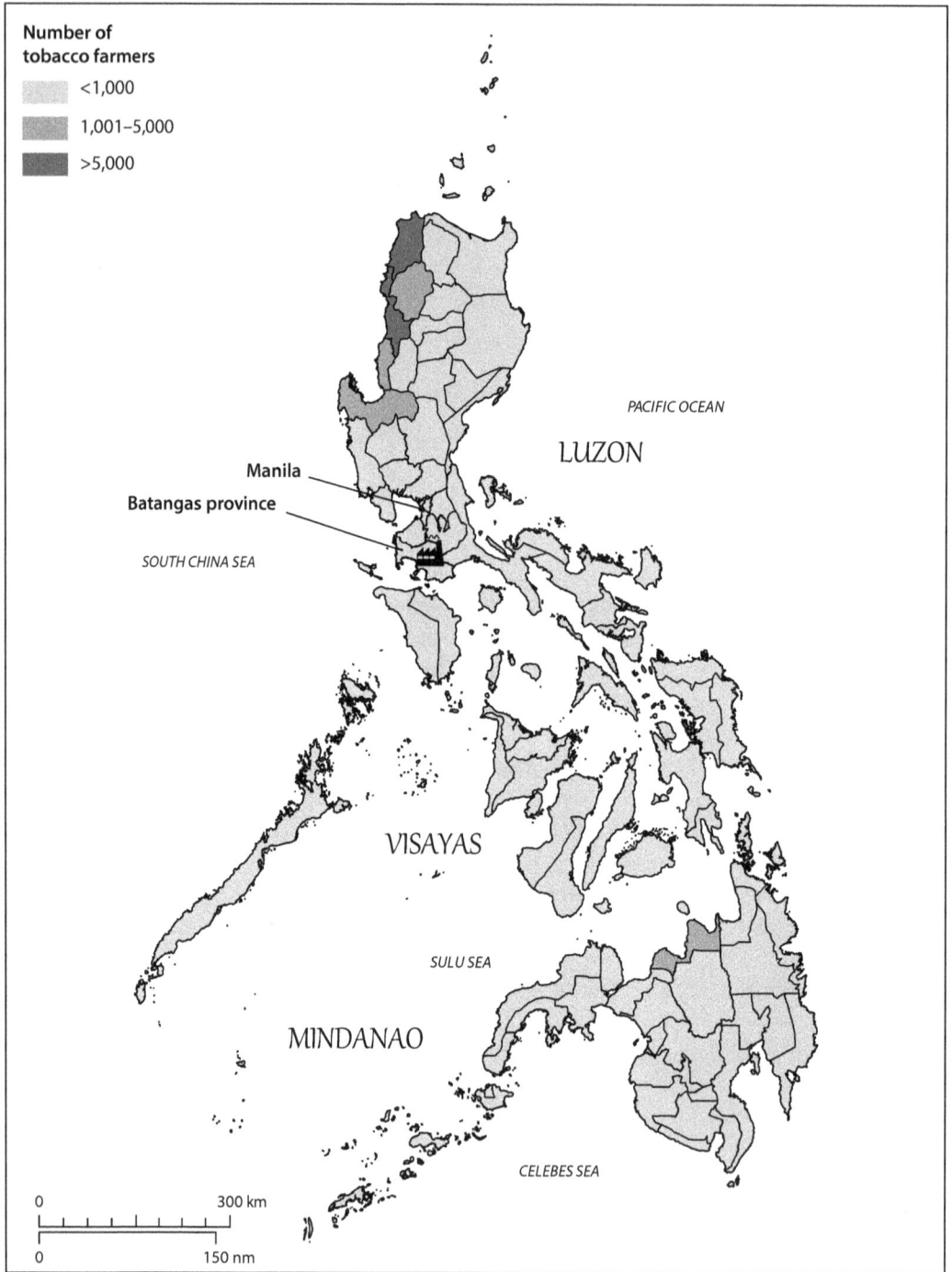

Source: Philippines Statistics Authority, Registry System for Basic Sectors in Agriculture; available via an open license from Global Administrative Areas, http://www.gadm.org.

Table 2.3 Projected Excise Incidence to Retail Prices of Cigarettes, Beer, and Spirits
percent

	Cigarettes (average of low-price segment)		Beer (average of low-price segment)		Spirits (Tanduay, the most-sold local brand)	
Year	2013	2016	2013	2016	2013	2016
Pre-STL (2011)	20.2	20.2	17.7	17.7	13.7	13.7
Amended House Bill No. 5727	50.2	64.1	21.9	23.2	17.7	17.7
Senate Bill No. 3299	46.0	61.6	33.2	34.8	25.3	27.6
STL (RA 10351)	50.3	65.1	24.0	29.6	25.3	27.6

Sources: House Bill No. 5727; Senate Bill No. 3299; Republic Act 10351.
Note: Calculations are for averages and currently representative leading brands in the low-price segment; excludes value added tax incidence of about 10.2 percent. Ratios are measured as excise tax as percent of sales price. RA = Republic Act; STL = Sin Tax Law.

the classification of different brands across tiers, and (3) the excise rate for any given classification. The practice of adding "annexes" to the laws meant that some brands were not classified based on their latest net retail price, but rather grandfathered into tiers based on their historical prices. These restrictions typically meant that excise tax incidence for a given brand was lower than it would have been under a "clean" tiering system. The STL removed this practice of grandfathering. Moving toward a unitary tax in 2017 was expected to further level the playing field in the cigarette industry and promote competition without the preexisting preferential treatment. With the net retail price tier cutoff set at ₱11.5 ($0.27), the possibility of downward reclassification has also been limited in practical terms, even though it has not been legislated against.[29]

The cigarette excise rates agreed by the House and Senate bills provided a reasonable starting point for a final STL, notably from a health perspective. The House bill did not include convergence to a unitary rate and the Senate bill proposed a continuation of three tiers and lower rates before eventually converging to a unitary rate. The bicameral reconciliation session resulted in a final bill that combined the best of both of the House and Senate bills: two tiers as a transitional measure to reach a unitary rate in 2017 and per-pack taxes that were higher than expected. Table 2.4 shows the rates that were agreed on in each chamber and in the final STL.

Because cigarettes are equally harmful regardless of price the unitary rate is an important feature for health purposes, especially given the large number of smokers in lower-income quintiles and smoking cheaper brands. In settling on the final rate structure, the technical analysis needed to focus closely on the interaction of excise rates and market structure (table 2.4 and figure 2.4), what the likely response functions of both consumers and producers would be, and what this implied for revenue forecasts.[30] Given the number of permutations of the bills, and the intense debate that surrounded them, the technical analysis had to provide continual "just-in-time" advice on the implications of all the options. The analysis was guided by health, governance, and revenue considerations. From a health perspective, the floor rate for cigarettes should be as high as possible. The rate structure should be kept as simple as possible to avoid firms trying to classify

Table 2.4 Final Cigarette Excise Tax Rates versus House and Senate Bills
₱ per pack

Bills/Sin Tax Law	2013	2014	2015	2016	2017	2018
House bill low	12	22	24	24	26	26
House bill high	28	30	32	32	35	35
Senate bill low	12	15	18	21	26	27
Senate bill mid	16	18	22	24		
Senate bill high	20	21	22	24		
STL low	12	17	21	25	30	31.2
STL high	25	27	28	29	30	31.2

Sources: House Bill No. 5727; Senate Bill No. 3299; Republic Act 10351.
Note: Cutoff of the House bill was ₱12 ($0.28); Sin Tax Law cutoff was ₱11.5 ($0.27). STL = Sin Tax Law.

brands in lower tax brackets, whether licitly or illicitly. Reclassification, or down-shifting, would not only erode revenues, but also erode health gains by making it cheaper to smoke. The transition to a unitary rate over five years was the cleanest way to do this. In this sense, the final STL picked the best from the Senate and House bills. It combined the minimum starting rate provided in both the House and Senate bills (i.e., ₱12) with the transition to unitary by 2017 (proposed in the Senate Bill), but starts at a higher excise tax rate (equivalent to the midpoint of the House rates).

Beer

As with cigarettes, the key feature of the Philippine beer market is concentration, and the market is dominated by San Miguel Brewery. Figure 2.6 shows the market's structure based on fewer than 40 brands monitored by the Bureau of Internal Revenue. Market estimates suggest that total domestic beer consumption was 1.6 billion liters in 2011. Bureau data indicate that volumes increased from 1.2 billion liters on average during 1999–2000 to about 1.5 billion liters in 2009–10, or 25 percent in a decade. This means industry growth rates have been below real GDP increases in this period.

The Senate bill was far more aggressive than the House bill on the taxation of beer, but the final law retained a cheaper tier. The Senate bill's excise bracket threshold rate of ₱22 ($0.51) for the net retail price per liter effectively put all beers into the upper tier of a nominal two-tier system. The final threshold of ₱50.6 ($1.18) proposed in the House bill gave some breathing space for cheaper beers, however. The important thing was that the STL did not allow for down-ward reclassification, such that some brands would still be taxed initially at the 2012 rates of ₱20.57 ($0.48) and ₱15.49 ($0.36) for the two tiers, above the 2013 rates of ₱20 ($0.46) and ₱15 ($0.35), owing to the change in tier classification cutoffs. Table 2.5 shows the final beer rates along with the House and Senate bills. From a revenue point of view, the definition of threshold levels was an important choice because it would distribute the market volume across the different price tiers.

Figure 2.6 Beer Market Structure, 2011

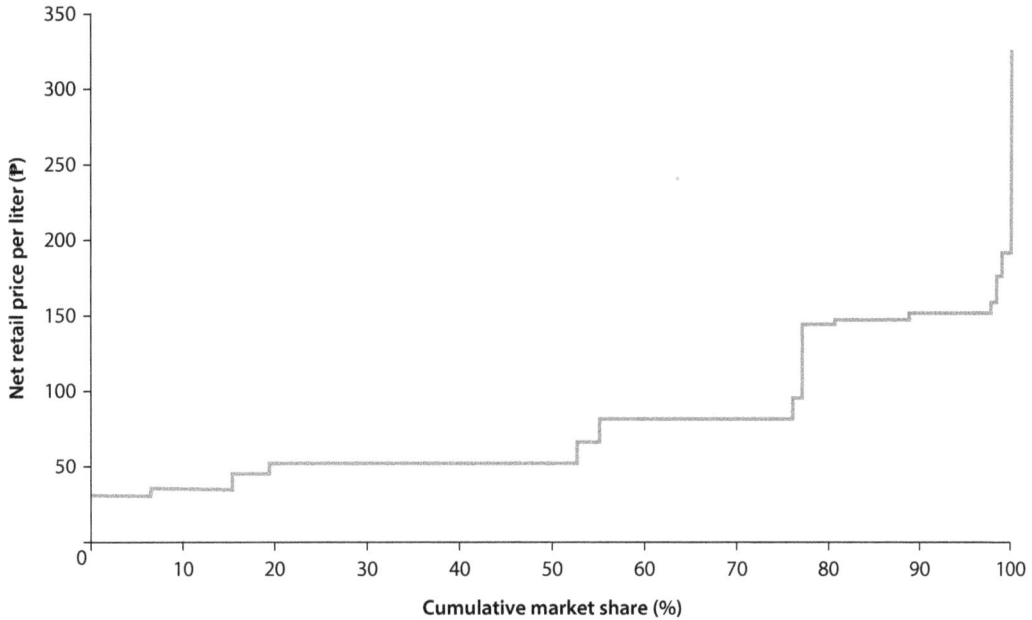

Source: Department of Finance.
Note: Excludes imports and products administered by the Bureau of Customs.

Table 2.5 Final Beer Excise Tax Rates versus House and Senate Bills

₱ per volume liter

Bills/Sin Tax Law	2013	2014	2015	2016	2017	2018
House bill low	13.75	13.75	14.85	14.85	16.04	16.04
House bill high	18.80	18.80	20.30	20.30	21.93	21.93
House bill outlier 1	15.49	15.49	16.73	16.73	18.07	18.07
House bill outlier 2	20.57	20.57	22.22	22.22	23.99	23.99
Senate bill low	20.00	20.80	21.63	22.50	23.4	24.33
Senate bill high	25.00	26.00	27.04	28.12	29.25	30.42
STL low	15.00	17.00	19.00	21.00	23.50	24.40
STL high	20.00	21.00	22.00	23.00	23.50	24.40

Sources: Senate and House bills; Republic Act 10351.
Note: STL = Sin Tax Law.

Distilled Spirits

The spirits market in the Philippines is dominated by low-end, domestically produced products. Market estimates suggest total domestic consumption was 689 million liters per year just before the sin tax reform. Figure 2.7 shows the prevailing market structure for the 30 domestic spirits monitored by the Bureau of Internal Revenue.[31] One producer, Ginebra San Miguel, also dominates the spirits market, but local competitors have made greater inroads into this market

Figure 2.7 Spirits Market Structure, 2011

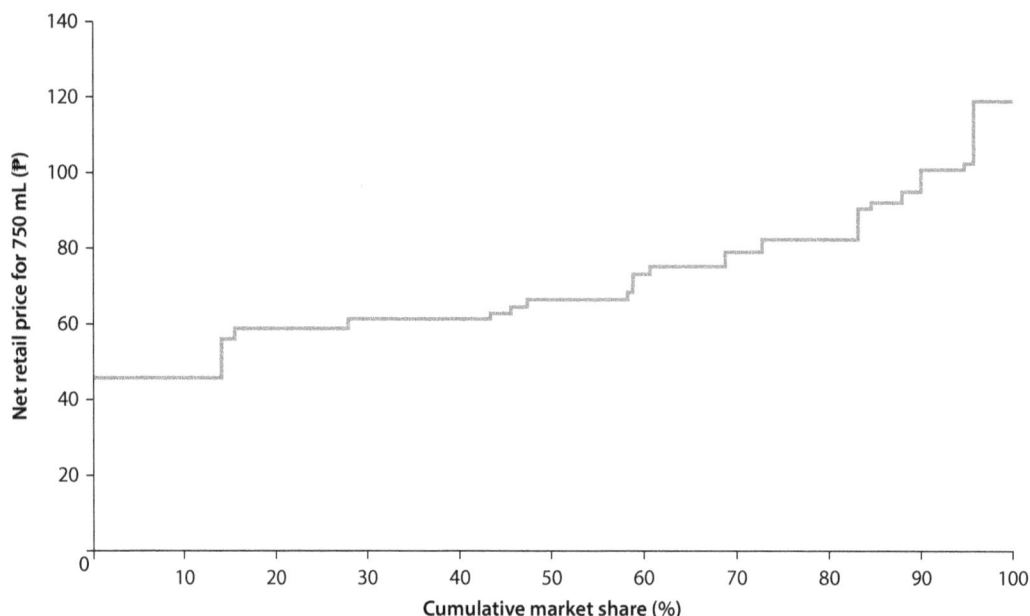

Source: Department of Finance.
Note: Excludes imports and products administered by the Bureau of Customs. mL = milliliter.

than into the beer and tobacco markets. Figure 2.7 excludes imported brands, which are far smaller in market share and subject to much higher prices.[32] The exact alcohol content (per volume) of individual spirits varies. Under the Philippines' excise tax system for alcohol, a proof liter means a liter of proof spirits, which is liquor containing one-half of its volume in alcohol of a specific gravity of 0.7939 at 15 degrees Celsius (NTRC 2010).

Preferential treatment of raw alcohol imports was an important feature of the Philippine spirits market. Consequently, most imports of spirits in 2011—83 percent by volume and 77 percent by value—were in the form of raw alcohol. Alcohol for "domestic" raw materials such as sugarcane enjoyed preferential treatment. However, local producers of spirits could source all raw materials at lower duty, even if the sugarcane alcohol came from, say, Brazil. Therefore, this preferential treatment did not really benefit lower input producers, but rather sellers of spirit that received the preferential treatment. The STL shifted excise taxation from one based on raw materials (ethyl alcohol) to one based on finished products.

In line with the Senate bill, the STL removed the WTO noncompliant, multitiered specific tax for end-product distilled spirits found in the previous system and in the House bill. Once again, the Senate bill was far more aggressive than the House bill. The debates on spirits were characterized by efforts to move to a hybrid regime of specific and ad valorem taxation. A specific system of taxes imposes an absolute amount of taxes per volume (for example, per liter or per liter of pure alcohol). In contrast, an ad valorem system is based on the product's price. Combining the two types of taxes allowed policy makers to balance concerns of revenue mobilization from the premium brands (through the ad valorem component) and ensure a minimum amount of taxation on the cheapest spirits (where a specific "floor" tax is preferred from a health perspective).

The introduction of the hybrid system required some changes to tax administration and excise assessments. Although this system is more complex to administer, it offers better protection from downshifting by introducing "floor pricing" as well as better revenue potential (especially from premium and luxury brands) without discriminating against imported brands. Table 2.6 summarizes the key features of the bills passed in both chambers of Congress and the final STL. Soon after the law was enacted, the Bureau of Internal Revenue issued a regulation to clarify how the taxes would be calculated.

Expenditure Earmarking for Health and Tobacco-Growing Regions

The public finance literature is typically skeptical about the earmarking of revenues. The universality principle argues that to ensure good overall fiscal control, as well as to ensure that when making allocation decisions, expenditure proposals should be considered in a transparent manner (Bird, Hemming, and Potter 2013; Bird 2015). Revenue earmarking also imposes administrative challenges and

Table 2.6 Final Excise Tax Proposals for Spirits versus House and Senate Bills

Distilled spirits			
House bill	*2013*	*2014*	*2015*	*2016*
NRP per 750mL < ₱90	₱20	₱20		
₱90 < NRP per 750 mL < ₱150	₱80	₱80	8% every two years	
NRP per 750 mL > ₱150	₱320	₱320		
Senate bill	*2013*	*2014*	*2015*	*2016*
NRP per 750mL < ₱90	₱40	₱40		
₱90 < NRP per 750 mL < ₱150	₱80	₱80		
₱150 < NRP per 750 mL < ₱250	₱160	₱160	8% every two years	
NRP > ₱250	₱320	₱320		
Final STL	*2013*	*2014*	*2015*	*2016*
₱ per proof-liter	₱20	₱20	₱20	4% annual increase
Ad valorem rate	15%	15%	20%	20%

Sources: House and Senate bills; Republic Act 10351.
Note: mL = milliliter; NRP = net retail price.

For the "House bill" and "Senate bill" sections of the table:

Ad valorem rates: 10% in excess of ₱90, 20% in excess of ₱160, 30% in excess of ₱250.
Ethyl alcohol: ₱40. Ethyl alcohol or imported substances used as raw material shall pay according to net retail of the final product.
For the "Final STL" section of the table:

Ethyl alcohol: Subject to same treatment on proof-liter basis.

requires enhanced collaboration among government agencies. Hard earmarking of an expenditure program to one revenue source also potentially makes it more vulnerable to volatility in that revenue source. Also, since revenue earmarking is typically done on the input side (that is, budget line items) rather than on a results basis (for example, individuals insured, patients treated, value for money), no guarantee exists that earmarked funds will achieve the goals that were used to justify them.

Yet, a political economy argument can be made for earmarking, and this was clearly relevant to the passage of the STL. The Philippines has a long-standing tradition of revenue earmarks. However, these have arguably done more to obfuscate the use of public finances and accountability for resources than secure predictable funding for "worthy" programs. Earmarking for tobacco-growing regions has had a long and controversial history (see box 2.2).[33] Abolishing earmarks for tobacco-growing regions would have introduced significant and well-coordinated opposition to any reform bill.[34] On the health side, Republic Act 9334 of 2004 also provided some precedent for health earmarking, although the extent to which this was actually implemented is unclear, and the Department of Health's annual budget also includes small earmarks from other sources, such as lotteries.

Box 2.2 Tobacco Earmarking: Use and Abuse

Excise taxation earmarking for tobacco-growing regions has played a prominent and controversial role in the political economy of the Philippines for decades. The first sin tax legislation, Republic Act (RA) 7171, was passed in 1992 during Corazon Aquino's presidency (1986–1992). The law's main proponent of earmarking was Luis Singson, at that time a lawmaker in the House of Representatives, who later became governor of Ilocos Sur, a tobacco-growing province.

RA 7171 earmarked 15 percent of the tax proceeds for four Virginia tobacco-growing provinces, of which Ilocos Sur province received the bulk (approximately 50 percent) for "eligible projects" aimed at improving farmers' livelihoods. RA 8240, which took effect in 1997, updated RA 7171 and included earmarks for regions producing Burley and Native tobaccos. Soon after, the use of earmarked funds came under closer scrutiny.

The Commission on Audit investigated Singson for allegedly using earmarked funds under RA 7171 for ineligible projects and for unaccounted funds during 1996–99. Singson was not prosecuted at the time. He was, however, the main witness in the trial of former president Joseph Estrada (1998–2001) in the Sandiganbayan, the country's anti-corruption court. In 2007, six years after the Philippines' second People Power Revolution removed Estrada from power,[35] he was convicted of plundering ₱130 million ($3.02 million) in tobacco tax earmarks (among other funds). Estrada's successor Gloria Macapagal-Arroyo (2001–10) pardoned him.

In October 2013, Singson and his successor as Ilocos Sur governor, Deogracias Savellano, were charged in the Sandiganbayan in a corruption case linked to the scandal over the Priority Development Assistance Fund. The charges were based on the Commission on Audit's findings from the late 1990s to the early 2000s (Cordon 2013; Rappler 2013).

Equity and social concerns are another reason for earmarking, but the validity of this hinges on implementation. Excise tax increases, especially in a country where smoking is concentrated among the poor, risk having a regressive effect because poor households will likely pay a greater share of their income in the form of tax than wealthier households. For poor households, tax outlays may also displace welfare-enhancing expenditure on other goods and services. Earmarking provides an opportunity to turn a potentially regressive reform into a progressive one by linking these taxes to an expenditure that benefits the poor, such as free health insurance. But realizing this potential depends on whether the earmarked health spending really does reach the poor.[36]

Earmarking the bulk of incremental sin tax revenues for universal health care really helped to make the case for sin tax reform. The earmarking explicitly linked sin tax reform to a popular priority of the administration, the "Social Contract with the Filipino People," promising the poor and the near-poor free health insurance in exchange for increased excise tax contributions.

The changes to the universal health care program under the STL also improved governance in the health sector. As previously discussed, a key feature of this was that the poor and near-poor, the main beneficiaries of universal health care earmarking, would be selected from the Department of Social Welfare and Development's National Household Targeting System for Poverty Reduction list of the poor. Doing this eliminated the previous practice whereby insurance subsidies were provided by local government units in a manner that was fragmented and subject to significant patronage. Thus, by earmarking funding for this national program, the STL both provided assurance that the financing for this pro-poor program would be sustained over the medium term, and also that it would not revert back to a patronage-based local entitlement.

Accountability for incremental revenues and their impacts will depend on the transparency and predictability of their associated earmarked financing envelopes. If the baseline parameters are not clearly defined, confusion in implementation could arise. For example, substantial funds from previous earmarks for tobacco regions were not released to eligible regions for many years because the definition of "incremental" was not made clear in Republic Act 8240 or its subsequent implementing rules and regulations. In November 2009, less than a year before the end of her term, President Arroyo issued two executive orders to release long-held funds earmarked under Republic Acts 7171 and 8240, which had been withheld from 2002 and 1997, respectively, due in part to unclear implementing rules and regulations. More recently, the Commission on Audit questioned the use of earmarked funds in Abra province, which receives 15 percent of Virginia-related earmarks, because only two of the 43 projects for 2010 went to tobacco farmer-related organizations, and no clear financial trail (separate accounts, for example) was available to account for the use of the earmarked funds (Salaverria 2011).

The STL and its implementing rules and regulations provided much more specificity regarding the earmarks for health and tobacco-producing regions. Yet, it is worth recalling that during the debates the emphases in the earmarking proposals differed.[37] None of the proposals deviated from the principle of maintaining the general earmarks for tobacco-producing regions in place under Republic Acts 7171 and 8240. Moreover, all of the proposals supported earmarking of revenues for health. Both the House and Senate bills proposed to continue to earmark 15 percent of tobacco revenues for producing regions, but differentiated between Virginia, Burley, and Native tobacco types.[38] The Senate bill was more explicit that there should be hard "nominal" earmarking, and allocated substantial amounts to cover apparent projected dislocations, such as loss of jobs in tobacco and alcohol manufacturing. The very hard earmarking contained in SEC. 10, section 289, of the Senate bill threatened to introduce rigidities into the system. Although the narratives that supported the earmarking proposals across the various bills may now seem like a secondary detail, they do underscore the careful analysis and consideration that earmarking provisions merit in these types of reforms. For excise earmarking, as in excise tax design, the devil is in the details.

How sin tax earmarking is assessed in hindsight will depend on how it is implemented and the effectiveness of accountability mechanisms. What is clear is that the success of the STL will be measured, to a large extent, by the performance of the earmarks—and the *perception* of their performance. There is no appetite to change the practice earmarking revenues for tobacco-growing regions. Still, it is hoped that the increase in revenue flows to these regions, coupled with efforts to put in place greater public transparency and scrutiny of these funding flows, will have demonstrable impacts on livelihoods and diversification in tobacco-growing regions. For health, the expectation is greater. The Department of Health and PhilHealth will undoubtedly face significant scrutiny in the coming years over their ability to spend the increased health financing secured by the STL—and to spend it well. If the law's periodic reviews serve to promote this accountability, even if the link between sin tax revenues and broader health outcomes will likely be indirect, then at least the use of health earmarking will have been justified from a political economy and governance point of view.

Conclusion

The STL story should be an inspiration for other reform efforts, but its wider relevance requires appreciating its specific framing, timing, and features. This chapter showed that sin tax reform was both a very long time in coming and precarious in that it could have failed but for the vote or abstention of just one senator. Framing the STL as a health measure, as well as one that made up for lost ground with regard to a creeping erosion of real revenues because of poor excise design, was central to the reform's success. Significant and just-in-time technical analysis, but above all strategic and tactical dexterity by the STL's champions in government and civil society, anchored in an adherence to key objectives, principles, and nonnegotiables, were also critical for the reform's success. Building a compelling reform narrative, coupled with requisite technical analysis, will be vital for realizing more victories like the STL.

The STL story is likely to continue to attract interest and be reinterpreted, not only among policy makers in the Philippines but also in other countries. For global health practitioners, the STL is one of the major successes of the decade in terms of increasing fiscal space for universal health care and guaranteeing free health insurance to almost half of the population of the Philippines, starting with the poorest. For public finance specialists, the STL represents the only major revenue reform in the Philippines in almost two decades, but also is an example for other developing countries grappling with the challenge of mobilizing revenues which, even when in the broad public interest, is always unpopular. For governance practitioners, the STL showed how the tireless efforts of a reform-minded government could bring about tangible successes, despite formidable opposition and adverse institutional and market structures.

An important part of the STL legacy—both demonstrational and transformational—will be how the challenges that will inevitably be encountered during its implementation will be overcome. Indeed, the story of the STL's implementation will be as critical to its legacy as the story of how the reform came about.

Notes

1. The STL was passed by the 15th Congress (2010–13).

2. Joseph Emilio Abaya was, at the time, a third-term member of the House of Representatives under the President Aquino's Liberal Party, and served in the 15th Congress as chair of the House Committee on Appropriations. He was appointed secretary of the Department of Transportation and Communications in 2012.

3. To many—and contrary to conventional wisdom—sin tax reform would not have happened but for the impetus from a case about taxes on distilled spirits that the Philippines "lost" at the WTO (ITIC and Oxford Economics 2014).

4. The World Bank's Country Partnership Strategy for the Republic of the Philippines for the fiscal years 2015–18 defines "transformational" as: "Does it address a binding constraint? Will it lead to changes in behavior and incentives that alter outcomes? Does it maximize impact? Does it have demonstration effects, including the potential for replication and influencing other actors, scaling up and spillover, or does it serve a catalytic role? Will it have lasting impact beyond the intervention horizon? Finally, does it offer a unique opportunity for the WBG [World Bank Group] based on comparative advantage?" (World Bank 2014, 140).

5. The grounds for shedding this reputation were emphasized by National Economic and Development Authority Secretary Arsenio Balisacan during the presentation of 2014's economic performance in January 2015, and also on numerous occasions by President Aquino himself.

6. A number of high-profile controversies saw the more fundamental relationships between the executive, judiciary, and legislative heavily debated. These included the impeachment of Supreme Court Justice Renato Corona at the end of 2011, as well as the Priority Development Assistance Fund and Disbursement Acceleration Program cases and rulings.

7. In describing the institutional development path beyond low-income to middle- and high-income status, Nobel Prize–winning economist Douglas North set out the need to transition from limited to open access orders (North, Wallis, and

Weingast 2009, 326; North et al. 2013). The framework identifies a set of threshold conditions whereby countries are able to control violence as political currency, but above all provide a level playing field to citizens and firms beyond the elite. Applying this framework to the Philippines, Montinola (2013) laments that the country seems farther away from this transition than two generations ago. See also, Studwell (2014).

8. Perhaps a surprising fact is that the Philippines, with a consumption of 265 million liters of gin in 2012, is the world's biggest gin market, beating the United States, Spain, United Kingdom, and India. For more information on the world's largest gin markets, see http://www.thespiritsbusiness.com/2014/02/worlds-largest-gin-markets/5/.

9. Alliance Global Group is another major group operating in the spirits sector, producing Emperador brandy. Among its other holdings are Megaworld property developers, and the McDonald's franchise for the Philippines.

10. In 2013, the Supreme Court ruled that the Priority Development Assistance Fund was unconstitutional. The section "Expenditure Earmarking for Health and Tobacco-Growing Regions" in this chapter discusses the impact this has had on the STL's implementing rules and regulations for these earmarks.

11. See Faustino (2014) for a succinct overview of the STL's promulgation in the context of tax reform in the Philippines.

12. The final bill that was passed (also known as the amended Abaya bill), however, projected just ₱30 billion ($698 million) from tobacco and ₱5 billion ($116 million) from alcohol in the first year of implementation.

13. For a highly accessible video of political dynasty dynamics in the Philippines, see https://www.youtube.com/watch?v=BBAA3IOZPkI. For background, see Mendoza et al. (2013).

14. See White (2015) for a recent summary of key strands of the literature.

15. Policy Note No. 2 of the Summary Technical Briefing Notes for Sin Tax Bicameral Deliberations provides a more exhaustive analysis of the implied revenue differences across the different bills. The simulations also provide a rough indication that some bills would be better on the health side—crudely proxied by a decline in consumption and some imputation of commensurate lives saved over time—than on the revenue side.

16. On objective constituency criteria, it should be noted that Senator Recto was previously a congressman from Batangas, where Philip Morris International, in 2003, established a major cigarette production facility, in Tanauan. He is also married to the current governor of Batangas.

17. See Inquirer.net (2012).

18. Both these papers focus primarily on special models of engagement that development partners can pursue to successfully advance pro-poor and development reforms in such politically challenging situations as the Philippines (for example, by the Australian Department of Foreign Affairs and Trade, USAID, and the Asia Foundation). The development entrepreneurship approach focuses on identifying technically sound and politically possible (also referred to as "second best" or "good enough" reforms). This means an entrepreneurial approach to pursuing reforms (rather than typically front-frontal, project-based approaches by major donors); and the need for local champions with strong personal motivations to pursue the reform (see Booth 2014, 5). The coalitions-for-change approach focuses on intermediaries that can help coalesce effective multisectoral coalitions around a reform.

19. While these exist at the national level, health is devolved in the Philippines. This puts the emphasis on implementation by local governments, notably at the province and city-municipality level.

20. These models were also closely coordinated with other agencies including the World Health Organization.

21. Note that the models did not capture excessive or youth drinking versus aggregate drinking.

22. At the lower net retail price tier for distilled spirits, the proposed new tax will be effectively ₱40 ($0.93) per liter of pure alcohol. Although there is no globally acceptable or benchmarked tax incidence per liter of pure alcohol, it is important to highlight that the lowest net retail price beer tax tier will have a tax incidence of ₱275 ($6.39) per liter of pure alcohol, or almost seven times higher than the cheapest distilled spirits. As such, with the ratio of taxes to alcohol so wide, some consumers may choose spirits more often, which can accelerate negative health effects. Monitoring should therefore focus ideally on examining the main associations between excessive and youth drinking and spirits, given that unit prices are far lower than on a per-unit alcohol basis.

23. See Policy Note No. 1: Consumer Impacts. For more information, see box 2.1.

24. See Policy Note No. 2: Revenue Forecasting. For more information, see box 2.1.

25. Average prices ranged from ₱13.46 ($0.31) for lower-priced cigarettes, ₱24 ($0.56) for medium-priced cigarettes, and ₱31.51 ($0.73) for premium cigarettes. The popular Marlboro brand was approximately ₱40 ($1.00).

26. Notably, a recent initiative by Philip Morris International to expand tobacco growing in Mindanao.

27. See Policy Note No. 3: Farmer Impacts. For more information, see box 2.1.

28. An interesting dynamic that emerged during the sin tax debates was Ilocos Sur Governor Luis Singson stating at a Department of Health event that the reform might actually benefit the north. He suggested that the market dominance of Philip Morris Fortune Tobacco had become such that farm gate prices might be depressed because of its monopolistic position. Similarly, British American Tobacco, having been largely excluded from the Philippine market because of preferential tax structures for the incumbents, favored STL reform.

29. The Senate bill proposed a provision of "no downward reclassification," which would have been more important had a middle-tier net retail price cutoff been adopted to prevent excess tax avoidance.

30. See Policy Notes No. 1: Consumer Impacts, and No. 4: Industry Response. For more information, see box 2.1.

31. A major question, however, is the size of the local market for informal spirits such as coconut and medicinal wines. The absence of good market information on this segment made the extent of possible downward substitution to this market difficult to assess.

32. The analysis of the import market was based on Bureau of Customs data. An initial concern of the analysis was that the reform would actually reduce excise revenues from imported spirits, albeit from a low quantity baseline. The analysis only assessed the static loss of the reform, but not the changes associated with a possible growth of the premium market in terms of actual taxation.

33. The comparative literature has paid some attention to typologies, as well as the pros and cons of hard versus soft earmarking (see WHO 2011). In moving beyond a focus

on defining revenue or expenditure program input boundaries, an important area for further analysis but above all policy innovation, should be to better link "earmarking compacts" to performance criteria. If agencies are able to deliver on results, these revenues are also more likely to be secured for greater medium-term-financing predictability. In settings that lack comprehensive program or performance-driven budgeting, earmarking could be a transitional measure for demonstrating and institutionalizing broader reforms in this direction (see WHO 2011).

34. Members of Congress from tobacco-producing regions are often referred to as the "northern bloc."

35. See, for example, ABS-CBN's 2009 investigative report http://www.abs-cbnnews .com/special-report /05/05 /09/p1-billion-tobacco-funds-misused.

36. See Policy Note No. 1: Consumer Impacts. For more information, see box 2.1.

37. Notably, the Senate bill contained a number of issues on earmarking. The House bill contained only soft earmarking for health (for universal health coverage), compared to the hard earmarking provided in SEC. 8, section 288, of the Senate bill ("funding gap...for universal health care," a list of programs, and an overall earmarked peso amount), followed by exceptionally hard earmarking in SEC. 10, section 289 (a list of programs, earmarked amounts per program, and eligible activities in each program). SEC. 8, section 288, was a more desirable articulation because it captures the spirit of the purpose of earmarking (that is, to cover the financing gaps in universal health coverage), and provides some legal assurance that the revenues raised will be used in a pro-poor manner (through listing the areas of focus and stipulating that PhilHealth allocations be for the premiums of households in the population's two poorest quintiles). Yet, SEC. 8, section 288, maintains flexibility by (1) allowing for the revenue allocation to be adjusted in subsequent years; and (2) instead of hard earmarking to programs, defining a process for allocating expenditure across programs (by the president, on the recommendation of the secretary of the Department of Health). The House bill maintained the flexibility needed for annual planning and budgeting, and provided that the annual budgeting process can be trusted to be pro-poor.

38. The House bill allowed for 85 percent of incremental revenues to be allocated to health compared to a maximum of 70 percent (but possibly less) in the Senate bill. This is because the House bill allocated 15 percent of incremental revenues to Burley and Native tobacco-growing regions, and the remainder to health. Meanwhile, Senate Bill No. 3299 allocated 15 percent of incremental revenues to Burley and Native tobacco-growing regions (SEC. 8, section 288); an additional 15 percent to Virginia-type tobacco-growing regions (SEC. 10, section 289); and defined allocations in pesos (rather than percentages) for health. The consequences would have been that the allocations to health were likely larger under the House rather than Senate bill because a greater percentage of incremental revenues were available to health.

References

Alechnowicz, K., and S. Chapman. 2004. "The Philippine Tobacco Industry: 'The Strongest Tobacco Lobby in Asia.'" *Tobacco Control* 13 (Supplement II): 71–8.

Bird, R. 2015. "Tobacco and Alcohol Excise Taxes for Public Health Financing: Marrying Sin and Virtue?" Policy Research Working Paper 7500, World Bank, Washington, DC.

Bird, R., R. Hemming, and R. Potter, eds. 2013. *The International Handbook of Public Financial Management*. New York: Palgrave Macmillan.

Booth, D. 2014. "Aiding Institutional Reform in Developing Countries: Lessons from the Philippines on What Works, What Doesn't and Why." Asia Foundation, San Francisco; Overseas Development Institute, London.

Cordon, J. C. 2013. "Singson Posts Bail in P24-M Graft Charges." *Manila Times*, October 16. http://www.manilatimes.net/singson-posts-bail-in-p24-m-graft-charges/45378.

Faustino, J. 2014. "Amid Staunch Opposition, 'Sin Taxes' Move Forward in Philippines." Asia Foundation. http://asiafoundation.org/in-asia/2012/12/19/amid-staunch-opposition-sin-taxes-move-forward-in-philippines.

Inquirer.net. 2012. "Santiago 'Gobsmacked' at Recto Sin Tax Bill Version." October 11. http://newsinfo.inquirer.net/287292/santiago-gobsmacked-at-recto-sin-tax-bill-version# ixzz3oIdZVDxu.

ITIC (International Tax and Investment Center) and Oxford Economics. 2014. *Asia-11: Illicit Tobacco Indicator 2013 Update for the Philippines*. Washington, DC: ITIC; Oxford: Oxford Economics.

Jha, P., J. Renu, D. Li, C. Gauvreau, I. Anderson, P. Moser, S. Bonu, I. Bhusha, and F. J. Chaloupka. 2012. *Tobacco Taxes: A Win-Win Measure for Fiscal Space and Health*. Manila: Asian Development Bank. http://www.adb.org/publications/tobacco-taxes-win-win-measure-fiscal-space-and-health.

Mendoza, R. U., E. Beja, V. Venida, and D. Yap. 2013. "An Empirical Analysis of Political Dynasties in the 15th Philippine Congress." Working Paper, Asian Institute of Management, Manila. http://www.kapatiranparty.org/wp-content/uploads/2013/02/SSRN-id1969605.pdf.

Montinola, G. 2013. "Change and Continuity in a Limited Access Order: The Philippines." In *The Shadow of Violence: Politics, Economics, and the Problems of Development*, edited by D. North, J. J. Wallis, S. B. Webb, and B. Weingast. Cambridge: Cambridge University Press.

North, D. C., J. J. Wallis, and B. Weingast. 2009. *Violence and Social Orders: A Conceptual Framework for Interpreting Recorded Human History*. Cambridge: Cambridge University Press.

North, D. C., J. J. Wallis, S. B. Webb, and B. Weingast, eds. 2013. *In the Shadow of Violence: Politics, Economics, and the Problems of Development*. Cambridge: Cambridge University Press.

NTRC (National Tax Research Center). 2010. *Short Guide to Philippine Taxes CY 2010*. http://www.ntrc.gov.ph/short-guide-to-philippine-taxes-cy-2010.html.

Rappler. 2013. "Chavit, Savellano Misused P26M Tobacco Funds—Ombudsman." Rappler.com, July 5. http://www.rappler.com/nation/32933-chavit-savellano-misused-tobacco-funds.

Salaverria, L. 2011. "COA Questions Abara's Use of Tobacco Excise Tax Share." *Philippine Daily Inquirer*, November 28. http://newsinfo.inquirer.net/101583/coa-questions-abra%E2%80%99s-use-of-tobacco-excise-tax-share.

Sidel, J. 2014. *Achieving Reforms in Oligarchical Democracies: The Role of Leadership and Coalitions in the Philippines*. Birmingham: Developmental Leadership Program.

Studwell, J. 2014. *How Asia Works*. London: Profile Books.

White, L. 2015. *Philippine Politics: Possibilities and Problems in a Localist Democracy.* Routledge.

WHO (World Health Organization). 2011. *WHO Technical Manual on Tobacco Tax Administration.* WHO: Geneva.

World Bank. 2011. "Philippines Quarterly Update: Sustaining Growth in Uncertain Times." World Bank, Washington, DC.

———. 2014. Country Partnership Strategy for the Republic of the Philippines FY 2015–18. Washington, DC: World Bank.

CHAPTER 3

Monitoring Implementation of the Sin Tax Law

Introduction

With effective implementation, the Sin Tax Law (STL) should deliver significant health, revenue, and good governance benefits. The health benefits will be derived partly from reduced domestic consumption as smokers adjust to the higher prices associated with the new excise tax rates.[1] The health benefits will also depend on the size, allocation, and efficiency of spending of the incremental STL revenues, about 85 percent of which are earmarked for universal health care and other health programs. Government revenues will be determined by the prevailing annual unit tax rates per product classification, legal production and sales volumes, and effective administration and revenue protection measures. Farmers in tobacco-growing regions should benefit from earmarked funding for projects to diversify their crops and incomes, translating into improved livelihoods. Finally, effective implementation of the STL should be a win for good governance, especially if accompanied by open and transparent evidence-based monitoring.

To help ensure the STL's effective implementation, as well as to track its accomplishments and any shortcomings, this chapter offers a monitoring framework for the law's implementation, an assessment of implementation progress to date, and recommendations to help ensure its objectives are achieved. The monitoring framework has 14 indicators—seven on the taxation side and seven on the expenditure side—and can be used by government, civil society, and the private sector (table 3.1).[2] One challenge is ensuring the availability of baseline and follow-up data. Where gaps exist, alternative information sources will be needed. Another challenge is to ensure the consistency with which indicators and related data are measured over time. Perhaps the biggest challenge is the sheer number of agencies and data sources involved in updating the indicators in the framework, and thus the coordination needed for effective monitoring.

Table 3.1 Overview of Sin Tax Law Monitoring Indicators

Seven indicators for taxes	Seven indicators for earmarks
Prices	Earmarked spending for tobacco-growing LGUs
Retail prices for cigarettes and alcoholic drinks	Budgets and disbursement to tobacco-producing LGUs
Sales/Tax Collection	Project selection, appraisal, and monitoring
Legal domestic sales	LGU reports on utilization and impact evaluation
Revenues (excise, VAT, customs)	Earmarked Spending for Health/UHC
Revenue Leakages/Tax Gap	Health budget, releases, and accountability
Consumption/Removals gap	Overall utilization of the amounts earmarked under
(Consumption/Removals)	Republic Act 10351
Tax avoidance mechanisms	Expansion of Universal Health Coverage
Consumption and Prevalence Behavior	NHIP sponsored enrollment and coverage
Prevalence and use of cigarettes/tobacco and alcohol	of poor/near poor
Tobacco farmer impacts	Improved access to, and use of, health services
Economic indicators concerning domestic tobacco	
farmers	

Source: Implementing rules and regulations of Republic Act 10351.
Note: LGU = local government unit; NHIP = National Health Insurance Program; VAT = value added tax; UHC = universal health care.

Sin Tax Monitoring Framework

Legal Mandate to Monitor the Implementation of the STL

The STL's implementing rules and regulations (IRRs) provide a governance framework for implementing the law, and have clear requirements regarding the monitoring of sin tax implementation. The STL mandated different government agencies to develop IRRs within 180 days of the law's passage. The revenue IRR was passed immediately to allow taxes to be increased from January 1, 2013. However, the IRRs required extensive consultations before they could be passed to ensure that they were clearly defined and all relevant agencies, as well as civil society, bought into them. Table 3.2 summarizes the administrative provisions, including mandated earmarks and the IRRs as specified in the law. These provide a solid basis for moving forward on a results compact for effectively delivering outcomes using the earmarked revenues.

The STL's IRRs specify monitoring indicators for expenditure earmarks for tobacco-growing regions and health. Table 3.3 gives an overview of the key provisions of the IRRs. The STL and its IRRs stipulate that the bulk of incremental excise revenues, after accounting for the revenue shares for local government units (LGUs) with tobacco farmers, should be allocated to health. Eighty percent of this allocation goes to universal health care, including health insurance for the poor and near-poor, programs supporting the health-related goals of the Millennium Development Goals, and health awareness, as well as implementation research to support universal health care. Twenty percent goes to medical assistance and investments in health facility construction and improvements under

Table 3.2 Sin Tax Law Administrative Provisions

Provision	Tobacco farmer protection	Universal health care premiums	Other health issues
Tax earmark	15% excise revenue of domestic cigarette production for Virginia tobacco regions, under Republic Act (RA) 7171 (1992); 15% of incremental revenues from tobacco products, in line with RA 8240 (1996), for Burley and Native tobacco-producing regions.	80% of balance of incremental revenues from RA 10351, after RA 8240 and RA 7171 deductions.	20% of balance of incremental revenues from RA 10351, after RA 8240 and RA 7171 deductions.
Implementing rules and regulations (IRRs) and reporting	Department of Agriculture, in coordination with Department of Budget and Management (DBM) and National Tobacco Administration, to issue guidelines identifying eligible and specific programs/projects in accordance with rule V and to require local government units (LGUs) to submit work and financial plans as funding a requirement, within 120 days upon implementation of RA 10351's IRRs (section 6, rule VI). DBM is responsible for the allocation and disbursement of funds to beneficiary LGUs (section 5, rule VI).	Secretary of Finance, on the recommendation of the Commissioner of Internal Revenue, and in consultation with Department of Health (DOH), must promulgate IRRs within 180 days. DOH and PhilHealth must submit to Congressional Oversight Committee a detailed annual report on use of funds.	
Key implementation concerns	Eligible projects need close monitoring at national and local levels to ensure funds are used effectively and in line with legislation.	Eligible projects need close monitoring at national and local levels to ensure funds are used effectively, especially as elements of the broader universal health care are already covered under existing national and local government programs and budgets.	
Congressional Oversight Committee	Continuation of committee per RA 8240: committee mandated to conduct an impact review of the revised taxes, but procedures for review are not specified. 2016 impact review: committee mandated to conduct an impact review of the revised taxes, but procedures for review are not specified.		

Source: Republic Act 10351.
Note: PhilHealth = Philippine Health Insurance Corporation.

Table 3.3 Highlights of STL Implementing Rules and Regulations from a Sin Tax Monitoring Perspective

Rule I: Preliminary provisions	Highlights rules pertaining to Department of Finance (DOF), Bureau of Internal Revenue (BIR), Bureau of Customs (BOC), Department of Health (DOH), PhilHealth, Department of Budget and Management (DBM), Department of Agriculture (DA), National Tobacco Administration (NTA), local government units (LGUs), and other involved government agencies.
Rule II: Computation and general allocation of incremental revenue	Defines baseline excise collections for incremental sin tax revenues, and specifies the earmark for tobacco growing regions by Virginia, Burley, and Native tobacco production, aligned with Republic Acts (RA) 7171 and 8240.
Rule III: Allocation for universal health care, Millennium Development Goals, and health awareness	Specifies the scope to allocations of incremental revenues to health care programs (accounting for 80% of incremental revenues, after deductions for tobacco-producing regions).
Rule IV: Allocation for medical assistance and health enhancement facilities	Specifies the scope of incremental revenue allocations to other health care programs (accounting for 20% of incremental revenues after deductions for tobacco-producing regions), including the Health Facilities Enhancement Program.
Rule V: Utilization of local government share	Specifies the earmark for tobacco-growing regions by Virginia, Burley, and Native products, aligned with RA 7171 and 8240.
Rule VI: Duties and responsibilities of concerned agencies	Further specifies responsibilities of DOF, BIR, BOC, DOH, PhilHealth, DBM, DA, and LGUs for guidelines and reporting.
Rule VII: Release of funds	Specifies release modalities from DBM through the Bureau of Treasury to DOH, PhilHealth, and tobacco-producing LGUs.
Rule VIII: Reporting and monitoring of performance and compliance	Specifies annual reporting requirements in the first week of August of each year, public disclosure provisions, and the role of civil society organizations. Sets special provisions for health outcome monitoring by DOH and PhilHealth. Sets special provision for a monitoring mechanism of the utilization and benefits of fund allocation to beneficiary LGUs by DA and NTA.
Rule IX: Final provisions	Notes DOF secretary leadership in any future amendments to the implementing rules and regulations.

Source: Implementing rules and regulations of Republic Act 10351.
Note: PhilHealth = Philippine Health Insurance Corporation; STL = Sin Tax Law.

the Health Facilities Enhancement Program. Funds for tobacco-producing regions focus on measures to promote crop diversification and protect livelihoods.

The STL's IRRs mandate that the Department of Budget and Management (DBM), Department of Agriculture (DA), and the Philippine Health Insurance Corporation (PhilHealth) submit a detailed report on the expenditure and utilization of earmarked funds in the first week of August each year (see box 3.1). The reports should be published in the *Official Gazette* and on the websites of these agencies. The DOH is responsible for formulating and implementing a unified framework to regularly monitor the consumption of tobacco and alcohol products within 60 days after the IRRs come into effect. One of the notable features of the STL IRRs is that they explicitly recognize the participation and assistance of civil society organizations in promoting and monitoring compliance with the STL and its IRRs.

Sin Tax Reform in the Philippines • http://dx.doi.org/10.1596/978-1-4648-0806-7

Box 3.1 Annual Reporting Requirements for Sin Tax Expenditure Earmarks

Section 10 of the Sin Tax Law (STL) mandates that the Department of Budget and Management, Department of Agriculture, Department of Health, and PhilHealth provide by the first week of August of every year a detailed report of earmarked expenditures linked to the incremental tobacco and alcohol excise revenues to the Congressional Oversight Committee. Under the STL, these reports must also be published in the *Official Gazette* and on the websites of these agencies. Section 11 provides for reporting by the Technical Education and Skills Development Authority to the Congressional Oversight Committee on transitional measures being put in place from 2014 to 2017 for workers displaced from the tobacco and alcohol industry, but it is unclear whether these reports are also subject to public disclosure. For earmarks to tobacco-growing regions, local government units are required to prepare quarterly reports of releases and project accomplishments in line with the Department of the Interior and Local Government's full disclosure policy.

The Congressional Oversight Committee is composed of the chairpersons of the Committees on Ways and Means of the Senate and House of Representatives and four additional members from each chamber designated by the Senate president and House speaker, respectively (see Section 11 of Republic Act 10351 (the STL) cross-referenced to Republic Act 8240). Republic Act 10351 includes the Agriculture and Health Committee chairpersons of the Senate and the House of Representatives as two of the four members from each chamber.

The emphasis on regular public disclosure of the use of earmarked funds is a progressive feature of the STL. The additional reporting requirements also echo the particular accountability expectations of the agencies benefiting from the automatic earmarked fund appropriations. However, it is not easy for interested individuals or entities, especially in civil society, to find all the required reports. To improve access to this information, we recommend that the Department of Finance and the Congressional Oversight Committee provide a one-stop website consolidating the links to these reports, or that the Department or Committee issue a short summary to the public on the main successes and concerns on the STL's implementation at the end of each calendar year.

Source: Republic Act 10351.

The Logic of the Monitoring Framework

Changes in excise tax rates and revenue-earmarking arrangements will have a number of health, revenue, and good governance implications. This direct chain of impact is no more than a simple tracing of how increased taxes will lead to the attainment of primary objectives of STL reform, namely reducing the consumption of "sin products" and raising revenues. At the conceptual level, STL implementation should deliver improved health through reduced consumption of tobacco and alcohol, and increased revenue for health spending. It should protect tobacco farmers from any adverse impacts through earmarking for programs to build local livelihoods. Figure 3.1 outlines the results chain catalyzed by the STL.

Figure 3.1 Chain of Expected STL Impacts, 2013–17 and Beyond

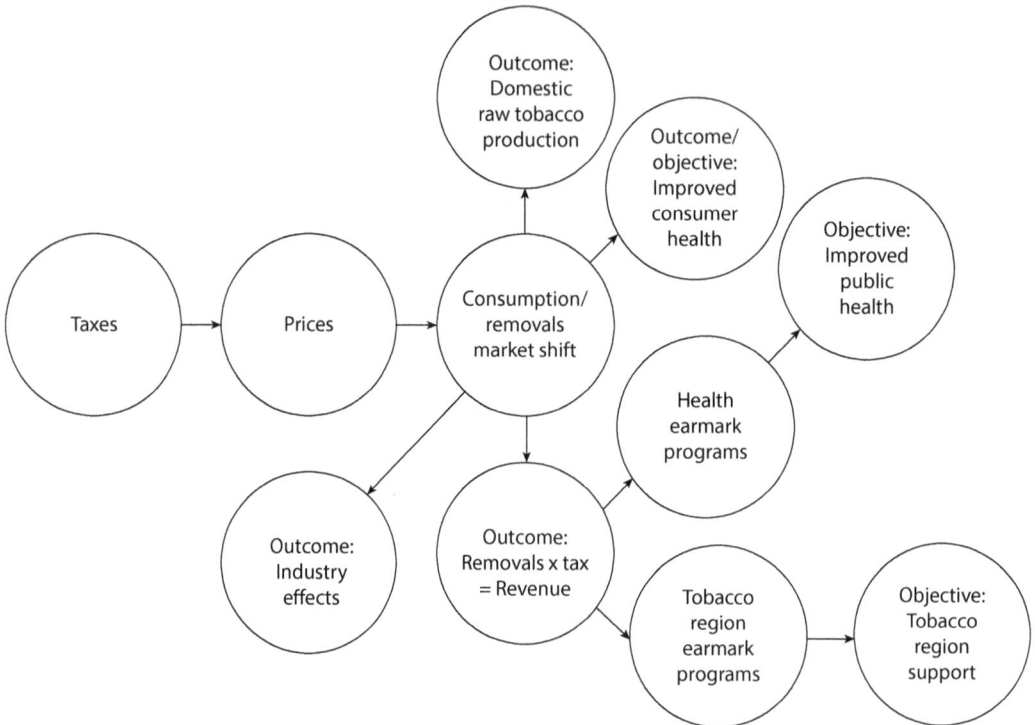

Note: STL = Sin Tax Law.

Tax and expenditure impacts can be tracked through a series of leading indicators. The framework pays close attention to the frequency, timeliness, and detail with which these indicators are measured in the Philippines. The indicators were selected for relevance; availability from standard sources (for example, the national statistical system and administrative data); tracking frequency; and links to formal reporting responsibilities described in the STL IRRs.

Excise tax increases should be felt through increased prices in the retail market. Especially for cigarettes, higher prices should decrease consumption among existing smokers or deter new smokers. Realized revenues will increase as long as unit tax increases exceed the decline in taxed volume (called removals). Market structure and timing will determine how tax changes translate into price changes. A tax increase of ₱4.9 ($0.11) per pack at the start of 2015 relative to 2014 (or ₱0.20 per cigarette) does not necessarily immediately get passed on to consumers (see figure 1.6 in chapter 1). On aggregate, however, producers are expected to increase prices to pass on the tax increases, but substantial variations in pricing changes may be seen by brand and market segment. If certain producers enjoyed high excess profits ("rents") before the reform, this would also mute price increases because producers (including new market entrants) devise strategies to maintain and capture new sales. With the introduction of new prices, consumption (or smoker and drinker demand) adjusts and settles into a balance with producer supply.[3]

The legal supply of cigarettes is equivalent to taxed removals from factory to warehouses for market distribution and retail sales to consumers. Through so-called frontloading, producers can benefit from the prevailing tax rate by bringing stock into the market just before an increase; for example, removals spiked before the 2015 low-tier cigarette tax rose from ₱17 ($0.37) to ₱21 ($0.46) per pack. But there are limits to this, including that stock may spoil. If consumption appears to perpetually exceed removals, this suggests some form of informal sales and revenue leakage. Reduced consumption and removals lead to three immediate outcomes: (1) improved health among consumers; (2) reduced demand for inputs, particularly domestic raw tobacco for cigarettes; and (3) increased revenues through the application of higher tax rates on the removal quantities.

An additional expected outcome from new revenues and earmarks legislated by the STL is government spending on programs to offset the potential negative impacts in affected farming regions, and additional spending on programs that provide health benefits. Moreover, with lower consumption, additional knock-on effects, such as lower health care costs due to less smoking and drinking, are also expected.

Proactive monitoring will help to ensure that sin tax reform will yield the desired health, revenue, and governance outcomes, as well as mitigate the risk of adverse outcomes. On governance, for example, incentives to engage in smuggling or illicit trade may increase; the demand for sin products may remain "sticky" if consumers are highly addicted; and government-supported programs for health and tobacco-growing regions may not be implemented effectively. Because STL reform represents a substantial tax-rate change that shocks the markets, especially for tobacco products, unforeseen industry strategies may emerge because of the dynamic and complex nature of the international tobacco industry. Retailers may also be affected, depending on how manufacturers negotiate margins, and "sari-sari" retailers (mom-and-pop shops) may feel the pinch on sales of cigarettes sold individually. In other words, the straightforward conceptual model may not play out in practice. Indeed, the anticipated outcomes of sin tax reform could be challenged in unexpected ways, both positive and negative. In the 2012 political debates on the STL, the tobacco industry predicted the collapse of sin tax revenues, but actual revenues in the first year of implementation far exceeded expectations. However, calls to roll back the tax may be made if the health results are not achieved, whether from reduced consumption or the effective implementation of earmarked programs. The successful expansion of universal health coverage will be a critical result against which the sin tax is measured.

Monitoring Excise Tax Implementation

Prices

The most obvious metric to track is whether the STL induced major shifts in the prices of cigarettes and alcohol products. From a health perspective, it is the prices of the cheapest cigarettes and alcohol products that matter because, short of quitting altogether, tax-induced price increases are likely to push consumers to cheaper brands. Producers would, in turn, try to keep the most price-insensitive segment of consumers in premium products, while encouraging emerging and price-sensitive consumers to take up smoking and drinking the lower-tier products. Tracking of price changes should therefore focus on levels and trends by general market segment (for example, using the current tiers for tax classification), but also ideally by brand, packaging, type of outlet, and location. Because cigarettes in the Philippines are mainly sold individually, and almost exclusively so among the poor, an analysis of both per cigarette and pack sales patterns is important.[4] Table 3.4 summarizes the price indicators that are being tracked, what underlying dynamics and strategic behavior by firms could explain observed patterns, and an analysis of what price changes may mean. Data on price changes from the Philippine Statistics Authority (PSA) and third-party sources, combined with a sense of market dynamics, give insight into the extent to which excise taxes are influencing frontline prices and will ultimately affect consumption.

The sin tax reform put an end to the one-peso cigarette. Figures 3.2 and 3.3 show cigarette price levels during 2011–15, using PSA data.[5] Recall that due to the STL, taxes on some brands increased by almost ₱0.50 ($0.01) per cigarette in 2012 and 2013, from ₱2.72 ($0.06) to ₱12.00 ($0.28) per pack (see section "The Final 2012 Sin Tax Law" in chapter 1), and will have gained ₱1 per cigarette by 2015 (₱21 or $0.46 per pack). Any cigarette selling for one peso would therefore either be receiving a subsidy from producers or not paying excise taxes. The tax for some lower-tier cigarettes would therefore have increased from ₱2.72 to ₱25 between 2011 and 2016, almost ten times (from $0.06 to $0.53 per pack).

Table 3.4 Price-Related Indicators and What They Reflect

Prices	Indicators measuring direct impact	Strategic behaviors	Indicators measuring strategic behaviors	Analysis
Prices of tobacco and alcohol products	Average price of the product, average price of upper-tier products, average price of lower-tier products.	Underpricing to gain market share, especially immediately after each rate increase.	Prices of cheaper brands, prices per cigarette of cheaper brands.	Normal or expected prices for 2013 should reflect the perfect pass-through of the tax increase in form of retail sale prices increases. Prices below or above reflect under- or overpricing.
		Overpricing for profit recovery.	Prices of premium brands.	
		Underpricing due to underreporting and tax evasion.	Sustained underpricing.	

Note: STL = Sin Tax Law.

Sin Tax Reform in the Philippines • http://dx.doi.org/10.1596/978-1-4648-0806-7

Figure 3.2 Cigarette Prices, 2012–15

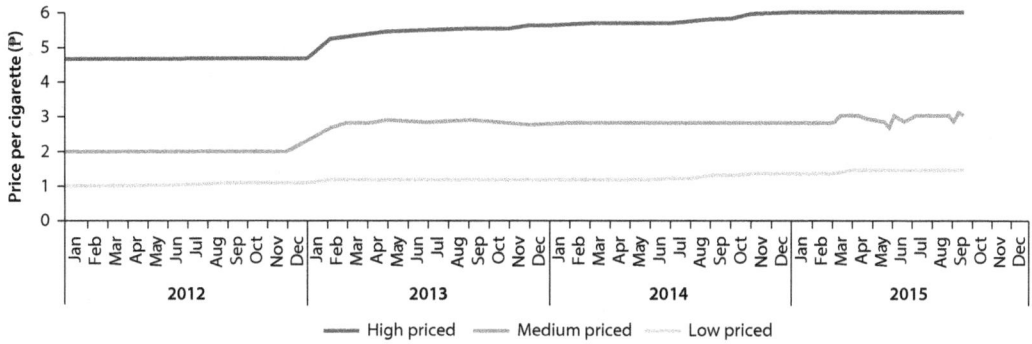

Sources: Philippine Statistics Authority; National Statistics Office.

Figure 3.3 Cigarette Prices per Pack, 2011–15

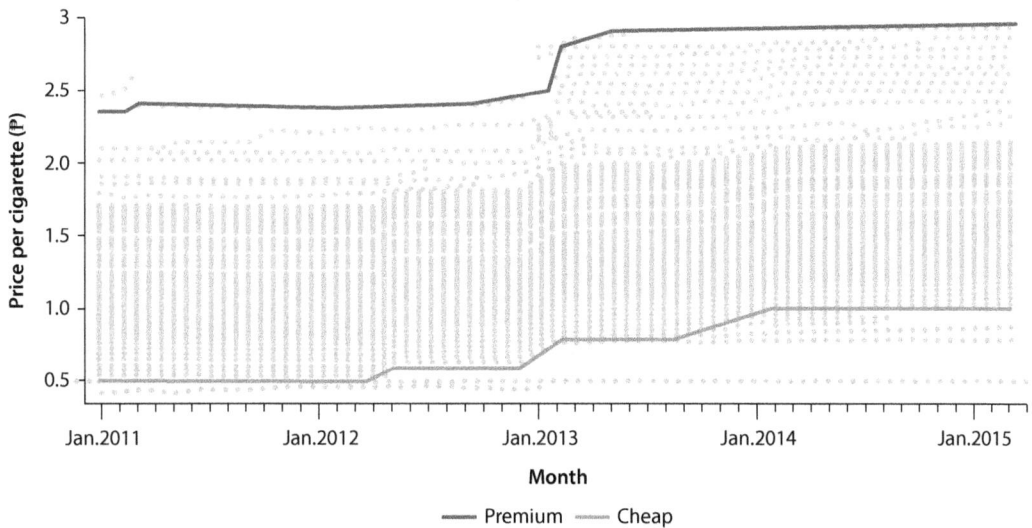

Sources: Philippine Statistics Authority; National Statistics Office.
Note: Packs normalized. ₱1 per cigarette for 2014–15 included Fortune, Plaza, and Mighty.

Cigarette prices initially increased less than expected, which sustained demand. Analysis of the STL's implementation over 2012–13 suggests that excise taxes for low-tier brands in particular were not fully passed through. Part of this can be explained by frontloading, the practice of avoiding tax increases by moving cigarettes or other products produced at the end of a tax year from the factory to the warehouse, for subsequent distribution to retail outlets and sales in the following tax year. In 2012, for example, producers managed to have a significant part of their 2013 sales taxed in 2012 through early warehouse releases. On the lower-end brands, most manufacturers passed on less than the full tax increase, and offered cheaper alternatives to encourage smokers to switch to lower quality, cheaper products or packaging rather than reduce the quantity smoked. In this market segment, a pack of 10 cigarettes was a cheaper alternative than packs of 20 for budget-constrained smokers.[6] This first phase of sin tax implementation also saw increased sales of Mighty Corporation's low-end brands.[7] Whether observed price trends may in part be explained by illicit behavior by cigarette manufacturers is examined in more detail later in the chapter. By 2015, frontloading had been significantly reduced, and floor prices were pushing above ₱1.5 ($0.03) per cigarette, supported by the successful rollout of a tax stamp to confirm payment of taxes.

The STL has made a massive difference to cigarette prices in the Philippines, but they are still not high by international standards. Figure 3.4 shows the international price trend for minimum and premium brand cigarette prices. In 2014, the cheapest pack of cigarettes in the Philippines cost about ₱30 (or ₱1.5 per cigarette). At prevailing exchange rates, this was equivalent to $0.70 per pack and $0.03 per cigarette. By this measure, the Philippines ranks 52 out of the 172 countries in the sample. Figure 3.4 suggests there is a lot of room to further increase cigarette taxes, and therefore prices, over the medium term to

Figure 3.4 International Cigarette Prices

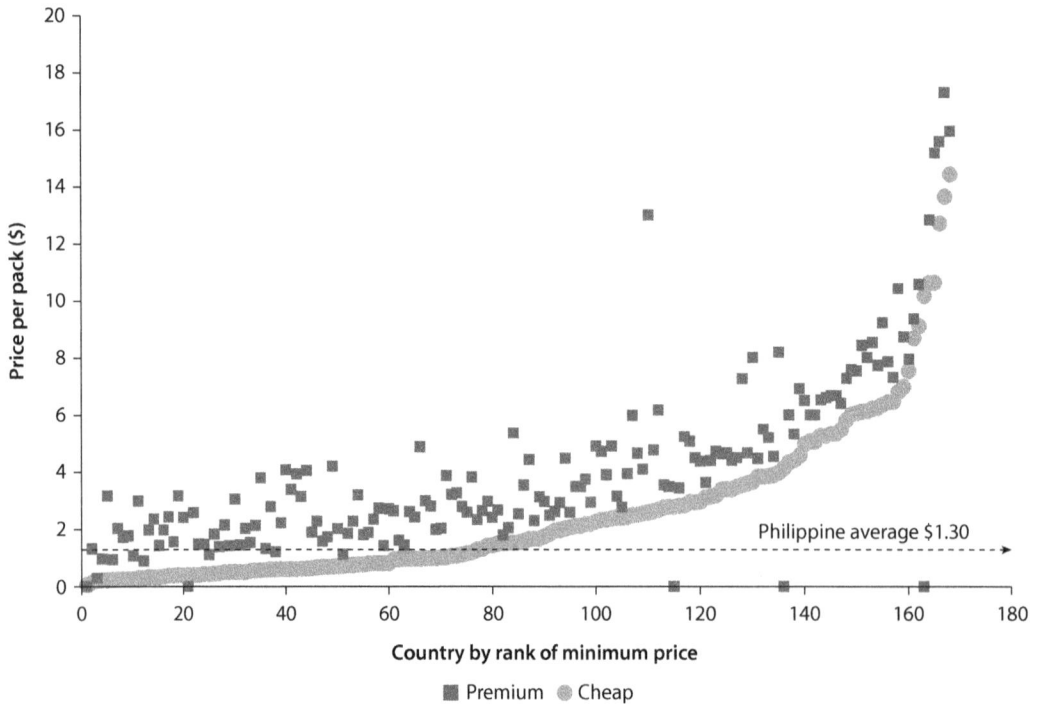

Source: WHO 2015.
Note: Conversion at official U.S. dollar exchange rate. 172 sample countries.

decrease the affordability of smoking. The recent robust performance of the economy should translate into higher incomes for Filipinos (see Cruz et al. 2016). Beyond looking at absolute prices or tax incidence, appropriate measures of especially cigarette price will therefore need to look at affordability based on different measures of disposable income to be spent on "sin" versus essential and "virtue" goods.

In contrast to cigarettes, beer and spirits did not show large price increases. Beer excise taxes are imposed on a gross liter of alcohol, equivalent to ₱19 ($0.42) or ₱22 ($0.48) per liter in 2015. Figure 3.5 describes the price of beer before and after the STL. Floor prices increased from just over ₱40 ($1) per liter before the STL to nearly ₱50 per liter by early 2015. The increase on some premium brands was greater, about 20 percent over two years.

Figure 3.6 shows selected spirits prices on a gross liter basis. The relative unit price of alcohol of spirits remains significantly lower than beer and has not increased by much over time. The excise tax incidence for spirits is more complex because of the hybrid specific and ad valorem structure. Also, the market is diverse, ranging from locally produced palm wine (tuba), coconut wine (lambanog), and medicinal wine to national brands such as Emperador brandy, San Miguel gin, and Tanduay rum, and international brands domestically produced or imported. The alcohol content of palm wine lies in the range of beer (at 4 percent), but coconut wine may have higher alcohol content. The low relative cost of alcohol from spirits means the Department of Finance (DOF) should continue to find ways to strengthen the taxation of spirits from both a revenue and health perspective if drinking is shown to present significant adverse health impacts (box 3.2).

Figure 3.5 Beer Prices, 2011–15

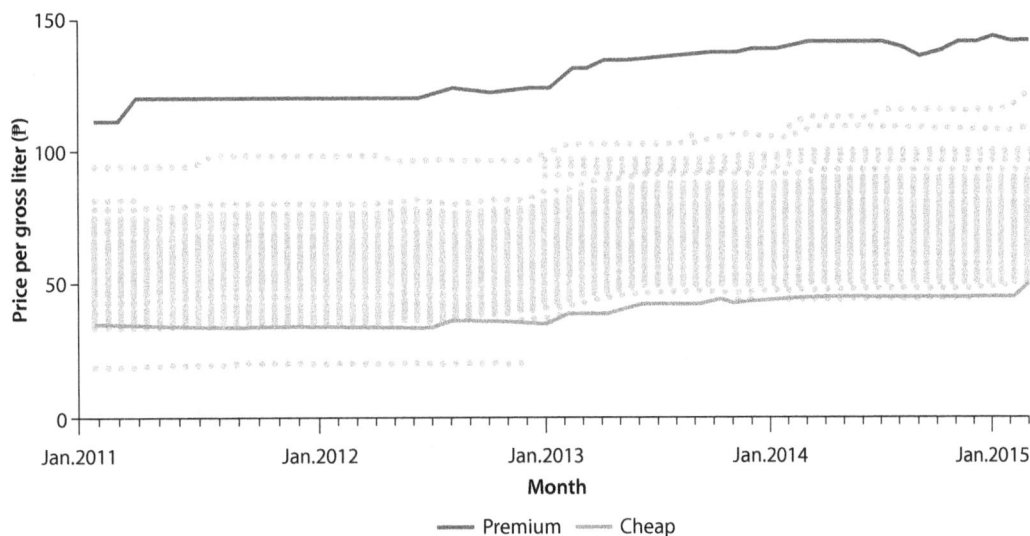

Sources: Philippine Statistics Authority; National Statistics Office.
Note: Note apparent outliers.

Sin Tax Reform in the Philippines • http://dx.doi.org/10.1596/978-1-4648-0806-7

Figure 3.6 Spirits Prices, 2011–15

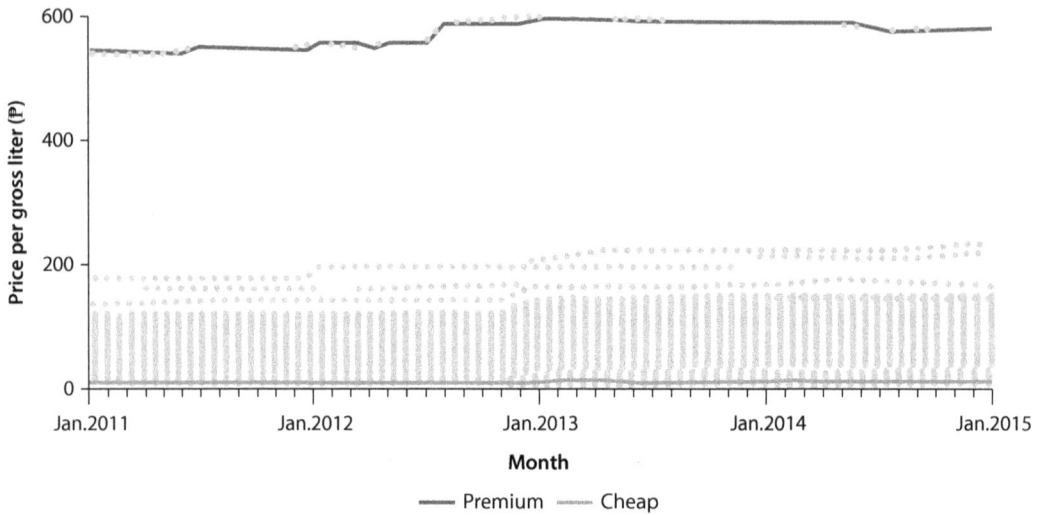

Sources: Philippine Statistics Authority; National Statistics Office.
Note: Outliers removed.

Box 3.2 Counting Alcohol

Excise taxes are imposed on alcohol because these products have traditionally been good revenue sources and because of growing concerns about excessive and youth drinking. Some brand segments are of particular concern because of their potency (alcohol percentages or proof levels) and form, such as sweeter tasting products catering to young drinkers. Because alcoholic beverages come in a variety of shapes and forms, deciding on the basis for taxation is challenging.

The excise tax on spirits in the Philippines is a combination of specific and ad valorem taxes. It is levied on a proof liter of alcohol, representing a 50 percent alcohol equivalent at a given room temperature. Most countries now use alcohol-by-volume measures, although historically the term proof has also commonly been used. A 100-proof bottle of rum represents about 57 percent alcohol by volume. In the Philippines, a proof liter of spirits was subject to a ₱20 ($0.44) specific excise in 2015 (plus an ad valorem component based on net retail price). A 100-proof liter bottle of rum would be subject to ₱23 ($0.51) of specific excise (57/50 percent), and a liter of alcohol-by-volume palm wine (tuba)—which has an alcohol content similar to beer—to ₱2 ($0.04) of specific excise.

The need to keep track of alcohol strength in the taxation of spirits in the Philippines, as opposed to beer, adds some complexity to the exercise. The ad valorem component also requires the Bureau of Internal Revenue to track net retail prices, through 2017 and beyond. The unitary specific rates for cigarettes and beer obviate the need to administer this part of the Sin Tax Law from 2017. The hybrid tax design for spirits, however, had a clear rationale based

box continues next page

Box 3.2 Counting Alcohol (continued)

on introducing a workable floor price (especially given how much of sales volume is at the low-end of the market), but also the need to generate revenues (notably from the growing share of premium brands). Effort should now be directed at understanding the actual incidence of excise taxes on a per unit of alcohol incidence. If the evidence suggests that both health and revenues merit it, the government should review excise policy and administration measures for spirits increasingly through the lens of tax incidence of de facto alcohol strength.

Source: Bird 2015.

While the regular price collections for tobacco and alcohol conducted as part of inflation monitoring by the PSA provided some insights to help track STL implementation, the data was subject to some limitations. The PSA is bound by disclosure restrictions concerning specific price data, and is focused on tracking a number of representative brands over time to help measure inflation. Since 2015, the World Bank has partnered with Premise, a San Francisco technology company that collects, indexes, and analyzes data captured by smartphone through a network of paid contributors.

Compensated crowdsourcing by mobile phone is a powerful way to gain rapid insights into frontline cigarette and alcohol prices in the Philippines. The Android app used allows for the capture of various types of data—photos of cigarette packs and individual cigarettes, geotagging, manual entry of prices and other information—ensuring comprehensive coverage with visual documentation and geographic coordinates (figure 3.7). Premise task managers assess the quality of contributions and optimize the sampling design in real time to ensure representativeness of the sample. Currently, several thousand prices are being collected across the Philippines every week, with statistical representation across major brands, locations, and packaging types. Powerful "big data" analytics allow for further analysis, including homing in on potential "hot spots" where final prices seem out of line with excise tax levels and changes. Premise data collectors enrich the STL data with information such as major brands, tax brackets (low and high), geographical location, and venue type. Thus, visualization and aggregation of the STL data is possible at many levels from national price distributions across all sin products to specific trends across a given product in a given region. In addition, the Premise network engages in a process they term "discovery" which involves investigations of specific issues, such as identifying the cheapest and most expensive brands found in sampled outlets, and providing continuous insights into market dynamics.

The Premise sin tax dashboard visualizes price trends across cigarettes, spirits, and staple products displaying price, tax stamp compliance, and observation volume across time and space. Specifically, the graph of cigarette, spirits, and staple goods price over time shows the lowest 5 percent average and the highest

Figure 3.7 Premise Geotagged Price Data Collection for Cigarettes

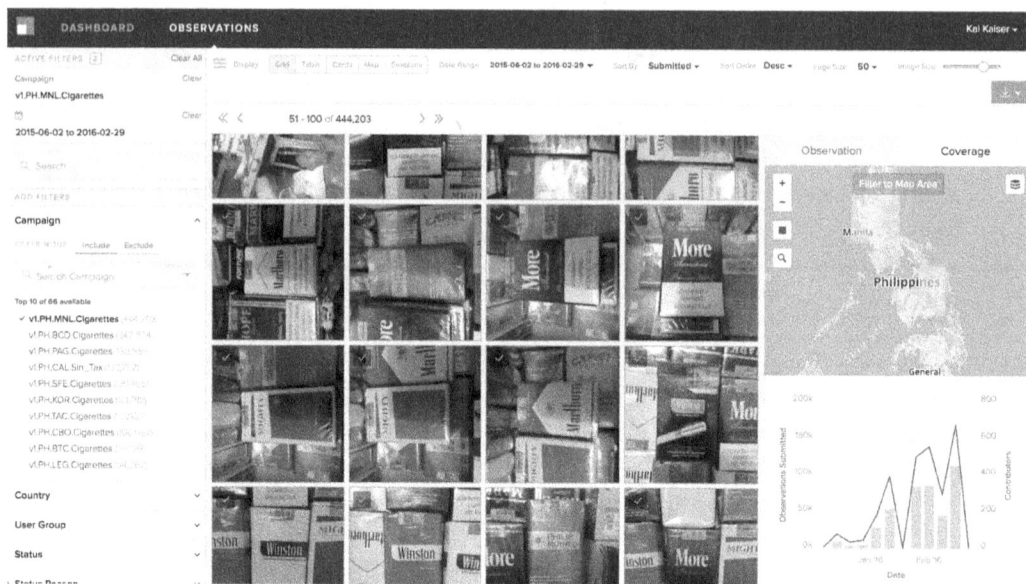

Source: Premise.

95 percent price of the different products by week, weighted by brand for each packaging variant (1 cigarette, pack of 20, carton). The data is also visualized by individual brand and geographic region. The microdata provided by the Premise network allows for further insights based on geographic location, venue type, brand, and tax stamp compliance allowing for policy making at both the aggregated and disaggregated scale.

Crowd-sourced data reveal that prices vary significantly between low-cost, low-entry level cigarette brands and premium ones. Figure 3.8 shows that prices varied from about ₱1.5 ($0.03) to over ₱5.0 ($0.11) per cigarette in September 2015. Per cigarette prices tended to be clustered in ₱0.50 ($0.01) increments.

From a health perspective, floor prices are the greatest concern. Figure 3.9 shows that during the first half of 2015, floor prices recorded by Premise contributors remained at ₱1.5 ($0.03), with ceiling prices just under ₱5 ($0.11) and some outliers at ₱6 ($0.13). This means that crowdsourced data were finding a floor price significantly higher than ₱1 per cigarette being found in the PSA data. The app is designed to track major brands, but contributors are also asked to seek out new brands as they enter the market. The DOF consequently posted a dashboard on its website with weekly updates of price trends, as well as the coverage of cigarette tax stamps.

The recent creation of the PSA provides an opportunity to significantly improve the availability of various types of tracking evidence, including for STL monitoring.[8] Moving forward, the DOF, Bureau of Internal Revenue (BIR),

Figure 3.8 Distribution of Cigarette Prices

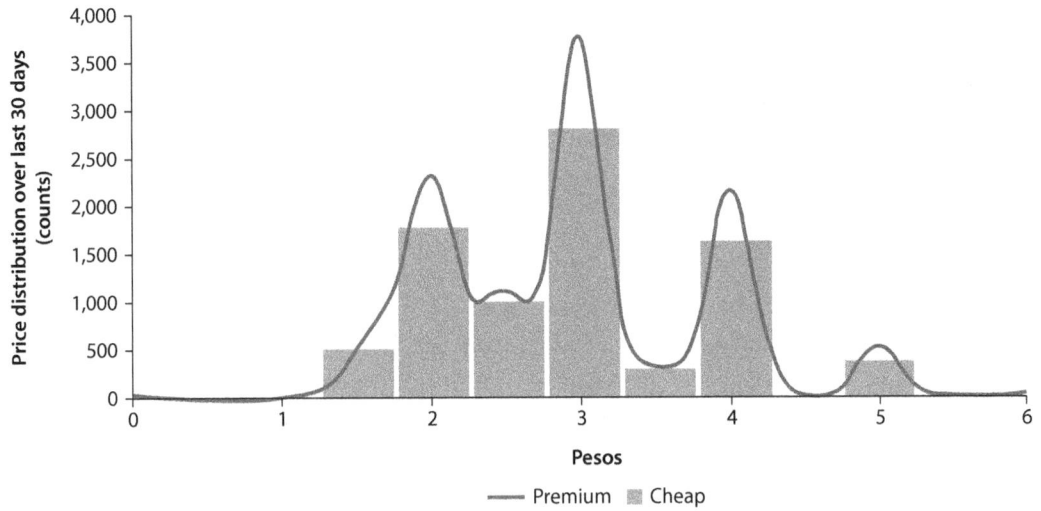

Source: Premise.

Figure 3.9 Prices Per Cigarette, April–September 2015

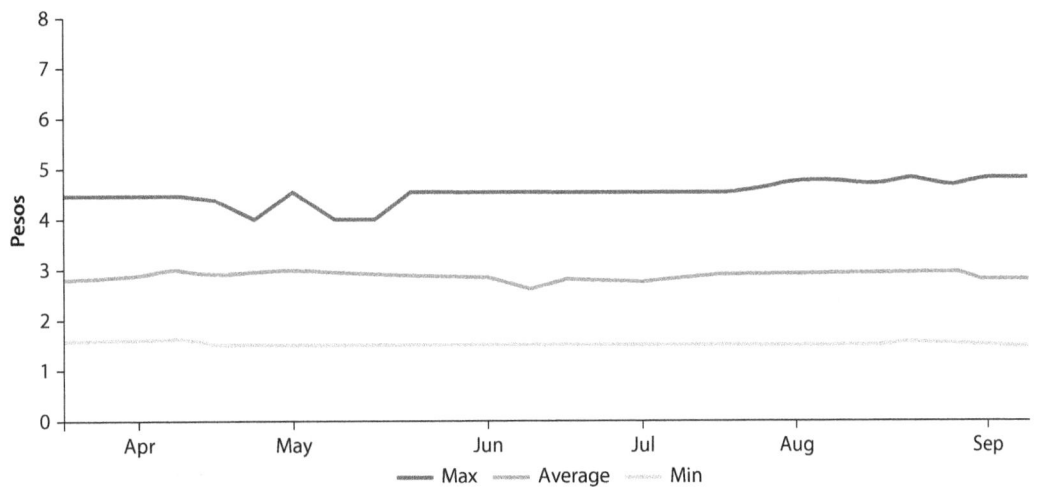

Source: Premise.

and PSA could further institutionalize better data access and analysis of tobacco and alcohol retail price dynamics. Although PSA data collection is adequate for collecting the Consumer Price Series, it is currently not set up to adequately capture cigarette market dynamics, including the entry of new brands.[9] The industry collects monthly price data through providers such as AC Nielsen, but this is used mainly to inform marketing strategies and for surveillance of competitors. Premise's price tracking provides one alternative monitoring mechanism

Sin Tax Reform in the Philippines • http://dx.doi.org/10.1596/978-1-4648-0806-7

for government that does not further burden the PSA's day-to-day work, but, instead, complements the longer-run price series. Premise price tracking will definitely continue until the end of the Aquino administration in June 2016. Thereafter, the government, in possible collaboration with development partners, will need to consider how this data collection will be sustained.[10] The spirits market is likely to see a significant transformation in the coming years, especially with the increased entry of foreign brands in the more premium segment. The PSA could use mainstream data collection, or rely on special survey innovations such as those conducted by World Bank-Premise, to also monitor alcohol prices. International experience suggests that price disclosure (see box 3.3) can help counter tax evasion and is an area in which the Philippines could serve as a global leader in good practice. To facilitate analysis by researchers and other stakeholders, these data should also be accessible in a machine-readable format; for example, by using guidelines established under the recently launched government statistics Open Government website, data.gov.ph. Building on the biannual World Health Organization Tobacco Monitor, countries in the Association of Southeast Asian Nations (ASEAN) could provide ongoing updates on cigarette floor and premium prices in their jurisdictions, as well as on the most popular brands that are traded, either licitly or illicitly, across borders. The achievement of a unitary cigarette tax in 2017 means the BIR no longer needs to be concerned

---

Box 3.3 Tobacco and Alcohol Price Disclosure in Chile and Colombia

Chile and Colombia, where retail prices form the basis of excise taxation, make prices public. In both countries, tax authorities draw on retail sale price information provided by their national statistics offices, and use this for tax determination and enforcement purposes.

Chile implements a mixed system, with ad valorem rates on retail sale prices with monthly adjustment of the tax base. The Chilean Internal Revenue Service publishes monthly data on average prices per brand, provided by the national statistics office. Once published on its website, these prices become the tax base for the removals of each type of brand the following month. This information also allows tax authorities to capture changes in the tax-based retail selling price in a particular month. The tax authorities then adjust the tax calculation once the information is public. For an example of this information from November 9, 2015, see http://www.sii.cl/pagina/valores/precios_cigarrillos.htm. The cigarette price index is made public on the website of the national statistics office at estadisticas_precios/ipc/nuevo_ipc /nuevo_ipc .php.

Colombia also implements a mixed system, with ad valorem rates on retail sales prices with annual adjustment. For the tax base definition, the statistics office publishes each December the average price of all brands from January to November of that year. This average price, adjusted by the expected inflation target for the coming year, forms the tax base applied during the following year. Tax authorities maintain this tax base for the whole year. See http://www.dane.gov.co/index.php/indices-de-precios-y-costos/cigarrillos-y-tabaco.

---

with special price surveys to classify cigarette brands, which is a distinct advantage of the simpler approach.

Revenues and Legal Sales

Removals reflect the official taxed volume of tobacco and alcohol products leaving the factory and entering the market. Companies are taxed when cigarettes are transferred to the warehouse from the factory; that is, on an ex-factory basis. Removals provide the most detailed and timely indicator of market trends and industry response. Overall cigarette removals have declined by almost a third since the 2012 baseline. The slight increase in removals from 2014 to 2015 can be explained by the high degree of frontloading prior to 2014. The incentives for frontloading will diminish as the unitary excise rate is achieved, and increases become more gradual (that is, 4 percent in excises per year). Because of market confidentiality the BIR cannot release detailed monthly removals data by product and brand, but this data can be analyzed in summary form to assess developments by market segments. Internally within the government, these confidential data should be made available, at least to the authorities in charge of monitoring the STL's implementation (table 3.5).[11]

Cigarette removals in particular have been subject to significant seasonality because of frontloading. Table 3.6 summarizes the indicators and issues related to the effects of removals. Since the STL, cigarette removals declined 32 percent over 2012–14, beer removals declined 10 percent, and spirits removals increased almost 45 percent.[12]

Figures 3.10, 3.11, and 3.12 show monthly removals for cigarettes, beer, and spirits during 2012–15. Note the spikes for cigarette removals in December of 2012, 2013, and 2014, which reflect frontloading. Detailed monthly removals by product type provide some insight into the overall structure of the market and consumption. Downshifting (consumers shifting to cheaper cigarettes), together with muted price increases, may have meant that aggregate removals did not drop as much as they would have without these two factors. The share of high-tier cigarettes rose to 19.8 percent in 2014, and to 33 percent in 2015. It should be noted that tax increases for the lower tier are higher, given the need to converge to a unitary rate in 2017, which may also explain the greater frontloading in the lower-tier market.

Table 3.5 Removals Before and After the STL Implementation

Product	Units	2012	2013	2014	2015	Change 2012–13 (%)	Change 2013–14 (%)	Change 2012–14 (%)	Change 2012–15 (%)
Cigarettes	Packs, billion	5.76	4.87	3.92	4.27	−15.45	−19.51	−31.94	−26.82
Beer	Liters, billion	1.57	1.40	1.41	1.43	−10.80	0.71	−10.19	−0.09
Distilled spirits	Proof liters, million	287.23	370.91	415.87	398.46	29.13	12.12	−4.19	38.73

Source: Bureau of Internal Revenue.
Note: STL = Sin Tax Law.

Table 3.6 Removals of Tobacco, Alcohol Products: Direct Impacts and Conditioning Behavior

Indicators measuring the direct impacts	Intervening behavior of industry and consumers	Monitoring indicators of conditioning behaviors	Analysis
Total removals, upper segment removals, lower segment removals.	Increasing removals of lower-priced cigarettes.	Bureau of Revenue (BIR) should provide a report on market-share changes per brand and company.	A comparison of expected removals, given actual prices collected by National Statistics Office, with actual removals should be conducted.
	Creating new cheaper brands.	BIR should provide a report on new brands.	A methodology to estimate expected removals for segments should be provided. BIR's confidential information on market segments and brands should be prepared and analyzed, but not published.
	Underreporting and smuggling.	Market volume indicator.	

Source: National Statistics Office.

Muted cigarette price increases relative to tax increases raised some concerns that tax evasion and smuggling were likely pronounced. However, other factors could have contributed, such as frontloading and companies delaying passing on the tax increases to consumers to protect market share. To maintain market share under the two-tier tax structure until 2017, companies also appear to have used strategies of cross-subsidizing cheaper brands with large increases on less price-sensitive premium brands. Because brand-level price and removals data for particular brands are not available, we could not assess whether muted prices of particular brands saw less than an expected increase in removals. Total brand demand would under these circumstances be the sum of licit (removals) and illicit sales (tax evasion and smuggling). In 2014, the government launched legal actions against specific low-cost cigarette producers suspected of breaching the STL.[13] The introduction of a tax stamp later that year made monitoring possible breaches clearer.

The market response to the STL will determine trends in cigarette and alcohol products. From a health perspective, our main concerns are the prices of cheaper products and the marketing strategies used. As already noted, the BIR reports on market shares per brand and new products are central to understanding firms' strategies to maintain consumption patterns. Given the size of the tax increases, the sales strategies of tobacco companies will certainly be more aggressive than those of alcohol companies. While maintaining confidentiality for the time being, BIR reports should include analysis of the removals data on close-substitute tobacco and alcohol products. From both a health and revenue perspective, the DOF and BIR should be concerned that the revenue gaps caused by currently licit measures, such as frontloading, and especially illicit ones, are minimized.

Figure 3.10 Cigarette Removals and Revenues, 2012–15

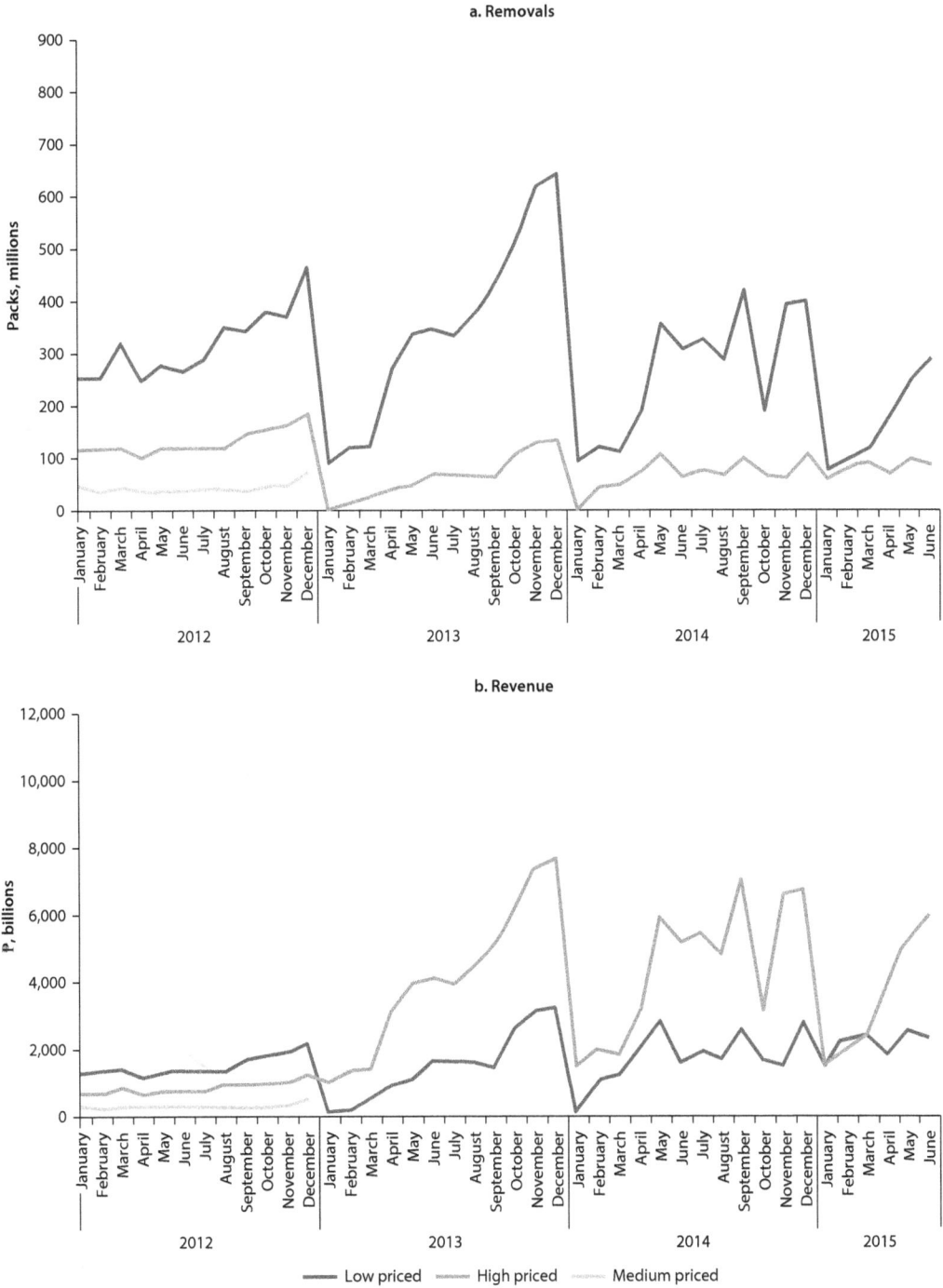

a. Removals

b. Revenue

Low priced ——— High priced ——— Medium priced

Source: Bureau of Internal Revenue.

Figure 3.11 Beer Removals and Revenues, 2012–15

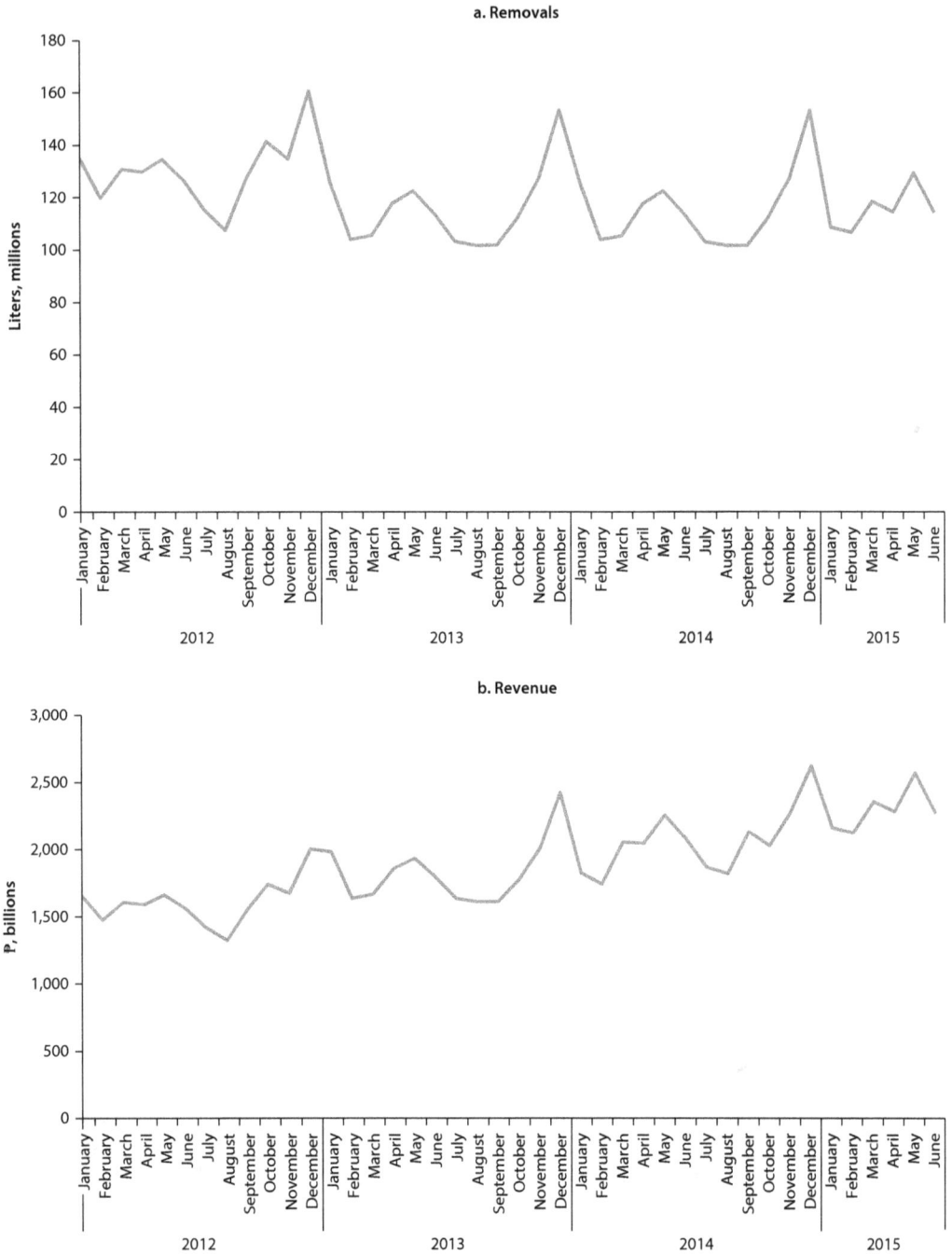

a. Removals

b. Revenue

Source: Bureau of Internal Revenue.

Figure 3.12 Spirits Removals and Revenues, 2012–15

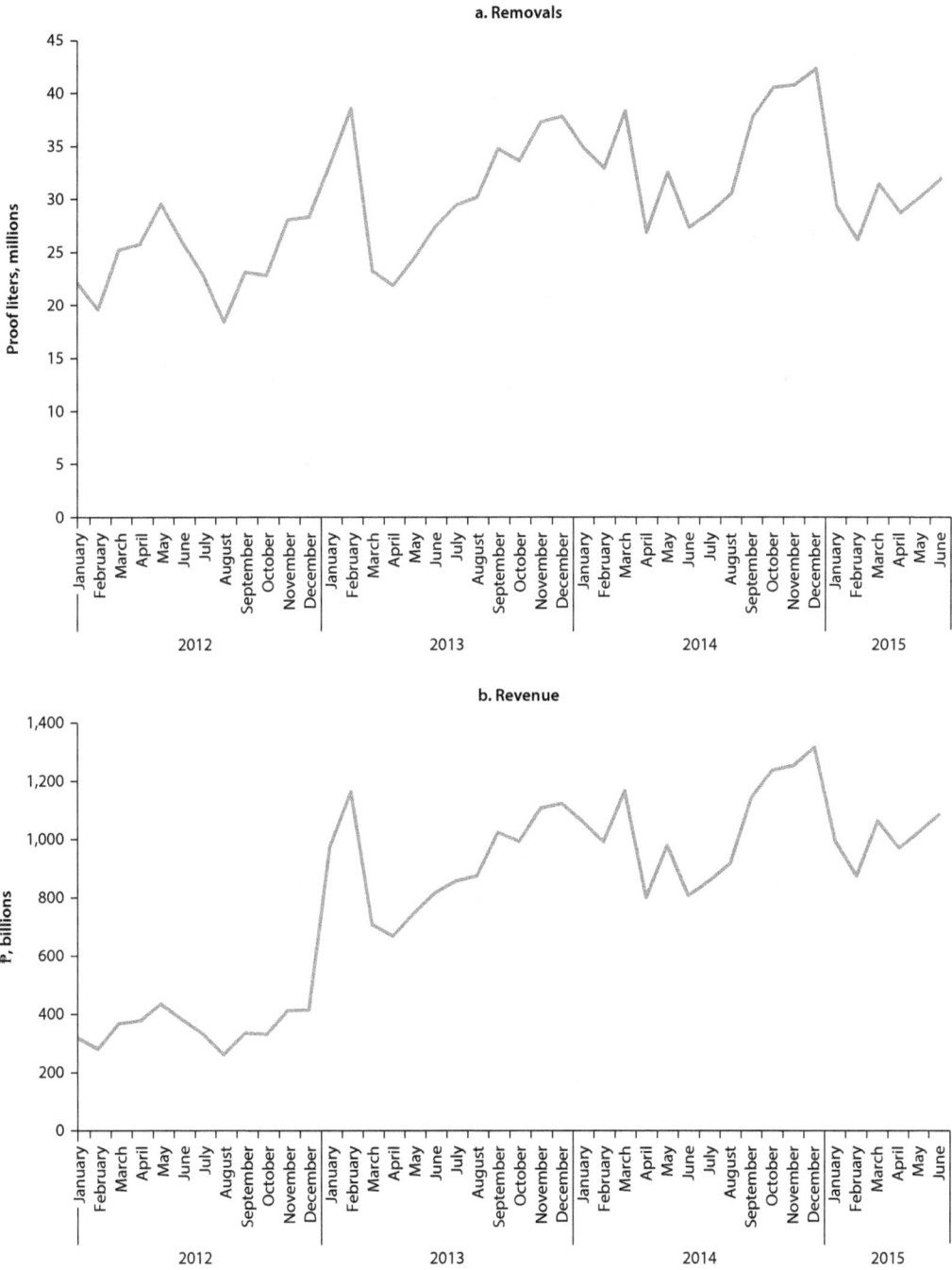

a. Removals

b. Revenue

Source: Bureau of Internal Revenue.

Revenue Gaps

Various sources and methodologies indicate the extent of the challenge of revenue leakage. A frequent industry assertion is that increases in taxes and retail prices lead to increased tax evasion and smuggling. This is hardly an argument for curtailing tax increases, but it does highlight the need for strengthened monitoring and evaluation and countervailing measures. The risk of revenue leakage can be assessed based on triangulating revenue, removals, and consumption levels, as well as changes. Levels refer to apparent discrepancies between consumption and tax sales. If tax increases do not seem to be translated into retail price increases this can be a cause for concern. As noted earlier, the lack of full excise tax pass through could be the result of competitive market dynamics: the pressure to maintain market share, and the ability to reduce production and distribution costs, could see the industry not fully pass through excise tax increases.

Revenue gaps—the difference between maximum collections against prevailing consumption and tax rates in any given year—can be licit (for example, through frontloading) or illicit, through tax evasion and smuggling. Revenue collection leakage measures rely on assessing the gaps between actual consumption and formal taxed sales. Smuggling and domestic tax evasion by producers and distributors may affect actual prices, decrease potential revenues, and increase tobacco and alcohol consumption. Revenue leakage raises a number of concerns. Untaxed sin tax goods blunt the reform's prospective health impacts, as the price signals to reduce consumption are undermined, and obviously also erode revenues. Pervasive smuggling and tax evasion undermines the STL's credibility because it creates a disparity between law-abiding and law-evading firms and consumers. However, detailed indicators on tax evasion and avoidance are not readily available.

Because of tax evasion and avoidance, retail prices end up being lower than they would be if taxes were included in the cost structure, and revenues are foregone. Broad measures of leakages rely on comparing removals with final consumption. Beyond accounting for legal duty-free quantities, the compared numbers should not show large discrepancies. However, knowledge of actual final consumption is typically gained through surveys, and thus aggregate measures are subject to a significant degree of measurement error. Special care needs to be taken to understand what factors lead to possible downward or upward biases in results, notably by types of cigarettes (cheap versus premium, for example). Other measures include cross-checking whether goods at final sales points have been subject to the relevant tax and duty payments, as well as bona fide supply chain validation (that is, tracking the actual movement of goods from factory through to the point of sale).

Box 3.4 suggests the main method to estimate removals discrepancies is to compare legal domestic sales net of exports and domestic consumption estimates, typically collected through surveys. Frontloading also needs to be accounted for. In a report commissioned by the tobacco industry, the International Tax and Investment Center and Oxford Economics estimated illicit cigarette sales in the Philippines in 2013 at 18.1 percent of total sales, above the average of 10.9 percent

---

Box 3.4 Measuring Illicit Consumption of Tobacco and Alcohol

A major concern in comparing annual final domestic consumption against estimates of removals as a measure of revenue leakage is controlling against biases and measurement errors (Merriman 2003). One challenge is to address the fact that survey respondents typically underreport their daily consumption of cigarettes. Another is to ensure adequate accounting for the lag between removals and when cigarettes are sold and consumed. If frontloading is large, major discrepancies between sales and consumption data are likely, but this bias can be controlled and easily calculated.

Many analysts follow the Merriman approach, which uses coefficients of consumption for underreporting in the past, and compares total consumption as measured through multiple surveys (Global Adult Tobacco Survey, Social Weather Stations, Family Income and Expenditure Survey) with actual removals figures for those years. The second part is to calculate actual consumption in a specific year (year T), using the following formula:

Actual total consumption in year T = self-reporting of total consumption in year T (using a special survey for examples/coefficients of underreporting (a number or interval of numbers) (1)

Using equation (1), we can estimate the market size for year T and compare it with actual removals for consumption in year T to see the existence of non-duty-paid cigarettes in smoking consumption, as shown by equation (2):

Non-duty-paid consumption = actual consumption in year T (using 1)—actual removals of duty-paid cigarettes in year T (excluding frontloading effects) (2)

Under the Sin Tax Law's implementing rules and regulations, the Department of Health is mandated to formulate a unified framework to regularly monitor the consumption of tobacco and alcohol products, using current monitoring mechanisms. Unfortunately, because of the timing of surveys, such as the ones already mentioned, the government did not have a survey covering self-reported consumption in 2013 for analysis in the annual sin tax report that was submitted in August 2014. Thus, a coefficient for past-year underreporting to calculate actual total consumption (applying the Merriman approach, for example) in the cigarette market is not currently possible.

---

for ASEAN-14 (ASEAN's 10 countries plus Australia; Hong Kong SAR, China; Pakistan; and Taiwan, China) (ITIC and Oxford Economics 2014). The report suggests the Philippines was among the top three countries in terms of illicit consumption in this group in 2013, along with Pakistan and Vietnam.[14] Updates for 2014 suggested that illicit cigarette use in the Philippines increased to 19.4 percent of the total sales (some 19.9 billion cigarettes), with over 95 percent coming from domestic production.[15] Market leader Philip Morris International[16] publicly flagged its concerns over revenue evasion by low-cost producers such as Mighty. By contrast, as we later show, big data analytics reveal illicit consumption of only about 5 percent.

The BIR has strengthened mechanisms for safeguarding revenues, including the rollout of a holographic tax stamp. In August 2013, the DOF ordered an investigation into alleged smuggling at Mighty; as a result, the Bureau of Customs closed one of Mighty's bonded warehouses in January 2014.[17] Starting in that year, the BIR introduced the affixture of internal revenue stamps with security features on imported and locally manufactured cigarettes through the Internal Revenue Stamps Integrated System. All packs sold in 2015 had to have this tax stamp—and those without were deemed illicit. Crowdsourced monitoring by phone through the Premise network was used to track the tax stamp's rollout, which approached 99.6 percent penetration levels by March 2016 (see figure 3.13). To put this in perspective, market cigarette removals were just under 4 billion packs in 2014, as table 3.5 indicates. With just 1 percent of this volume representing 40 million packs, and multiplied by the lowest tax tier of ₱21 ($0.47) in 2015, this would represent a revenue loss of ₱840 million (or just under $20 million).

Closed-circuit TV cameras were installed at one major cigarette manufacturer as part of the BIR's efforts to strictly safeguard revenues, and the same measure will soon be implemented at all cigarette manufacturers. The cameras aim to monitor whether factories are declaring all production for tax purposes. Monitoring and accounting for all packs on the market will provide a high return.[18] We recommend that the DOF, BIR, private sector, and civil society use monitoring initiatives such as Premise or other field-based observations to ensure maximum tax stamp compliance. The BIR can also use targeted information on brands and geographic areas with low tax stamp penetration for further action.

Transparency in international trade can further curtail tax and duty evasion. While the bulk of Philippine tobacco is produced domestically, domestic sales of cigarettes are subject to international inputs. Figure 3.14 shows the key components of a cigarette. As it turns out, acetate filters used in the production of cigarettes in the Philippines are wholly imported. Some tobacco, including for flavoring, is also imported.

Figure 3.13 Cigarette Tax Stamp Coverage

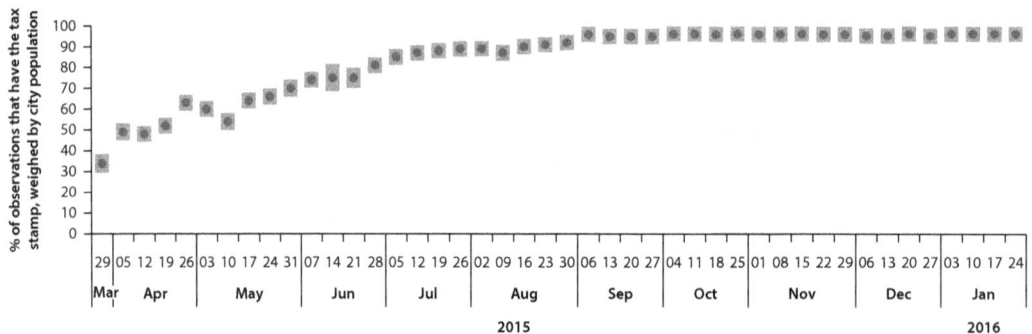

Source: Premise.

To enhance scrutiny on producers, the DOF publishes data on tobacco and acetate imports in newspapers, as shown in figures 3.15 and 3.16. Because the data allowed for a unit-cost analysis of declared inputs, this information could be used to take action against producers where the value of declared inputs was not in line with the tax being paid on units of cigarettes produced. We recommend

Figure 3.14 Anatomy of a Cigarette

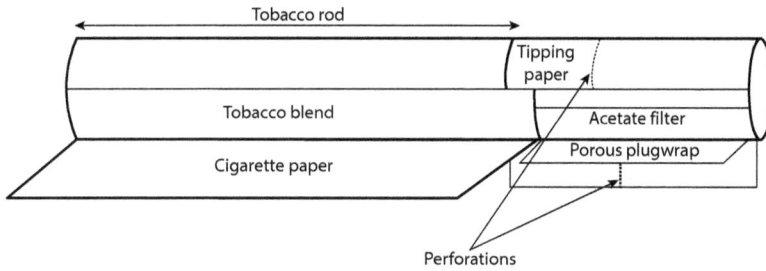

Source: Adapted from the United Kingdom Parliament webpage, http://www.parliament.the-stationery -office.co.uk/pa/cm199900/cmselect/cmhealth/27/0011323.htm.

Figure 3.15 Tax Watch Tobacco Imports Public Disclosure

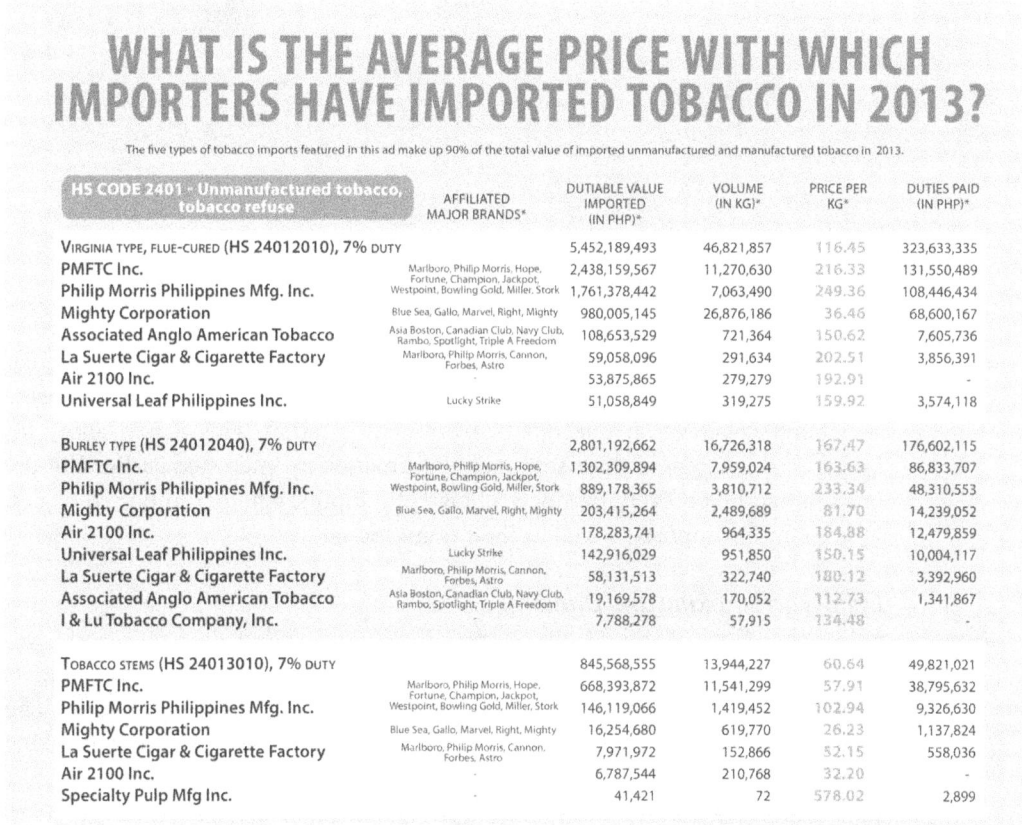

WHAT IS THE AVERAGE PRICE WITH WHICH IMPORTERS HAVE IMPORTED TOBACCO IN 2013?

The five types of tobacco imports featured in this ad make up 90% of the total value of imported unmanufactured and manufactured tobacco in 2013.

HS CODE 2401 - Unmanufactured tobacco, tobacco refuse	AFFILIATED MAJOR BRANDS*	DUTIABLE VALUE IMPORTED (IN PHP)*	VOLUME (IN KG)*	PRICE PER KG*	DUTIES PAID (IN PHP)*
Virginia type, flue-cured (HS 24012010), 7% duty		5,452,189,493	46,821,857	116.45	323,633,335
PMFTC Inc.	Marlboro, Philip Morris, Hope, Fortune, Champion, Jackpot, Westpoint, Bowling Gold, Miller, Stork	2,438,159,567	11,270,630	216.33	131,550,489
Philip Morris Philippines Mfg. Inc.		1,761,378,442	7,063,490	249.36	108,446,434
Mighty Corporation	Blue Sea, Gallo, Marvel, Right, Mighty	980,005,145	26,876,186	36.46	68,600,167
Associated Anglo American Tobacco	Asia Boston, Canadian Club, Navy Club, Rambo, Spotlight, Triple A Freedom	108,653,529	721,364	150.62	7,605,736
La Suerte Cigar & Cigarette Factory	Marlboro, Philip Morris, Cannon, Forbes, Astro	59,058,096	291,634	202.51	3,856,391
Air 2100 Inc.	-	53,875,865	279,279	192.91	-
Universal Leaf Philippines Inc.	Lucky Strike	51,058,849	319,275	159.92	3,574,118
Burley type (HS 24012040), 7% duty		2,801,192,662	16,726,318	167.47	176,602,115
PMFTC Inc.	Marlboro, Philip Morris, Hope, Fortune, Champion, Jackpot, Westpoint, Bowling Gold, Miller, Stork	1,302,309,894	7,959,024	163.63	86,833,707
Philip Morris Philippines Mfg. Inc.		889,178,365	3,810,712	233.34	48,310,553
Mighty Corporation	Blue Sea, Gallo, Marvel, Right, Mighty	203,415,264	2,489,689	81.70	14,239,052
Air 2100 Inc.	-	178,283,741	964,335	184.88	12,479,859
Universal Leaf Philippines Inc.	Lucky Strike	142,916,029	951,850	150.15	10,004,117
La Suerte Cigar & Cigarette Factory	Marlboro, Philip Morris, Cannon, Forbes, Astro	58,131,513	322,740	180.12	3,392,960
Associated Anglo American Tobacco	Asia Boston, Canadian Club, Navy Club, Rambo, Spotlight, Triple A Freedom	19,169,578	170,052	112.73	1,341,867
I & Lu Tobacco Company, Inc.	-	7,788,278	57,915	134.48	-
Tobacco stems (HS 24013010), 7% duty		845,568,555	13,944,227	60.64	49,821,021
PMFTC Inc.	Marlboro, Philip Morris, Hope, Fortune, Champion, Jackpot, Westpoint, Bowling Gold, Miller, Stork	668,393,872	11,541,299	57.91	38,795,632
Philip Morris Philippines Mfg. Inc.		146,119,066	1,419,452	102.94	9,326,630
Mighty Corporation	Blue Sea, Gallo, Marvel, Right, Mighty	16,254,680	619,770	26.23	1,137,824
La Suerte Cigar & Cigarette Factory	Marlboro, Philip Morris, Cannon, Forbes, Astro	7,971,972	152,866	52.15	558,036
Air 2100 Inc.	-	6,787,544	210,768	32.20	-
Specialty Pulp Mfg Inc.	-	41,421	72	578.02	2,899

figure continues next page

Figure 3.15 Tax Watch Tobacco Imports Public Disclosure (continued)

Other, not flue-cured (HS 24011090), 7% duty		1,361,187,420	7,004,361	194.33	62,563,192
PMFTC Inc.	Marlboro, Philip Morris, Hope, Fortune, Champion, Jackpot, Westpoint, Bowling Gold, Miller, Stork	719,856,706	4,297,177	167.52	36,789,515
Philip Morris Philippines Mfg. Inc.	Asia Boston, Canadian Club, Navy Club, Rambo, Spotlight, Triple A Freedom	595,009,375	2,245,066	265.03	22,531,189
Associated Anglo American Tobacco		35,456,109	256,172	138.41	2,481,923
Mighty Corporation	Blue Sea, Gallo, Marvel, Right, Mighty	5,780,402	198,026	29.19	404,628
Universal Leaf Philippines Inc.	Lucky Strike	5,084,828	7,920	642.02	355,937

HS CODE 2402 - Cigars, cheroots, cigarillos and cigarettes, of tobacco or of tobacco substitutes

Cigarettes containing tobacco (HS 240220), 10% duty		1,146,420,917	3,090,942	370.90	25,240,237
British American Tobacco (Phils) Ltd.	Lucky Strike, Dunhill, Kent, Pall Mall	742,559,923	1,731,068	428.96	14,862,659
JT International (Philippines) Inc.	Winston, Camel, Mild Seven	280,740,578	590,639	475.32	7,895
Goldlink Intl. (Subic) Inc.	-	38,211,766	403,282	94.75	3,821,173
Prudence Dev't and Mgmt. Corp.		25,536,444	67,504	378.30	2,620,843
Realway International Phil. Corp.		15,513,550	62,655	247.60	1,551,353
Richie Import & Export Trading		15,004,522	47,882	313.37	1,112
Subic Bay Global Intl Corporation		9,085,410	133,000	68.31	908,541
Bumi Jaya International Corporation		7,472,752	47,526	157.23	747,274
Philip Morris Philippines Mfg. Inc.	Marlboro, Philip Morris, Hope, Fortune, Champion, Jackpot, Westpoint, Bowling Gold, Miller, Stork	5,464,210	1,064	5,137.85	546,419
Duty Free Philippines Corporation		5,101,982	3,797	1,343.68	-
PMFTC Inc.	Marlboro, Philip Morris, Hope, Fortune, Champion, Jackpot, Westpoint, Bowling Gold, Miller, Stork	1,014,213	336	3,021.19	101,414
Jade Crown Philippines Corp.		389,937	1,485	262.58	38,993
Tabaqueria De Filipinas Inc.	Flor de Filipinas, Flor de Filipinas Reserva, Antonio Gimenez, Independencia 1898	183,289	150	1,221.93	18,328
Golden Tobacco Corporation	Chancellor	109,025	510	213.77	10,902
Columbia Transport Inc.		33,316	45	734.80	3,331

*Data is extracted from the e2M database and hence, does not include manual assessments. Low duties paid are caused by the availment of free trade agreements ssuch as the ASEAN Free Trade Area (AFTA) and ASEAN China Free Trade Area (ACFTA). The HS Code can be considered the "identification number" of commodities in customs procedures. Dutiable value = Cost of goods + Freight + Insurance + Other Charges and Costs Customs duty (CUD) paid - Customs duty is levied on goods entering the country, and is derived by multiplying the dutiable value with duty rate and converted to peso value (using the applicable foreign exchange rate). Duty rate varies depending on the classification of goods under the 2012 ASEAN Harmonized Tariff Nomenclature (AHTN) and various Philippines Trade Agreements Does not include payments in January 2014 for importations assessed in 2013. Common ingredients for a cigarette stick are composed of the following: cutfiller, cigarette paper, tipping paper, filter rods, wrapper and stamp. aluminum foil, cellophane/BOPP, tear tape, corrugated cardboard boxes and gummed tapes, paste Sources for affiliated major brands: http://www.bir.gov.ph/lumangweb/oic/nir_annx_d.html http://www.bat.com/group/sites/uk__3mnfen.nsf/vwPagesWebLive/DO52ADIQ?opendocument&SKN=1 http://www.pmi.com/marketpages/pages/market_en_ph.aspx ftp://ftp.bir.gov.ph/webadmin1/pdf/67478Annex%200-1_RMO%2090-2012.pdf

Visit the new Customs website (www.customs.gov.ph) and the Customs ng Bayan microsite (www.dof.gov.ph/customsngbayan), and follow @Customs PH for information and data on BOC activity. Check out the BOC dashboard in the Open Data Portal (data.gov.ph).

Got a report on smuggling activity? Submit it through www.perangbayan.com.

DOF.GOV.PH   CUSTOMS.GOV.PH

Source: Bureau of Customs.

that the DOF, working with the BIR and Bureau of Customs, consolidate regular information updates on tobacco- and alcohol-related trade, as well as domestic tax stamp coverage, in one open-government location. This would allow for broad-based analysis of these sources of information by interested parties. But the onus should be on every producer of cigarette inputs, whether imported or not, to account for imports as well as their domestic sales.

Impact on Smoking and Drinking

While the effect of the sin tax reform on cigarette and alcohol sales and revenues can be measured on a monthly basis using administrative data, assessing its effect on actual smoking and drinking behavior requires household surveys. The main health outcomes of interest are the prevalence of smoking and drinking (among both men and women), the intensity of smoking and drinking, and quitting behavior. From an equity perspective, and since the STL is supposed to benefit the poor most of all, the government also needs to measure how the

Figure 3.16 Customs Watch Comparison of Declared Tobacco Import Values

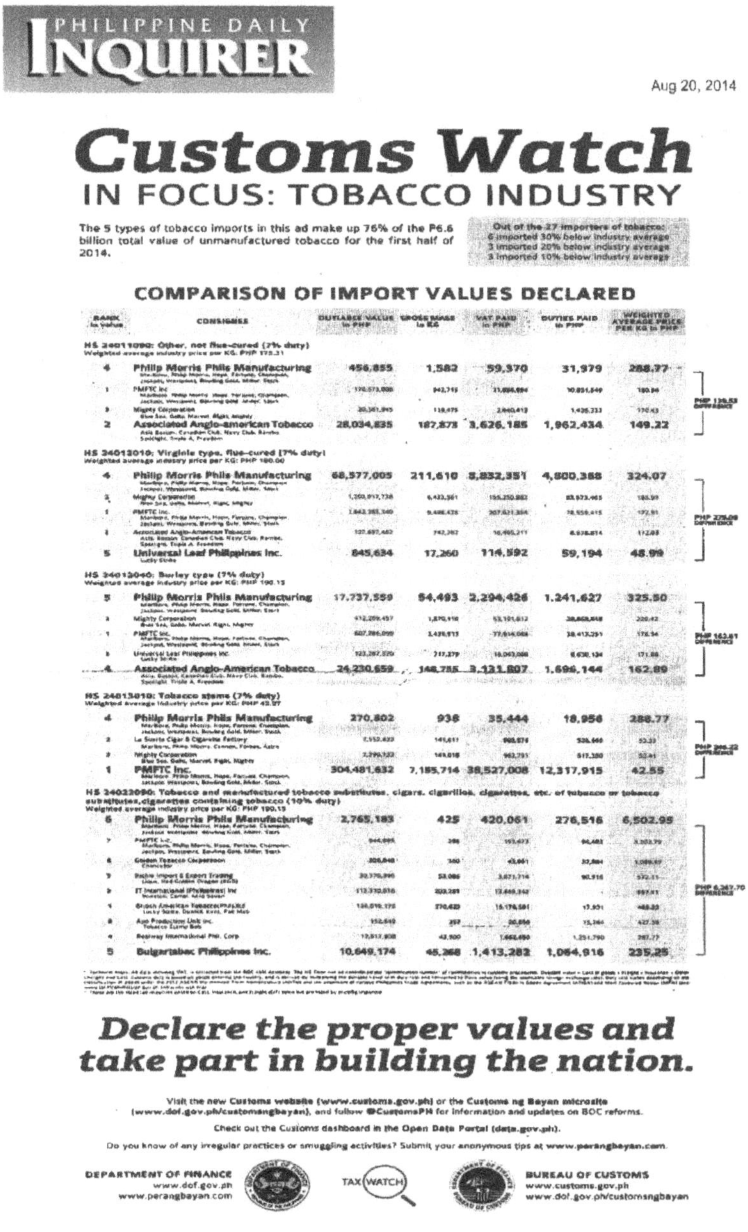
PHILIPPINE DAILY INQUIRER

Aug 20, 2014

Customs Watch

IN FOCUS: TOBACCO INDUSTRY

The 5 types of tobacco imports in this ad make up 76% of the P6.6 billion total value of unmanufactured tobacco for the first half of 2014.

Out of the 27 importers of tobacco:
6 imported 30% below industry average
3 imported 20% below industry average
3 imported 10% below industry average

COMPARISON OF IMPORT VALUES DECLARED

RANK in value	CONSIGNEES	DUTIABLE VALUE in PHP	GROSS MASS in KG	VAT PAID in PHP	DUTIES PAID in PHP	WEIGHTED AVERAGE PRICE PER KG in PHP
	HS 24011090: Other, not flue-cured (7% duty) Weighted average industry price per KG: PHP 175.31					
4	**Philip Morris Phils Manufacturing**	456,855	1,582	59,370	31,979	288.77
1	PMFTC Inc	[illegible]	[illegible]	[illegible]	[illegible]	[illegible]
3	Mighty Corporation	[illegible]	[illegible]	[illegible]	[illegible]	[illegible]
2	**Associated Anglo-american Tobacco**	28,034,835	187,873	3,626,185	1,962,434	149.22
	PHP 139.55 DIFFERENCE					
	HS 24012010: Virginia type, flue-cured (7% duty) Weighted average industry price per KG: PHP 180.00					
4	**Philip Morris Phils Manufacturing**	68,577,005	211,610	8,832,351	4,800,388	324.07
2	Mighty Corporation	[illegible]	[illegible]	[illegible]	[illegible]	[illegible]
1	PMFTC Inc.	[illegible]	[illegible]	[illegible]	[illegible]	[illegible]
3	Associated Anglo-American Tobacco	[illegible]	[illegible]	[illegible]	[illegible]	[illegible]
5	**Universal Leaf Philippines Inc.**	845,634	17,260	114,592	59,194	48.99
	PHP 275.08 DIFFERENCE					
	HS 24012040: Burley type (7% duty) Weighted average industry price per KG: PHP 190.15					
5	**Philip Morris Phils Manufacturing**	17,737,559	54,493	2,294,426	1,241,627	325.50
2	Mighty Corporation	[illegible]	[illegible]	[illegible]	[illegible]	[illegible]
1	PMFTC Inc.	[illegible]	[illegible]	[illegible]	[illegible]	[illegible]
3	Universal Leaf Philippines Inc	[illegible]	[illegible]	[illegible]	[illegible]	[illegible]
4	**Associated Anglo-American Tobacco**	24,230,659	148,785	3,131,807	1,696,144	162.89
	PHP 162.61 DIFFERENCE					
	HS 24013010: Tobacco stems (7% duty) Weighted average industry price per KG: PHP 42.97					
4	**Philip Morris Phils Manufacturing**	270,802	938	35,444	18,956	288.77
2	La Suerte Cigar & Cigarette Factory	[illegible]	[illegible]	[illegible]	[illegible]	[illegible]
3	Mighty Corporation	[illegible]	[illegible]	[illegible]	[illegible]	[illegible]
1	**PMFTC Inc.**	304,481,632	7,185,714	38,527,008	12,317,915	42.55
	PHP 246.22 DIFFERENCE					
	HS 24022090: Tobacco and manufactured tobacco substitutes, cigars, cigarillos, cigarettes, etc. of tobacco or tobacco substitutes, cigarettes containing tobacco (10% duty) Weighted average industry price per KG: PHP 190.15					
6	**Philip Morris Phils Manufacturing**	2,765,183	425	420,061	276,516	6,502.95
7	PMFTC Inc.	[illegible]	[illegible]	[illegible]	[illegible]	[illegible]
8	Golden Tobacco Corporation	[illegible]	[illegible]	[illegible]	[illegible]	[illegible]
3	Richie Import & Export Trading	[illegible]	[illegible]	[illegible]	[illegible]	[illegible]
2	JT International (Philippines) Inc	[illegible]	[illegible]	[illegible]	[illegible]	[illegible]
1	British American Tobacco (Phils) Ltd	[illegible]	[illegible]	[illegible]	[illegible]	[illegible]
8	Ace Production Unit Inc.	[illegible]	[illegible]	[illegible]	[illegible]	[illegible]
4	Bestway International Phil. Corp	[illegible]	[illegible]	[illegible]	[illegible]	[illegible]
5	**Bulgartabac Philippines Inc.**	10,649,174	45,268	1,413,282	1,064,916	235.25
	PHP 6,267.70 DIFFERENCE					

Declare the proper values and take part in building the nation.

Visit the new Customs website (www.customs.gov.ph) or the Customs ng Bayan microsite (www.dof.gov.ph/customsngbayan), and follow @CustomsPH for information and updates on BOC reforms.

Check out the Customs dashboard in the Open Data Portal (data.gov.ph).

Do you know of any irregular practices or smuggling activities? Submit your anonymous tips at www.perangbayan.com.

DEPARTMENT OF FINANCE
www.dof.gov.ph
www.perangbayan.com

TAX WATCH

BUREAU OF CUSTOMS
www.customs.gov.ph
www.dof.gov.ph/customsngbayan

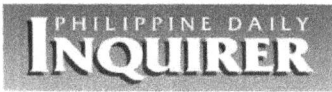

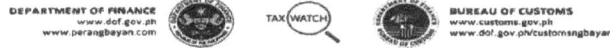

Source: Philippine Daily Inquirer.

changes in these indicators vary across poor and nonpoor groups. Special attention should be given to the consumption behavior of youth, because this group is one of the most sensitive to price changes, and this is where lifelong smoking and drinking starts.

A number of regularly scheduled household surveys collect much of the information needed to monitor smoking behavior. The 2008 and 2013 National Demographic and Health Survey (NDHS) as well as a 2011 Family Health Survey which has a similar structure, provides information on the prevalence and intensity of smoking across different ages, income groups, and regions—but only among women. The 2008 and 2013 National Nutrition and Health Survey (NNHS), managed by the Department of Science and Technology, also provides information on smoking, and allows disaggregation by gender, income group, and age. Its findings are made available to other government agencies and to the public, but the underlying data are not. A 2009 Global Adult Tobacco Survey (GATS), with a follow-up GATS anticipated in 2016, complements the NDHS by providing substantially more detailed information on smoking behavior (including prevalence, intensity, and quitting) with results disaggregated by literacy, gender, age, and location. Together, these surveys provide a picture of pre- and post-SLT smoking behavior. Of course, it is not possible to attribute any observed change in smoking behavior directly to sin tax reform because other factors affect smoking trends, such as DOH and LGU regulations and changes in peoples' attitudes. Another limitation, typical of household surveys, is that the results are often only available with a considerable lag owing to the time needed for data cleaning, compilation, and analysis.

An important data gap is that none of the routinely collected, nationally representative surveys contain questions that allow for alcohol use and abuse to be monitored. The quantity of alcohol products bought by households and related expenditures is captured in the triennial Family Income and Expenditure Survey (FIES), together with information on the quantity and expenditure on tobacco products. From this, some inferences about drinking behavior can possibly be made. However, the FIES, last conducted in 2012,[19] only tells us what households buy, and not how much alcohol individual household members drink, and certainly not whether they engage in chronic or binge drinking. In other words, it tells us nothing about health. Information on drinking behavior was last available in 2004, in the World Health Organization's World Health Survey, which was also conducted in the Philippines. Thus, a good baseline for monitoring alcohol use does not exist, and there is unlikely to be information on this in future routinely collected surveys.

To fill the gaps in the scope and frequency of routinely-collected data, the DOH is implementing additional surveys formulated to measure the effect of the sin tax reform. In 2012, in the first quarter of 2014, and in the third quarter of 2015, the department funded a module of questions on smoking in the Social Weather Stations' (SWS) quarterly poverty survey, including information on tobacco consumption, price per cigarette, and cigarette marketing strategies. While not as comprehensive as the GATS questions, the smoking questions in the SWS survey are solid and have been widely quoted as an indication of the early effects of the STL. The 2015 survey also included information on consumption of alcohol products, drinking behavior, and health insurance coverage—all of which were important data gaps.

To complement the efforts of the DOH, the UPecon Foundation and World Bank collaborated on a 2015 survey covering questions related to smoking, drinking, and insurance coverage, as well as other health-related behavior. Since this nationally-representative survey reinterviews the same households who took part in a similar 2011 survey,[20] it provides the special opportunity of following a panel of households over time.

Analysis of the available survey data on the STL's impact shows that smoking has been declining. Drawing together all available data, smoking prevalence appears to have fallen steadily from 31 percent in 2008 (NNHS) to 28 percent in 2009 (GATS), 30 percent in 2011, 29 percent in 2012 (SWS/DOH), 25 percent in 2013 (NNHS), 26 percent in 2014 (SWS/DOH) and 25 percent in 2015 (SWS/DOH) (figure 3.17). The sample sizes and sampling approaches in the surveys are not comparable, and confidence intervals may overlap, but all claim to be nationally representative. The 2014 and 2015 SWS/DOH surveys also find a reduction in the median number of cigarettes smoked per day from 10 to 9. One caveat to this good news is that smoking was already on the decline before the STL, suggesting that at least part of the reduction in smoking observed since 2012 may be part of a longer term trend and likely due to other factors.

The reduction in smoking has been greatest among the youth and has varied across income groups. The pair of SWS surveys conducted in the last quarter of 2012 (just before the STL was implemented) and mid-2015 (two-and-a-half years after STL implementation) show the reduction in smoking was greater among the youth (18 to 24 years), from 35 percent to 22 percent, than among the general population, 29 percent to 25 percent. Further analysis of these data are needed to determine whether this is due to quitting smoking or noninitiation of smoking. Among the wealthiest people in the Philippines (income classes A,

Figure 3.17 Smoking Trends

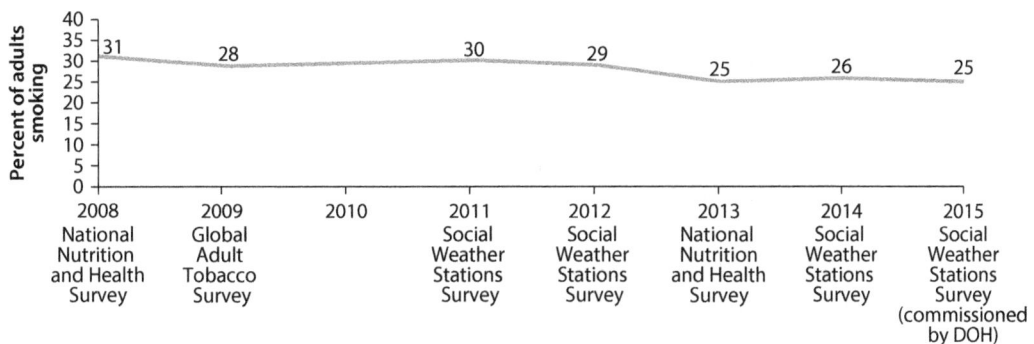

Sources: As shown in the figure.
Note: DOH = Department of Health.

B, and C[21]), smoking prevalence fell from 25 percent to 14 percent; among the middle class it stayed the same at 26 percent, and among the poorest 60 percent of the population it fell from 38 percent to 27 percent.

On drinking prevalence, the available data are not particularly informative. The 2015 SWS/DOH surveys show that 43 percent of Filipinos, and 66 percent of Filipino men, describe themselves as drinkers. However, only 4 percent of these people report that they drink on a daily basis, with a further 39 percent reporting that they drink several times per week. Because of the lack of drinking information in previous surveys, trends cannot be assessed. It is also not clear what percentage of the population are heavy drinkers. While the lack of good data to examine this question in more detail is unfortunate, these numbers are sufficiently low to suggest that it is the problem of smoking rather than drinking that is the more important one for tax policy to address.

Changes in smoking behavior, especially when analyzed across different subgroups (rich and poor, youth and adults), provide some insight into the important question of "who bears the burden of excise taxation." Indeed, the equity implications of the increase in taxation, especially in a country where smoking rates are higher among the poor, was one of the major issues raised during the STL congressional hearings. Background analysis prepared for this report using the 2009 FIES anticipated that tax incidence would be slightly more regressive after the reform than before. Before the reform, the poor spent a greater share of their income on alcohol and tobacco taxes than the rich (that is, tax incidence was already regressive). After the reform, the share of income that the poor spent on these taxes was expected to increase by more than the share spent by the rich, implying a more regressive tax system. However, the absolute amount of excise tax paid by the rich would be greater than the amount paid by the poor. It will only be possible to assess whether these predictions were correct once the 2015 FIES survey data become available for analysis. This is because this analysis requires information on the quantity and type of tobacco and alcohol products bought by different types of households, which can only be obtained through household surveys; it cannot be calculated from the aggregate sales and tax data collected monthly by the BIR because the characteristics (especially income) of the people purchasing alcohol and tobacco products needs to be known. As well as measuring tax incidence, these data will be useful for assessing the extent to which expenditure on the "sin products" is displacing "good" expenditure on health, education, and other family needs. The ultimate question to be answered, though, would be whether the benefits accruing to the poor as a result of the new earmarked allocations to health insurance subsidies and facility investments would fully offset the increase in taxes that they would pay.

Tobacco Farmer Impacts—Prices and Volumes

Domestic tobacco farmers were identified as a potential loser in the sin tax reform, and so its impact on this group requires close monitoring. The main concern was that a reduction in domestic tobacco demand/removals would reduce prices and volumes for tobacco-growing farmers, without adequate time to adjust by shifting to alternative crops or livelihoods. Tobacco production in the Philippines, concentrated in northern Luzon (with some emerging production in Northern Mindanao), is subject to both domestic and export demand, covering different types of leaf—Virginia, Burley, and Native—and varying qualities of dried leaf. International export demand for Philippine tobacco is likely to provide a buffer against the effects of projected declines in the local market.

In the absence of repeated household surveys of potentially affected tobacco farmers, a series of readily available tracking indicators suggest that the impact of the STL on tobacco farmers has not led to inordinate distortions. During 2013–15, estimated production levels declined by 23 percent, according to National Tobacco Administration (NTA) data on industry performance. Both tobacco exports, and input imports, remained highly significant to the market, suggesting that international market dynamics rather than the STL as such were the principal drivers of tobacco farmer fortunes.

Close monitoring of tobacco prices and demand will confirm whether this is indeed the case. Tobacco farmer impacts are captured by Indicator No. 7 of the STL monitoring indicators on the tax side (table 3.1). The indicator focuses on domestic tobacco demand and prices. The principal sources of data on the economic situation of tobacco farmers are the DA and NTA. The principal variables to be monitored are tobacco leaf production and price levels, number of farmers, and tobacco leaf exports and imports. These variables are already regularly monitored by the NTA and the figures are released annually. The main challenge will be to link this work with more periodic farmer surveys, as these farmers often produce multiple crops.

The early years of the STL's implementation showed no evidence of major adverse shocks to farmers' livelihoods through changes to domestic tobacco prices, production levels, and acreage. DA and NTA data show that most tobacco farmers have access to domestic and international markets, which likely muted the impact of any changes in domestic tobacco demand that might have occurred following the STL's implementation. There also does not appear to have been a significant drop in the prices paid to producers, or a decline in tobacco leaf volume demand, during the early-2013 harvest. According to Bureau of Agricultural Statistics, average farm gate prices per kilogram of Virginia-type leaf fetched ₱65.0 ($1.50) in 2011–12 and ₱67.3 ($1.56) in 2013. Burley-type leaf did decline slightly, from ₱74 ($1.72) to ₱68 ($1.58) from 2012 to 2013, but since most of this production is exported the price movement reflects international rather than domestic demand. Farm gate prices of the Native-type leaf decreased, but 2013 average prices were still above 2011 levels, so the drop is unlikely to be attributable to the implementation of the STL. The government has also begun identifying alternatives for tobacco crop demand, including as inputs to fish pond and paper products production.

Despite this generally favorable trend, ongoing monitoring is needed for tobacco-growing regions, especially for farmer livelihoods. The last major survey of tobacco farmers was in 2009 (Espino, Evangalista, and Dorotheo 2009).[22]

A farmer registry was put together in 2012–13, but data on livelihoods are either not available or have not yet been analyzed. Monitoring of production and employment trends should be accompanied by evaluations of the impacts of this spending because STL revenues are being allocated to tobacco-producing LGUs to promote alternative livelihoods and diversification. Currently, however, no plans seem to be in place—either among government agencies or development partners—to conduct a further targeted survey for tobacco-growing regions to follow on the 2009 baseline.

Monitoring Expenditure Earmarking

The prominence given to revenue earmarks for tobacco-growing regions and universal health coverage calls for a careful assessment of the extent of the increases in financing and the appropriateness of the use of funds. Indicators of the disbursement and use of funds in tobacco-growing regions (indicators Nos. 1–3 on the earmarking side) and on the disbursement and use of funds for the expansion of universal health coverage (Nos. 4–7 on the earmarking side)—needed to be defined and monitored. This is to ensure that disbursements adhere to the intended use of funds described in the STL and IRRs, and also to assess the impact of this spending on tobacco farmers' livelihoods and health goals. The experience of the tobacco earmarks in place under previous legislation had highlighted the varying capacities of LGUs to use earmarked funds appropriately, as well as the likelihood of spending on noneligible projects and unaccounted funds, making a clear monitoring framework essential for achieving transparency in public spending and results on the ground.

An emphasis on transparency and public disclosure is a hallmark of the STL's IRRs. Under IRR rule VIII, the DBM, DA, DOH, and PhilHealth are required to submit detailed reports on the expenditure and utilization of earmarked funds by the first week of August each year and these reports are to be published simultaneously in the *Official Gazette* and on the websites of these agencies, and are subject to formal government audit. The IRRs also explicitly recognize the participation and assistance of civil society organizations in promoting and monitoring compliance with the STL and its IRRs. The indicators selected for the monitoring framework are aligned with the STL's IRRs, including the areas on which government agencies are supposed to report.

Transfers to Tobacco-Growing Regions

Transfers to tobacco-growing regions will almost double in the wake of the STL, but this was only budgeted to LGUs in these regions in 2015 because earmarked transfers were based on 2013 realized revenues. Similar to how the main national-to-local transfer of funds under the Internal Revenue Allotment is calculated, transfers are based on realized revenues, hence the transfer was lagged by two years.[23] Figure 3.18 summarizes projected allocations, suggesting an increase of ₱6 billion ($143 million) over the year of the passage of the STL. Actual fund disbursements by the DBM to tobacco-growing regions was delayed until 2016,

Figure 3.18 Allocations to Tobacco-Growing LGUs, 2010–15

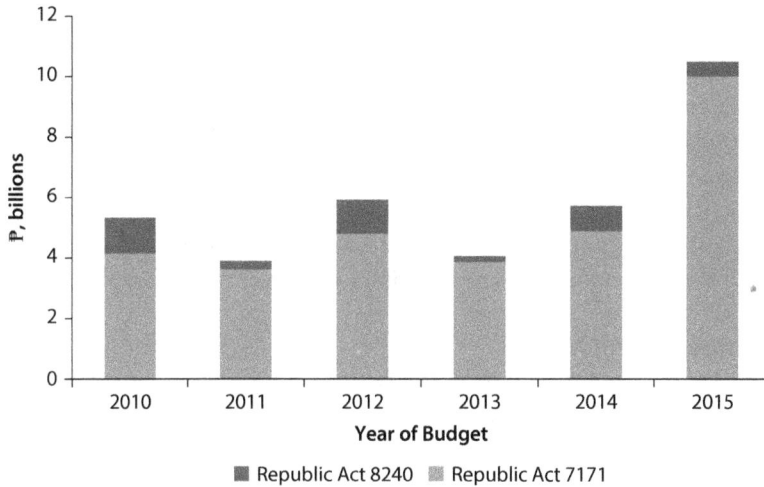

Source: National Tobacco Administration.
Note: LGU = local government unit.

however.[24] This delay was associated with the Supreme Court's ruling in November 2013 banning the Priority Development Assistance Fund. These were funds allocated to members of the House of Representatives and senators to use for special projects of their choice, and had been broadly referred to as "pork barrel" funds because of their political and discretionary nature. Because the Supreme Court declared Priority Development Assistance Fund lump-sum transfers unconstitutional, all other lump-sum transfers were also brought into question, with the result that additional clarification on how the tobacco earmarked funds should be disbursed was needed before the funds could actually flow.[25]

The STL's IRRs created transparent procedures for disbursing funds to tobacco-producing regions. The STL stipulated that the DA issue guidelines identifying eligible programs and projects to be financed by earmarked funds to tobacco-growing regions, and a certified list of beneficiary tobacco-producing LGUs each year. Under the guidelines, LGUs must notify the DBM of their intended use of these funds and provide quarterly reports of accomplishments, including objective and verifiable indicators of project progress. The LGUs are responsible for implementing the projects and programs, and using their revenue shares in a way that observes applicable budgeting, accounting, and auditing laws, rules, and regulations. The STL's IRRs oblige the DBM to compute, allocate, and distribute the individual shares of entitled LGUs; issue local budget memorandums informing LGUs of their respective shares; and release the revenue shares of beneficiary LGUs. The guidelines are a clear break with the opacity of past implementation of tobacco earmark fund releases and their use. However, the capacity and commitment of recipient LGUs should be a significant concern of the national government in its monitoring responsibilities, including formal auditing by the Commission on Audit.

Pending the flow of these funds, dedicated monitoring will be needed to assess whether tobacco farmers are benefiting from earmarked transfers. Intended to offset the potential negative effects of the STL on tobacco-growing regions from a reduced demand for tobacco leaf, these allocations should be spent on income-generating and welfare programs in the community. Information on these projects is not yet easily available, but should be able to be compiled from the information submitted to each LGU by the DBM. In 2016, it will be important to undertake an analysis of whether these funds have been committed to projects, which types of projects are being implemented, and the results achieved. Civil society engagement will also be important in monitoring LGU-level project implementation.[26]

Expenditure on Health

A major thrust of the Aquino administration has been to provide financial protection from health shocks and adequate health care for the poor and vulnerable through its universal health care program. The STL's tax increases, coupled with the earmarking of these revenues for health, were designed to fill the financing gap for this program. Recall from the previous chapters that 85 percent of the incremental revenues from the STL are earmarked for health. Of this, 80 percent is supposed to be used to provide free health insurance for poor and near-poor families through the National Health Insurance Program (NHIP) managed by PhilHealth, programs intended to speed progress to achieving health-related Millennium Development Goals, and health awareness schemes. The remaining 20 percent seeks to expand the service delivery network by providing additional financing to the DOH's Health Facilities Enhancement Program (HFEP), through which the DOH supplements local government investments in health facilities, and augments the financing of the DOH's Medical Assistance Program, a hospital fund (in the name of mayors, representatives to congress, and DOH officials) that can be used by the facility to cover the medical costs of those who cannot afford to pay. The first earmarked allocations flowed to the health sector in 2014, based on sin tax collections in 2013. Indicator No. 4 on the earmarking side captures budget allocation and releases for health; indicator No. 5 on the earmarking side captures utilization of these budgetary allocations.

The STL and its IRRs describe how the incremental sin tax revenues will be earmarked for health, as well as the accountability arrangements. The incremental revenues are assigned to the Universal Health Care Expenditure Program, approved by the Development Budget Coordination Committee (rule III section 1, and rule IV section 1).[27] The annual requirements are reviewed by the DBM as part of the annual budget process. Thus, the earmarking for health is not "hard" but subject to the annual budgetary process.[28] As required by the STL, the DOH produced a medium-term expenditure program as part of the 2015 and 2016 budget preparation processes to show how the expanded budget allocation would be used. These did not receive the approval of the Development Budget Coordination Committee as required, but they were used by the DOH for planning purposes.

The Department of Health's budget has increased dramatically since the start of the Aquino administration in 2010 and, with the additional revenues coming from the STL, reached almost five times its 2010 level by 2016. Specifically, the DOH budget doubled from ₱24.6 billion ($581 million) in 2010 to ₱50.4 billion ($1.19 billion) in 2013, and then increased sharply to ₱83.7 billion ($1.89 billion) in 2014 (which was the first year with sin tax earmarks), reaching ₱122.6 billion ($2.62 billion) in the 2016 budget. These numbers show that allocations to health were already increasing in anticipation of sin tax revenues; that is, even before the first actual earmarking for health was implemented in 2014.[29]

Total new appropriations for the DOH in the 2013 General Appropriations Act totaled ₱53.23 billion ($1.13 billion).[30] Under the DOH 2013 budget, ₱12.6 billion ($293 million) was slated to cover the health insurance premiums of the indigent population that had already been benefitting from the NHIP before the STL, and ₱2.79 billion ($59 million) was for the HFEP.[31] As a transitional measure, an unprogrammed amount of ₱13.6 billion ($316 million) was allocated to the NHIP in 2013, but this budget was not used. The 2014 General Appropriations Act saw further significant increases in financing for health care, including a marked rise in allocations to the NHIP to also include additional indigent members and the poor. New appropriations for the DOH increased to ₱83.7 billion ($1.95 billion), driven mainly by the expansion of the NHIP to ₱35.3 billion ($821 million), and the HFEP to ₱13.5 billion ($304 million).

The 2014 government budget, for the first time, also provided explicit expenditure results targets for all government departments. The key results area for the DOH was "poverty reduction and empowerment of the poor and vulnerable." Since then, this area has also included a set of organizational outcomes associated with improving access to quality primary health care, hospital services, health commodities, and health insurance. In subsequent years, the overall DOH budget continued to increase, as did the funds going to the program financed by the STL (figure 3.19).

The funds allocated to the DOH for the NHIP are released by the Bureau of Treasury to PhilHealth, an attached agency of DOH, only once provisions designed to promote accountability are satisfied. Specifically, PhilHealth must first submit to the DBM the number of poor and near-poor beneficiaries (indigent members), together with a financial statement and special budget. This procedure creates an important accountability mechanism because information on the number of eligible beneficiaries is required before funds are released. The accountability mechanism could be even stronger if it depended on, for example, evidence that eligible beneficiaries had received their member data record (which in the absence of health insurance cards for the poor is the primary form of proof of membership) or information on whether the poor have enlisted with their primary care providers. This would ensure that all the subsidized poor know of their coverage, are aware of their benefits, and empowered to use them.

The monitoring framework also captures the extent to which the increased public resources allocated for health (from sin tax revenues) are actually used and, moreover, used for their intended purpose (indicator No. 5 on the earmarking side). One source of information is the budget report for the Commission on Audit and DBM that should be prepared by the DOH and PhilHealth for the

Figure 3.19 DOH Budget Allocations, 2010–16

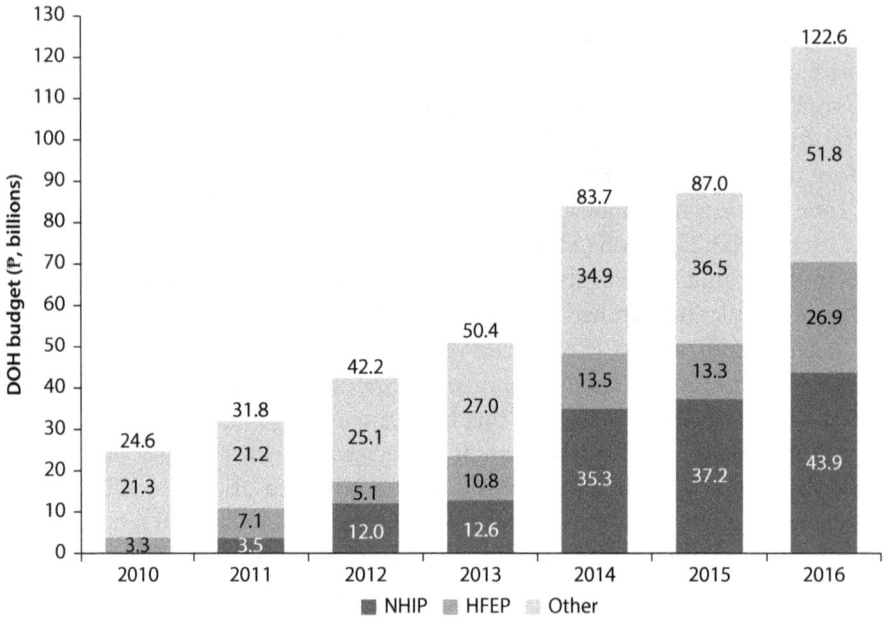

Source: DBM online budget documentation.
Note: Does not include additional allocation of ₱2.79 billion ($65 million) for the HFEP under the DPWH in 2013. See DBM, DPWH Joint Circular No. 1, August 2, 2013 at http://www.dbm.gov.ph/wp-content/uploads/Issuances/2013/Joint%20 Circular%202013/JC2013-1(DBM-DOH-DPWH).pdf. DBM = Department of Budget and Management; DOH = Department of Health; DPWH = Department of Public Works and Highways; HFEP = Health Facilities Enhancement Program; NHIP = National Health Insurance Program.

release of health funds. There is also the annual report to the Congressional Oversight Committee created under Republic Act 8240, which the DOH prepared and submitted in 2014 and 2015.

Budget execution rates provide some insights into the extent to which earmarked sin tax revenues are being effectively utilized. In 2014, the most recent year for which data are available, the DOH's overall budget execution rate was about 89 percent, but budget execution of line items supported by funds from the STL was considerably lower—81 percent for the Medical Assistance Program, 78 percent for attainment of Millennium Development Goals and health awareness, and only 57 percent for the HFEP (table 3.7). The practice of continuing appropriations means that these resources will still be available for use in subsequent years, but it does raise questions about absorptive capacity and whether STL revenues can be spent—and spent well. Some of these line items, such as the HFEP, have always been low-disbursing, and the additional STL revenues may have aggravated the situation.

What budget execution rates do not tell us is the extent to which the funds allocated to these line items are being put to the best possible use. Program guidelines, public financial management rules, and audits will help to ensure that funds are not misused, but what cannot be assessed is whether resources are

Table 3.7 Budget Execution Rates of Selected DOH Line Items Supported by the STL

	2013			2014		
DOH programs	Obligation (₱, billions)	Adjusted allotment (₱, billions)	Utilization (%)	Obligation (₱, billions)	Adjusted allotment (₱, billions)	Utilization (%)
National Health Insurance Program	12.55	12.63	99	35.34	35.34	100
Attainment of MDGs and health awareness programs	5.21	6.12	85	6.63	8.54	78
Health Facilities Enhancement Program	2.81	6.52	43	3.72	6.48	57
Medical Assistance Program	n.a.	n.a.	n.a.	0.69	0.85	81
Total DOH appropriations	45.82	51.44	89	72.19	80.97	89

Sources: Department of Health; Department of Budget and Management.
Note: DOH = Department of Health; MDGs = Millennium Development Goals; STL = Sin Tax Law; n.a. = not applicable.

allocated most appropriately, efficiently, and effectively. For example, are HFEP resources going to the most under-served LGUs (allocative efficiency and equity) and are health awareness funds being spent on the most promising interventions? To assess this, in-depth evaluations of the HFEP, Medical Assistance Program, and health awareness programs are recommended.

Universal Health Care—Insurance Coverage and Access to Services
The monitoring framework includes two indicators to monitor the impact of the STL on the expansion of universal health coverage. Indicator No. 6 on the earmarking side measures the change in the number of poor people enrolled in the NHIP. This information is available on a quarterly basis on the PhilHealth website in the "PhilHealth Stats and Charts" and is also presented, together with trend data, in PhilHealth's annual reports. Indicator No. 7 on the earmarking side goes even further down the results chain, looking at changes in the use of health services. The latter has to do with both the increase in the availability of health facilities (supply-side), which would be expected as a result of the increased funds going to the HFEP, as well as the increase in demand for health services resulting from the expansion of health insurance coverage among the poor.

The STL contributed to institutionalizing a more accurate, transparent, and less discretionary means of identifying which poor families should receive subsidized health insurance. Before 2011, LGUs were charged with identifying the poor families to be sponsored by the NHIP. Since each LGU had complete discretion to decide who should be subsidized, the identification process was fragmented and inherently politicized. From 2011, the national government-subsidized NHIP program started to use the National Household Targeting Survey for Poverty Reduction—originally developed for identifying beneficiaries of the government's conditional cash transfer program—for identifying the poor households who would receive subsidized health insurance. Parallel to this, LGUs retained the right to sponsor additional families from their respective constituencies based on their own targeting mechanisms, with the national government (through PhilHealth) providing a 50 percent enrollment subsidy. In 2011, those receiving national government subsidies for health insurance included 18.9 million individuals identified by National Household Targeting Survey for Poverty Reduction as well as the 19.6 million individuals identified by LGUs in that year. This number was substantially higher than the 22 million "poor" individuals who had received free health insurance in 2010 under the LGU-sponsored program.

PhilHealth Stats and Charts show that from 2013 to 2014, the number of poor families enrolled in the NHIP—and identified by the National Household Targeting Survey for Poverty Reduction—increased from 5.2 million to 14.7 million. This grew to 15.3 million poor families by the end of 2015,[32] almost tripling the coverage of the poor since the passage of the STL, and equivalent to a total of 45.4 million poor ("indigent") beneficiaries. LGUs, meanwhile, continue to retain the right to subsidize other families that they deem deserving under a new "sponsored" program of PhilHealth.

In November 2014, the law on mandatory PhilHealth coverage for all senior citizens was passed (Republic Act 10645). This allowed sin tax revenues, which had been well in excess of projections, to also be used to fully subsidize the health insurance of senior citizens (that is, those older than 60) who were not already covered by other PhilHealth programs. Republic Act 10645 amended to the Senior Citizen Act, effectively removing the requirement of a senior citizen to be indigent before being covered by PhilHealth. By the end of 2015, membership in the new senior citizen program was equivalent to 5.9 million families (or a total of 7.1 million beneficiaries).[33] Thus, from 2015, the proceeds of the STL were being used to cover the health insurance of both poor and elderly Filipinos.

Together with beneficiaries of other PhilHealth membership categories, including the formally employed, individually paying members, "lifetime members" (elderly members exempt from premiums because of contribution history) and overseas workers, the total number of people covered by PhilHealth in 2015 was 93.4 million in a population estimated at 101.5 million people, or 92 percent of Filipinos (figure 3.20).

The drawback of using PhilHealth administrative data to monitor health insurance coverage is that it only captures the number of people *entitled* to free health insurance (that is, de jure coverage), and on whose behalf PhilHealth is allocated premium subsidies by the DBM, and not the number of people who know that they have subsidized coverage (that is, de facto coverage). If PhilHealth issued health insurance cards to indigent program members, counting the number of cards issued to beneficiaries could have offered some insight into the number of people who know of their coverage. However, this is not the case. Consequently, the only a way to assess whether people know of their entitlement to PhilHealth is to ask them through household surveys. Routinely collected household surveys already provide information on self-reported coverage by PhilHealth. These include the NDHS and the Family Health Survey, which were most recently carried out in 2011 (Family Health Survey) and 2013 (NDHS).

Figure 3.20 Enrollment of the Poor in PhilHealth Sponsored and Indigent Programs, 2010–15

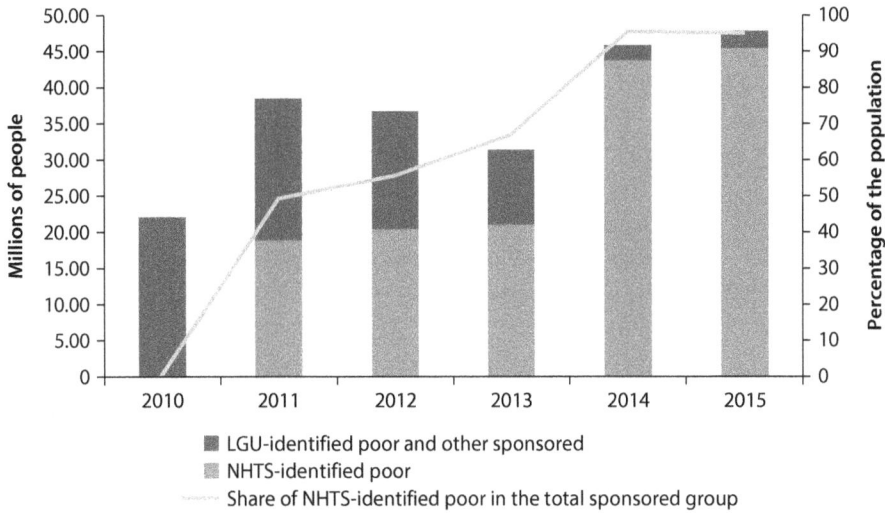

LGU-identified poor and other sponsored
NHTS-identified poor
Share of NHTS-identified poor in the total sponsored group

Source: PhilHealth.

Note: Before 2014 the term "sponsored" was used for all PhilHealth members who had their premiums subsidized by either the national government (if they identified as poor per the NHTS-PR) or by LGUs. From 2014, the term "indigent" was adopted to refer to the poor or near-poor members subsidized by national government, while the term "sponsored" was reserved for those whose premiums were paid by another entity, such as LGUs, charities, or charitable individuals. LGU = local government unit; NHTS = National Household Targeting Survey (for Poverty Reduction).

The 2015 DOH/SWS special survey, carried out specifically to monitor sin tax implementation, also asks about insurance coverage.

Data from the 2013 NDHS (before the expansion of health insurance coverage from the STL) shows why asking people about their coverage is a critical complement to administrative data: in 2013, when the PhilHealth database was reporting about 83 million beneficiaries, equivalent to 83 percent of the population, these survey data showed a coverage rate of only 61 percent of the population (Bredenkamp and Buisman 2015). The results of the mid-2015 DOH/SWS are a little more encouraging, but not by much. Carried out in the middle of the year, when PhilHealth Stats and Charts (mid-year estimates) were reporting national coverage rates of 89 percent, the DOH/SWS survey found that 67 percent of respondents reported having PhilHealth coverage. This is exactly the same percentage coverage that the SWS survey reported in 2013 and in 2011.[34]

The availability of, and access to, health services is also important to measure since it mediates whether the increased demand for health services (through the expansion of health insurance) translates into increased utilization. Indeed, the allocation of STL resources to the HFEP, with which the national government supports health facility construction and renovations at national and local levels, is intended precisely for this purpose. Information on the number of facilities constructed and rehabilitated under the HFEP program since the STL earmarks started was not available at the time of writing, and this information was not included in the DOH's 2015 annual report on the use of sin tax funds.[35]

What we do know is that the number of facilities accredited to deliver PhilHealth benefits has increased. Between December 2013 and December 2014, the percentage of towns and municipalities with at least one outpatient clinic (government or private) accredited by PhilHealth to deliver the primary care benefit package increased from 79 percent to 93 percent. By December 2015, PhilHealth was reporting availability of the primary care benefit package in almost all LGUs—as many as 99 percent of towns and municipalities had at least one accredited facility.[36] For the maternity care package, the share increased from 62 percent to 71 percent between 2013 and 2014, and reached 80 percent by the end of 2015. Availability of the TB DOTS package for tuberculosis increased from 67 percent in 2013 to 75 percent in 2014, and by 2015 was reportedly available in at least one facility in 81 percent of LGUs.

The final question is how to monitor whether the expansion of health care insurance to the poor is translating into more pro-poor health care utilization patterns. Health care utilization must be measured through household surveys and, luckily, can be captured by the universal health care module of the NDHS and Family Health Survey. However, as with information on self-reported health insurance coverage, no post-STL estimates are available since the last NDHS was conducted in 2013 before the sin tax allocations to health insurance. We need to wait until either the next NDHS which, given past survey periodicity, is likely to next be in 2018, or, alternatively, an interim Family Health Survey funded by development partners.

Another measure of PhilHealth utilization, and convenient for monitoring purposes given the frequency of data availability, is PhilHealth administrative data on benefit payments and the frequency of members' contacts with health care providers. When the sin tax monitoring framework was first developed, the percentage of indigent PhilHealth members enrolled with a primary care provider for the primary care benefit package was identified as a good indicator, as was the percentage of inpatient admissions. The appeal of these measures was that they were included in the 2014 DOH budget as monitoring indicators, together with the following associated performance targets: greater than 80 percent for admissions and greater than 85 percent for primary care enrollment. By the end of 2014, 10.7 million of the 14.7 million indigent families were enrolled with a primary care provider, falling short of the 85 percent target set in the 2014 budget. Updated estimates for 2015 are not yet available, but will hopefully be included in the 2015 PhilHealth annual report. The STL's IRR rule VIII, section 3, also required that PhilHealth measure the benefit delivery rate— a composite measure of insurance coverage, service utilization, and share of health care costs covered by insurance[37]—to gauge the progress of the implementation of universal health care. It is not clear where and how this is being reported, though. The benefit delivery rate was not reported in the 2014 PhilHealth annual report or the DOH's report on the utilization of incremental sin tax revenues.

Figure 3.21 PhilHealth Benefit Claims by Membership Group

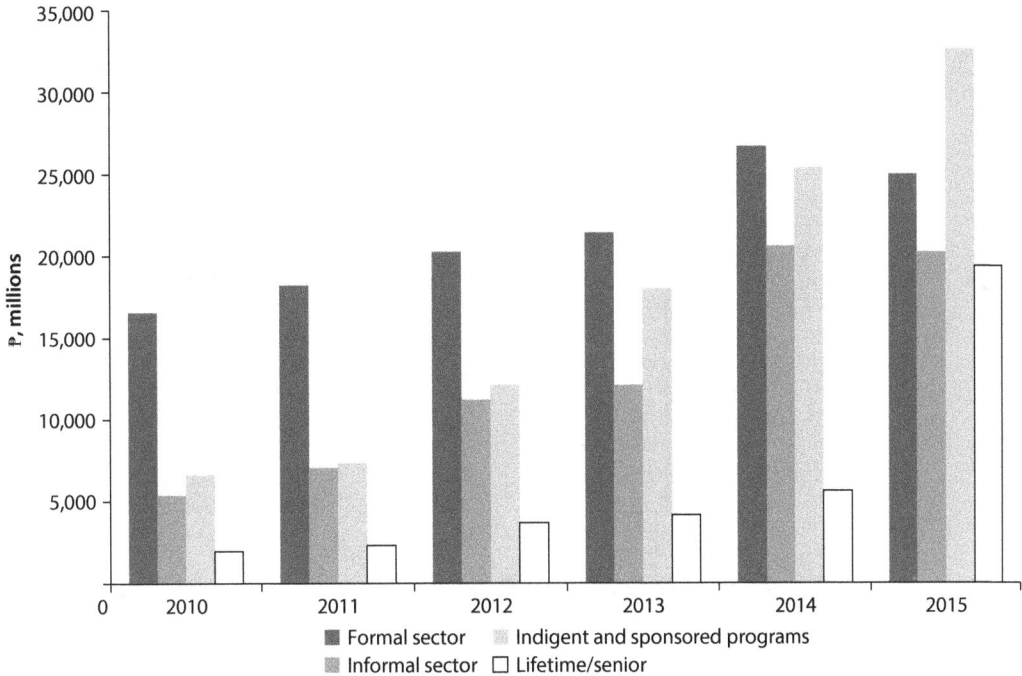

Source: PhilHealth.

PhilHealth benefit payments also provide an indication of the extent to which PhilHealth members, including the poor, are benefiting from their coverage—and the findings are quite encouraging. The monetary value of PhilHealth claims has been increasing, growing from ₱56.5 billion ($1.33 billion) in 2013 to ₱95.5 billion ($2.10 billion) in 2015. In fact, 2015 benefit payments exceeded premium income by about ₱1 billion ($2.20 million). This increase was seen across all membership groups, although payments to formal and informal sector members levelled off from 2014 to 2015 (figure 3.21). For indigent and sponsored[38] membership groups, the value of claims increased from ₱18 billion ($42.4 million) to ₱32.6 billion ($71.6 million) from 2013 to 2015 when, for the first time, the value of the claims of this group exceeded the claims of any other member group. The groups whose claims increased most of all were the senior citizens and lifetime[39] members whose share increased from ₱5.6 billion ($13.2 million) in 2013 to ₱19.3 billion ($42.4 million) in 2015.

However, it seems that PhilHealth benefit payments still accrue disproportionately to nonpoor members (figure 3.22). In other words, the share of the indigent and sponsored members and beneficiaries in the total value of claims is substantially lower than their membership share. Figure 3.20 confirms the increased enrollment of the poor in PhilHealth by showing how, from 2013 to 2014, the share of the indigent and sponsored program members and dependents in total PhilHealth membership increased from just over 40 percent to just over

Figure 3.22 PhilHealth Membership and Benefit Payment Shares by Membership Category, 2010–15

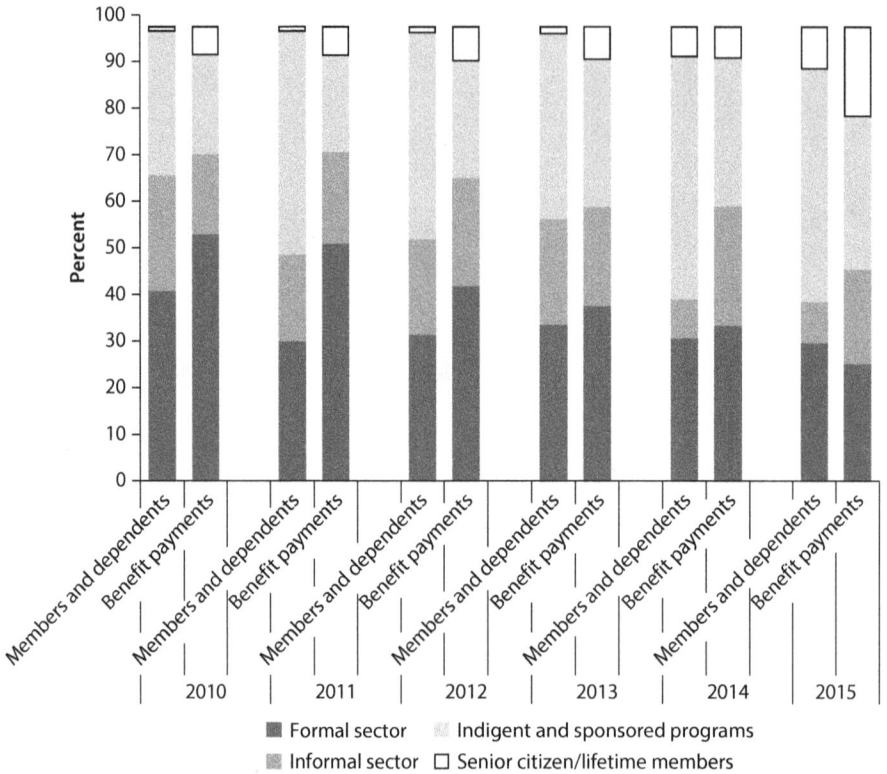

Source: PhilHealth annual reports, 2010–15.

50 percent. In 2015, the share of these two groups was 51 percent; that is, more than half of all PhilHealth beneficiaries. However, benefit payments to this group remained more or less constant at about a third of PhilHealth benefit payments by value—substantially lower than their membership share. From 2013 to 2015, the increase in their share of claims was only two percentage points. On the latter point, the geographic availability of facilities, especially higher-level hospitals where claims tend to be more expensive, may be an important determining factor that limits the access of the poor.

By contrast, the creation of a new category of senior citizen members (funded by the STL), has been associated not only with an increase in the membership share of this group, but also with a sharp increase in the share of this group in total claims value. Specifically, the expansion of coverage of senior citizens increased the membership share of those over 60 (lifetime and senior citizen groups combined) from 2 percent in 2013 to 9 percent in 2015. Some of this increase was likely due to movements of these beneficiaries from being dependents (for example, of their spouses or other family members) in other member categories to being primary members in the senior citizen category. What is most notable, though, is by how much the share of this group in total claims grew, from 7 percent to 20 percent. This suggests that those over 60, especially those who had previously not had health insurance coverage, were some of the major beneficiaries of the sin tax reform.

Beyond the overarching recommendation to carefully monitor health insurance coverage and the availability and use of health facilities (both through the DOH and PhilHealth administrative records and through household surveys), a number of additional policy actions would help to ensure that those receiving free health insurance (funded by the proceeds of the STL) are able to benefit from the services to which they are entitled. First and foremost, efforts need to be made to ensure that all PhilHealth members (and especially the poor and near-poor) know that they are covered and are aware of the full range of benefits. PhilHealth is currently implementing various measures to improve benefit awareness. These include radio, television, and newspaper advertisements, information sessions for beneficiaries of the conditional cash transfer program, outreach campaigns at the "barangay" (community) level, and hospital-based interventions such as signboards and patient outreach officers. An additional measure to consider is issuing health insurance cards to all indigent members. Second, the expansion of health insurance needs to be matched with supply-side readiness; in other words, ensuring that good-quality PhilHealth-accredited health facilities are within the close reach of all members. LGUs, which in the Philippines' decentralized health delivery context are responsible for building, equipping, and staffing facilities, could invest more in the quality of local health facilities, both primary care and hospital. This effort must also be complemented by more careful targeting and speedier implementation of the resources of the HFEP. Without quality accredited health facilities within easy reach, PhilHealth membership would be an empty promise.

Conclusions

The Government of the Philippines is to be commended for laying out a clear and evidence-based implementation framework for the STL. The law and its IRRs commit all relevant government to providing annual implementation updates. It obliges the DOH to submit a study of the effects and impact of the universal health care program supported by the STL to the Congressional Oversight Committee by 2016 (IRR rule V section 3e).[40] The publication of Tax Watch in January 2014 (and subsequently), as well as the attainment of near 100 percent tax stamp rollout, highlights the DOF's commitment to transparency and to advancing the efficiency of customs and tax revenue collection. The emphasis in the IRRs on public disclosure and participation by civil society organizations stand out as international best practice in transparency and demand-side accountability.

However, the timely availability of data to track implementation is a challenge. A first step to gradually overcome the lack of data is to identify priority baseline and tracking indicators, and then assess where and why evidence is lacking.

For indicators to reveal relevant and useful data, monitoring officials must be aware of the risks to achieving expected outcomes, as well as the difficulties in collecting and assessing data.

The STL has continued to yield increasing revenues, particularly from cigarettes. An absolute decline in removals, especially for lower-tier cigarettes, was dampened during the first years of the reform as not all price increases were passed to consumers. Annual frontloading served to defer some of the excise tax increases. However, as floor prices for cigarettes continue to rise with the progressive increases toward a unitary excise rate for cigarettes in 2017, we expect the STL health impacts to further increase.

To date, it appears that the health impact of the STL—both direct and indirect effects—is positive, though it may be too early to assess the full impact. This is due to a mix of factors, including the lag between intervention and effect, the fact that the full tax increase was not passed on to consumers in the form of price increases, delays in the availability of survey data, and because there will still be further tax increases in 2017. The 2015 DOH/SWS survey shows the prevalence of smoking fell from 29 percent in 2012 to 25 percent in 2015, while the percentage of those who had never smoked increased from 50 percent to 59 percent over the same period. A similar trend was observed in the NNHS data, which show that the prevalence of smoking fell from 31 percent in 2008 to 25 percent in 2013. In addition, revenues generated from the new excise taxes allowed the national government to increase the number of families provided with free health insurance from 5.2 million families to 14.7 million families, as well as subsidize 5.9 million senior citizens, bringing the country close to achieving universal coverage of health insurance.

Other countries can learn a lot from the design and implementation of the STL—and they are watching. At the same time, the reform's high profile raises the stakes: the STL reform needs to demonstrate success in improving health, revenue, and earmarking outcomes or else potential sin tax reforms in other contexts may not get the support they need. The prominence of the STL's earmarking provisions means that the measure will be judged as much on the success of programs such as universal health coverage and local programs to support farmer livelihoods as on its direct impacts on smoking and excessive drinking.

The STL clearly ranks as one of the most decisive and significant policy reforms in the Philippines in the past decade. Not only domestically but also internationally, it is viewed as a landmark reform for the way it reformed tobacco taxation and expanded free health insurance to the poorest 40 percent of the population. A cross-cutting question of this report is the extent to which the STL has been both demonstrational and transformational. By demonstrational, we mean whether key aspects of its technical design, as well as the political reform process, can provide lessons for reforms in similarly challenging situations—whether related to tax or otherwise—in the Philippines and elsewhere. By transformational, we mean the extent to which the STL is part of a deeper institutional transformation in the Philippines, from policies and programs driven primarily by patronage and personalism to ones anchored in principles, evidence, and citizen entitlement.

The STL clearly provides a set of demonstrational lessons. The achievement of a robust unitary tobacco excise tax rate in 2017, following a five-year phase-in period, has delivered results in terms of revenues and discouraging smoking due to higher prices. By removing excessive complexity in its structure, the excise tax policy is also easier to administer and monitor. A commitment to consistently track implementation has been made, including by using new data collection technologies, as well as ensuring the public disclosure of results to buttress the reform. Capturing the full extent of the health and expenditure impacts of the STL's earmarked revenues will require additional investments in information systems. Through regular reviews of its achievements and challenges, the sin tax reform will continue to serve as point of reference for other national government programs and for excise tax reform globally.

If the Philippines is to realize its ambition of inclusive growth, the STL will need to be followed by other reforms, both big and small, that embody the principles of good governance and pro-poor social policy that the STL stands for. The STL showed it is possible to escape a low-level equilibrium clouded by patronage and personalism to pursue goals whose benefits are more broadly shared, are based on clear principles, and are informed by evidence. Reform champions across a host of other policy domains will hopefully draw inspiration from the STL experience. But it is only if the STL becomes the precursor of a wider set of successful reforms aimed at enhancing inclusive growth that it will prove itself to be truly transformational.

Notes

1. This includes reduced smoking or quitting by existing smokers, as well as those not starting to smoke (including youth and women). Projections suggest cigarette demand may go down by as much as 50 percent between 2012 and 2017. A central concern for alcohol from a health perspective is monitoring excessive and youth drinking, rather than the aggregate consumption.

2. A key technical audience for specific indicators would be selected government agencies (Department of Finance, Department of Budget and Management, Department of Health, Department of Agriculture–National Tobacco Administration, and Department of the Interior and Local Government), the Philippine Statistics Authority, and international development partners, as well as civil society and the private sector concerned with third-party validation.

3. The STL requires the Bureau of Internal Revenue (BIR) to conduct formal price surveys to set tax tiers. With the current two-tier taxation structure, net retail prices must be assessed by the BIR based on sales in major stores. The applicability of the new excise rates on specific products in 2013 are based on a 2010 BIR price survey, or, for new products, sworn statements by producers. See ftp://ftp.bir.gov.ph/webadmin1/pdf/ for copies of BIR circulars.

4. A significant share of end-consumer purchases, especially by the poor, in the Philippines is made by single-cigarette purchases through street vendors and sari-sari stores. Per-pack retail price gaps between these vendors and other distribution channels such as supermarkets are worth noting in terms of how much consumers actually pay. Because the Philippines is an archipelago there may be important regional price

differences across the country (as well as brand differences). In addition, consumption behavior by the poor is likely to bring about a different marketing structure than for more affluent consumers. Rural and urban differences are also important.

5. The PSA collects monthly retail prices for brands, packs, and units of cigarettes; brands of spirits; and beers. The data are collected as part of consumer price index and general retail price index monitoring. This allows for the selection of a 2012 baseline comparison for monitoring. However, the National Statistics Office (NSO), now unified with other data agencies into the PSA, does not allow the public release of individual price data. The main weaknesses of the NSO's cigarette sample are the lack of enough information on prices for individual cigarette sales, and data on new best sellers in the cheaper market segment. Our analysis, therefore, is limited to an aggregate perspective or to the use of commercial data, and thus uses average price per tax and market segment for cigarette packs, beer, and spirits. This information is made available 30 days after the end of each month. The NSO collects prices of 14 cigarette brands monthly. Under these brands, it also collects several varieties for a total of almost 60 brand presentations. The NSO also collects the price-per-cigarette of eight brand presentations. The sample has a poor representation of cheaper brands, such as Mighty and La Suerte. Of course, it does not have a good representation of the most-sold cheap brands, or provides updates by new market entrants, as the market shifted faster than the NSO's capacity to adjust its data collection methodology. For beer, the NSO collects prices of nine brand presentations. For spirits, prices of 10 brandy presentations, 10 gin presentations, and seven rum presentations are collected. See http://www.census.gov.ph/business/price-indices.

6. A traditional way for producers and distributors to cushion higher prices with tax increases is to emphasize consumer discounts for larger volumes, and change product packaging or other product marketing details. Assessing these practices could be done through special surveys focusing on the discount strategies (such as selling products in bundles of three) that companies and retailers may have been using to maintain consumption levels. The purpose of collecting this sort of information is to connect brand price levels, their discount strategies, and market shares. This can help elucidate pricing patterns in relation to tax increases.

7. It is also important to note that the standard deviation recorded during the NSO price surveys increased, showing that price dispersion around the mean increased after the sin tax reform, reflecting different price changes for different brands. Gin and rum prices remain about an eighth that of beer (see Policy Note No. 2 of the Summary Technical Briefing Notes for Sin Tax Bicameral Deliberations). For more information, see box 2.1 in chapter 2.

8. Republic Act 10625, known as the Philippine Statistical Act, was signed into law by President Benigno Aquino on September 12, 2013. The National Economic Development Authority chairs the PSA board; the DOF is represented as one of the agencies on the board.

9. Future updates of the consumer price index base should also capture some of the changes to market structure and leading brands since the last base year and the STL.

10. To produce prices per tax segment, the BIR should assist the PSA in the tax classification of the products that form the basket of tobacco and alcohol products.

11. In fact, this type of analysis should be part of the regular obligations of the statistical unit, the large taxpayer, or the BIR's audit division. What the country experience indicates is that any of these units could be responsible for the analysis of these figures and for the preparation of confidential reports to the heads of the tax authority and DOF.

12. The increase in spirits in this series appears to be partly because imported spirits were previously taxed through the Bureau of Customs. The 2013 data seem to include the early Bureau of Customs collections. Figure 3.12 suggests that most of the increase in levels was during 2012–13.

13. In early 2014, the Bureau of Customs and DOF shut down one of Mighty Corporation's importation warehouses over alleged smuggling. For further details, see ABS-CBN's report at http://www.abs-cbnnews.com/business/01/23/14/customs -orders-suspension-mightys-bonded-warehouse, and the *Philippine Star* at http:// www.philstar.com/headlines/2014/06/10/1333084/bir-probes-cigarette-maker -mighty.

14. In connection with the Philippines, see http://business.inquirer.net/199962/sin-taxes -blow-out-smoking-in-ph-but-gives-life-to-illicit-cigarette-trade on Inquirer.net.

15. To enhance the discussion on using administrative data to pinpoint undeclared and illicit imports (inputs and final product), domestic production (inputs and final product), and market volumes (to pinpoint final sales), a public hearing could be held to request an explanation of AC Nielsen's statistical survey methodology and its evaluation by independent specialists from Philippine universities. The dialogue would also assess the extent to which the data is likely to overreport or underreport consumption by various market segments.

16. As a listed company, Philip Morris International provides public documentation of its financial position. Its 2013 results report (http://investors.pmi.com/phoenix.zhtml?c =146476&p=irol-irhome, p. 15) provides a detailed analysis of Philippine market developments. In that year, overall demand decreased by 15.6 percent. The report notes that the company's market share dropped from 90.7 to 79.3 percent over 2012–13. The report notes that consumers downshifted to cheaper brands, also fueled by Philip Morris International's main brand competitor—Mighty—for allegedly under-declaring tax revenues, therefore undercutting prices.

17. For further information, see ABS-CBN's report at http://www.abs-cbnnews.com /business/01/23/14/customs-orders-suspension-mightys-bonded-warehouse.

18. This analysis assumes that holographic tax stamps are not counterfeited. However, the technology allows for further validation in this regard.

19. There is also a 2015 FIES, but the results are not yet available.

20. The 2011 survey was conducted by UPecon Foundation, a private, nonprofit research institution of faculty members of the University of the Philippines School of Economics, in collaboration with Erasmus University, Rotterdam, and the World Bank, and funded by the European Union.

21. Social Weather Stations and other market research firms use an A, B, C, D, and E income classification for survey respondents. The A, B, C group is reported to roughly correspond to the wealthiest 10 percent of the population, D to the next 30 percent, and E to the poorest 60 percent. Commentators loosely refer to these three groups as the upper, middle, and lower-income classes.

22. The Registry of Sector of Basic Sectors in Agriculture was conducted after 2011. It lists 38,149 farmer households engaged in tobacco growing.

23. Under Republic Act 7171 of 1991, transfers would increase in 2015 to about ₱10 billion ($233 million) from ₱5 billion ($116 million). Under Republic Act 8240 of 1996, allocations may decline to ₱0.5 billion ($11.6 million).

24. See Local Budget Memorandum, No. 68, February 18, 2015.

25. For the Supreme Court ruling, see http://www.lawphil.net/judjuris/juri2013/nov2013 /gr_208566_2013.html.

26. Section 9 of the STL also provided for "special financial support for displaced workers in the alcohol and tobacco industries" to be included in the budgets of the Department of Labor and Employment and the Technical Education and Skills Development Authority. While likely smaller in scale than the earmarks for tobacco-growing regions, these should also be assessed as part of the STL's actual transitional impacts.

27. Under STL section 8/C "eighty percent (80%) of the remaining balance of the incremental revenue derived from this Act shall be allocated for the Universal Health Care under the National Health Insurance Program, the attainment of the Millennium Development Goals and health awareness programs; and twenty percent (20%) shall be allocated nationwide, based on political and district subdivisions, for medical assistance and health enhancement facilities program, the annual requirements of which shall be determined by the Department of Health."

28. The international literature typically distinguishes between "hard" and "soft" earmarking of revenues.

29. In anticipation of revenue increases, the 2013 General Appropriations Act allocated unprogrammed funds of ₱13.6 billion ($316 million) to the DOH. However, they were not used. See http://www.dbm.gov.ph/wp-content/uploads/GAA/GAA2013 /DOH/DOH.pdf.

30. The total reported budget was ₱53.23, but a particular feature of the Philippine budgeting system is that it has both new and continuing appropriations for each year. For 2013, the DOH's continuing appropriations were quite limited at ₱175 million ($4.1 million), as stated by the DBM's Statement of Allotment, Obligations, and Balances for the first quarter of 2013 (see http://www.dbm.gov.ph/wp-content /uploads/e-Fund_Releases/SAOB2013/SAOB_1stQ_2013.html). The DBM's statement included allocations to the Commission on Population and National Nutrition Council. In 2013, ₱2.786 billion of the HFEP budget is lodged to DPWH.

31. See p. 596 of the *Official Gazette*, December 12, 2008, at http://www.dbm.gov.ph /wp-content/uploads/GAA/GAA2013/DOH/DOH.pdf.

32. A family consists of the principal PhilHealth member, spouse (if any), and dependents aged under 21 who do not have children of their own; if they have children, they are listed as a separate indigent family.

33. For the senior citizen program, a family is defined slightly differently in that a spouse of the principal member older than 60 is counted as a separate family.

34. The SWS survey of 2012 reported a PhilHealth coverage rate of 61 percent; the 2014 survey reported a coverage rate of 69 percent.

35. Sin Tax Law Incremental Revenues for Health Annual Report, produced by the DOH, as required by the STL's IRRs.

36. PhilHealth administrative records note that PhilHealth regional offices requested certain LGUs be excluded when this statistic is calculated for reasons that are not clear. This means that only 1,584 of 1,634 LGUs figure in this calculation, suggesting that the overall increase in the accreditation rate must be less than the 99 percent statistic implies.

37. See Quimbo et al. (2013) for a detailed description of the benefit delivery rate and its development.

38. Unfortunately, changes over time in the way membership groups are categorized in PhilHealth Stats and Charts mean the share of the indigent and sponsored groups cannot be examined separately.

39. The categorization of membership groups in PhilHealth data means that the share of senior citizens and lifetime members cannot be examined separately.

40. The Congressional Oversight Committee was initially created under Republic Act 8240.

References

Bird, R. 2015. "Tobacco and Alcohol Excise Taxes for Public Health Financing: Marrying Sin and Virtue?" Policy Research Working Paper 7500, World Bank, Washington, DC.

Bredenkamp, C., and L. R. Buisman. 2015. "Universal Health Coverage in the Philippines: Progress on Financial Protection Goals." Policy Research Working Paper 7258, World Bank, Washington, DC. http://documents.worldbank.org/curated/en/2015/05 /24450100/universal-health-coverage-philippines-progress-financial-protection-goals.

Cruz, Kevin Thomas Garcia, Joseph Louie C. Limkin, Noel Borja Del Castillo, Karl Kendrick Tiu Chua, Rogier J. E. Van Den Brink, and Roberto Martin Nolan Galang. 2016. "Philippine Economic Update: Moving Full Speed Ahead—Accelerating Reforms to Create More and Better Jobs." Working Paper 104611, World Bank, Washington, DC.

Espino, R. R., D. L. Evangalista, and E. U. Dorotheo. 2009. *Survey of Tobacco Growing Areas in the Philippines*. Los Baños: University of the Philippines Los Baños, p. 82.

ITIC (International Tax and Investment Center) and Oxford Economics. 2014. *Asia-14 Illicit Tobacco Indicator 2013*. Oxford: ITIC, Oxford Economics.

Merriman, David. 2003. *Understanding, Measuring and Controlling Illicit Trade*. Washington: DC, World Bank.

Quimbo, S., A. Kraft, J. Capuno, and C. Tan. 2013. *How Much Protection Does PhilHealth Provide Filipinos?* Manila: Philippines Center for Economic Development, p. 11.

WHO (World Health Organization). 2015. *WHO Report on the Global Tobacco Epidemic, 2015: Raising Taxes on Tobacco*. Geneva, World Health Organization. http://apps.who .int/iris /bitstream/10665/178574/1/9789240694606_eng.pdf?ua=1: 103.

Sin Tax Law Earmarking for Tobacco-Growing Regions

Provision	Republic Act (RA) 7171 (1992) and Memorandum Circular No. 61-A (1993)	RA 8240 (1996) (reiterated under RA 9334, 2004) Revenue Regulation No. 15-2008 and Joint Circulars No. 2009-1 and 2009-1A	RA 10351 (2012) and implementing rules and regulations, and Department of Budget and Management Local Budget Memorandum 2016-72
Earmark purpose	Support Virginia tobacco regions.	Support Burley and Native tobacco.	Reinforce existing tobacco region earmarks and expansion of eligible projects.
	15 percent of the excise taxes on locally manufactured Virginia-type cigarettes.	RA 8240 (section 8) stipulates that 15 percent of the incremental revenue collected from the excise tax on tobacco products be divided among the provinces producing Burley and Native tobacco in accordance with the volume of tobacco leaf production.	Tobacco earmarks stay the same as before (RA 10351 section 8), with additional earmarking for health in incremental revenues (following deduction set out in RA 7171 and RA 8240). Specifies use of Burley and Native tobacco funds for "programs to promote economically viable alternatives for tobacco farmers."
Qualification for earmarked projects	Provinces producing Virginia tobacco to be designated beneficiary provinces under RA 7171 provided they have average annual production of Virginia leaf of not less than 1 million kilos. The amount to be divided on a pro-rata basis among beneficiary provinces based on the respective annual volume of adjusted Virginia tobacco acceptances for the immediate past year as certified by the National Tobacco Administration.	Under Joint Circular No. 2009-1A (amended January 12, 2010), for a local government unit to qualify as a beneficiary under RA 8240, its annual Burley and Native tobacco production and acceptances must not be less than 1,000 kilos (the qualifying benchmark was previously set at 100,000 kilos under Joint Circular No. 2009-1).	Local Budget Memorandum Circular No. 72 dated March 8, 2016, downloadable under the Department of Budget and Management's (DBM) website http:// www.dbm.gov.ph/?page _ id=2801.

table continues next page

Provision	Republic Act (RA) 7171 (1992) and Memorandum Circular No. 61-A (1993)	RA 8240 (1996) (reiterated under RA 9334, 2004) Revenue Regulation No. 15-2008 and Joint Circulars No. 2009-1 and 2009-1A	RA 10351 (2012) and implementing rules and regulations, and Department of Budget and Management Local Budget Memorandum 2016-72
	For determining the pro-rata shares, immediate past year means the two years preceding the budget year. For example, if 1994 is the budget year, two years preceding is 1992.		
Eligible programs	Cooperative projects that will enhance better quality products, increase productivity, guarantee the market, and, as a whole, increase farmers' incomes. Livelihood projects, particularly the development of alternative farming systems, to enhance farmers' incomes. Agro-industrial projects that will enable tobacco farmers in the Virginia tobacco producing provinces to be involved in the management and subsequent ownership of these projects, such as postharvest and secondary processing (for example, cigarette manufacturing and by-product utilization). Infrastructure projects such as farm-to-market roads.	Cooperative projects that will enhance the quality of agricultural products and increase incomes and productivity of farmers. Livelihood projects, particularly the development of alternative farming systems, to enhance farmers' incomes. Agro-industrial projects that will enable tobacco farmers to be involved in the management and subsequent ownership of projects, such as postharvest and secondary processing (for example, cigarette manufacturing and by-product utilization).	The fund to be exclusively utilized for programs to promote economically viable alternatives for tobacco farmers and workers such as: Programs that will provide inputs, training, and other support for tobacco farmers who shift production to agricultural products other than tobacco including, but not limited to, high-value crops, spices, rice, corn, sugarcane, coconut, livestock, and fisheries. Programs that will provide financial support for tobacco farmers who are displaced or who cease to produce tobacco. Cooperative programs to assist tobacco farmers in planting alternative crops or implementing other livelihood projects. Livelihood programs and projects that will promote, enhance, and develop the tourism potential of tobacco-growing provinces. Infrastructure projects such as farm-to-market roads, schools, hospitals, and rural health facilities. Agro-industrial projects that will enable tobacco farmers to be involved in the management and subsequent ownership of projects, such as postharvest and secondary processing (for example, cigarette manufacturing and by-product utilization).

table continues next page

Provision	Republic Act (RA) 7171 (1992) and Memorandum Circular No. 61-A (1993)	RA 8240 (1996) (reiterated under RA 9334, 2004) Revenue Regulation No. 15-2008 and Joint Circulars No. 2009-1 and 2009-1A	RA 10351 (2012) and implementing rules and regulations, and Department of Budget and Management Local Budget Memorandum 2016-72
Allocation to growing regions	30 percent to the provincial government of the beneficiary province. 40 percent to the municipalities and cities to be further distributed with the following subdivisions: 50 percent to be divided equally among all municipalities and cities of the beneficiary province, 50 percent to be divided according to volume of their respective tobacco production. 30 percent to the municipalities and cities in the congressional districts of a beneficiary province in consultation with the representatives of the congressional districts of the province. Under this component, the share of each congressional district is based on the volume of tobacco production within each district provided that 50 percent of all the shares accruing to local government units are used for "barangay" (community) economic development projects.	Under Joint Circular No. 2009-1: 80 percent to the municipalities and cities in the congressional districts of a beneficiary province. 10 percent to the provincial government of the beneficiary province, provided that the beneficiaries of the projects to be implemented by the province are local government units producing Burley and Native tobacco products. 10 percent to the municipalities and cities, provided that the beneficiaries of the projects to be implemented are local government units producing Burley and Native tobacco products.	RA 10351 does not specify allocation percentages. DBM Local Budget Memorandum 2016-72 specifies the guidelines on the release and utilization of local government unit transfers for 2013, and emphasizes the concomitant posting and reporting requirements to enhance transparency and accountability. These include mandatory postings of fund utilization and status of program/project implementation following specified formats each quarter, within 20 days, on a DBM-established website and by individual local government units. The guidelines also address the issues raised by the November 2013 Supreme Court rulings declaring Priority Development Assistance Fund ("pork barrel") allocations unconstitutional.
Incremental revenue calculation	Not applicable	Under Revenue Regulation No. 15-2008 and Joint Circular No. 2009-1, incremental revenues defined as "equivalent to the excess of the actual calculation of excise taxes from tobacco products for the year under consideration over calendar year 1996 as the base year, net of the incremental revenue collected from the increase in excise tax rates under RA No. 9334."	Pending confirmation by forthcoming implementing rules and regulations, and congressional committee concerns, incremental revenue calculations for tobacco should remain the same as before. The exact calculations, however, are not readily available.

table continues next page

Provision	Republic Act (RA) 7171 (1992) and Memorandum Circular No. 61-A (1993)	RA 8240 (1996) (reiterated under RA 9334, 2004) Revenue Regulation No. 15-2008 and Joint Circulars No. 2009-1 and 2009-1A	RA 10351 (2012) and implementing rules and regulations, and Department of Budget and Management Local Budget Memorandum 2016-72
Notable issues for discussion for implementation of RA 10351	Revenue Resolution No. 12-2008 (September) was issued to clarify that domestic production of Virginia-type cigarettes with domestic or imported Virginia tobacco inputs are subject to excise tax earmarks. Executive Order No. 846 (November 16, 2009) was required to release funds collected from 2002 to 2009 that were not disbursed in a timely manner.	Revenue Regulation No. 15-2008 indicated the problem associated with defining "incremental revenues," a problem that took over a decade to resolve, as follows: "In the absence of the corresponding rules and regulations governing the determination of what constitutes 'incremental revenue,' the above legislative requirement covered under the said Act could not be implemented." In line with RA 9334, which states: "The Department of Budget and Management, in consultation with the Oversight Committee created under said RA 8240, shall issue the corresponding rules and regulations governing the allocation and disbursement of this fund." The Oversight Committee issued resolutions prior to Joint Circular No. 2009-1, and its amendment in 2010, which provides guidelines on sharing and releasing of incremental funds. Executive Order No. 843 (November 9, 2009) was required to release funds collected from 1997 to 2007 that were not disbursed in a timely manner.	The exact methods for calculating allocations and disbursements of previous sin tax revenues should be analyzed and reconfirmed for accuracy and guidance in determining future calculations. The following terminology under Joint Circular No 2009-1, for example, is not clear: "net of the incremental revenue collected from the increase in excise tax rates under RA 9334." Public issuance of timely, clear, and simple calculations including detailed examples of earmarks and their distribution to tobacco farming regions will enhance transparency and accountability of the use of public funds. A new baseline for incremental revenues must be set for health program earmarks, but tobacco earmarks should not be affected if baseline and distributional percentages remain the same. Release of tobacco funds should not be stalled due to the health earmark baseline requirement. In a change from RA 9334, the Congressional Oversight Committee is not cited for consultation on tobacco earmark implementing rules and regulations: "The Department of Budget and Management, in consultation with the Department of Agriculture, shall issue rules and regulations governing the allocation and disbursement of this fund, not later than one hundred eighty (180) days from the effectivity of this Act." However, the committee's role is defined in a number of other ways in RA 10351. Under Executive Memorandum Circular No. 188 (February 26, 2010) the status of work for Cabinet Officers for Regional Development for inspection, monitoring, and evaluation of projects funded by sin tax revenues should be clarified and updated under RA 10351.

Source: The republic acts and proclamations cited in this table.

Sin Tax Law Earmarking for Health

Provision	Republic Act 9334 (2004)	Republic Act 10351 (2012) and its implementing rules and regulations
Earmark purpose	Precedent set for health earmarking (2005–09).	Significant health earmarking.
Tax earmarks	2.5 percent of the incremental revenue from the excise tax on alcohol and tobacco products starting January 2005 to be remitted directly to the Philippine Health Insurance Corporation for meeting and sustaining the National Health Insurance Program's goal of universal health coverage. 2.5 percent of the incremental revenue from the excise tax on alcohol and tobacco products starting January 2005 to be credited to the Department of Health and constituted as a trust fund for its disease prevention program. RA 9334, in amending RA 7660, also earmarked partially some revenues from documentary stamp taxes for health purposes.	After deducting the allocations under Republic Acts (RA) 7171 and 8240, 80 percent of the remaining balance of the incremental revenue derived from this act to be allocated for universal health care under the National Health Insurance Program, attaining Millennium Development Goals, and health awareness programs; and 20 percent to be allocated nationwide, based on political and district subdivisions, for medical assistance and the Health Facilities Enhancement Program (the annual requirements of the latter to be determined by the Department of Health).
Qualification for earmarked projects	Not applicable.	Annual funding requirements for universal health care (UHC), meeting Millennium Development Goals, and health awareness programs to be determined and allocated by the Department of Health (DOH) and reviewed by the Department of Budget and Management (DBM) for inclusion in the national budget in accordance with the UHC Medium-Term Expenditure Program, as approved by the Development Budget Coordination Committee (DBCC). The list of indigent families is to be provided by the Department of Social Welfare and Development in coordination with PhilHealth, and updated at least once every four years.

table continues next page

Provision	Republic Act 9334 (2004)	Republic Act 10351 (2012) and its implementing rules and regulations
		Annual funding requirements for medical assistance and health facilities enhancement to be determined by the DOH and reviewed by the DBM for inclusion in the national budget in accordance with the UHC Medium-Term Expenditure Program, as approved by the DBCC.
Eligible programs	National Health Insurance Program, DOH's disease prevention program.	Under the implementing rules and regulations, eligible programs are: (1) the National Health Insurance Program, DOH programs intended to attain the Millennium Development Goals, DOH health awareness programs, and DOH implementation research on UHC (80 percent); and (2) DOH's Medical Assistance Program, DOH's Health Facilities Enhancement Program, and DOH service delivery networks. In addition, the tobacco earmarks for Burley and Native tobacco regions include the potential for excise tax funds to be used on rural health facilities infrastructure.
Incremental revenue calculation	Not applicable.	Under the IRRs, the incremental revenue is computed as the difference between the total actual excise collections from alcohol and tobacco products for the year under consideration under RA 10351, and the baseline excise collections (without RA 10351) for the same year. Considering that some local government units (LGU) are entitled to a portion of this incremental revenue under RA 7171 and RA 8240, the LGU share is deducted first from the incremental revenue to determine the net amount earmarked for UHC.

Source: Republic Act 9334, as amended; Republic Act 10351 and its implementing rules and regulations.

Environmental Benefits Statement

The World Bank Group is committed to reducing its environmental footprint. In support of this commitment, the Publishing and Knowledge Division leverages electronic publishing options and print-on-demand technology, which is located in regional hubs worldwide. Together, these initiatives enable print runs to be lowered and shipping distances decreased, resulting in reduced paper consumption, chemical use, greenhouse gas emissions, and waste.

The Publishing and Knowledge Division follows the recommended standards for paper use set by the Green Press Initiative. The majority of our books are printed on Forest Stewardship Council (FSC)–certified paper, with nearly all containing 50–100 percent recycled content. The recycled fiber in our book paper is either unbleached or bleached using totally chlorine-free (TCF), processed chlorine-free (PCF), or enhanced elemental chlorine-free (EECF) processes.

More information about the Bank's environmental philosophy can be found at http://www.worldbank.org/corporateresponsibility.